# *The Narcissist on Instagram:*

# *Epigrams and Observations*

# *The Fifth Book*

by

## Sam Vaknin, Ph.D.

Professor of Psychology

Southern Federal University, Rostov-on-Don, Russian Federation and SIAS-CIAPS

Centre for International Advanced Professional Studies (SIAS Outreach)

The author is NOT a Mental Health Practitioner

The book is based on interviews since 1996 with 2000 people diagnosed with

Narcissistic and Antisocial Personality Disorders (narcissists and psychopaths)

and with thousands of family members, friends, therapists, and colleagues.

Editing and Design:

**Lidija Rangelovska**

*A Narcissus Publications Imprint*

*Prague & Haifa 2023*

To get FREE updates of this book JOIN the Narcissism Study List.
To JOIN, visit our Web sites:
http://www.narcissistic-abuse.com/narclist.html or
http://groups.yahoo.com/group/narcissisticabuse

**Visit the Author's Web site**   http://www.narcissistic-abuse.com

**Facebook**   http://www.facebook.com/samvaknin

http://www.facebook.com/narcissismwithvaknin

**YouTube channel**   http://www.youtube.com/samvaknin

**Instagram**   https://www.instagram.com/vakninsamnarcissist/ (archive)

https://www.instagram.com/narcissismwithvaknin/

**Buy other books and video lectures about pathological narcissism and relationships with abusive narcissists and psychopaths here:**

http://www.narcissistic-abuse.com/thebook.html

**Buy Kindle books here:**

http://www.amazon.com/s/ref=ntt_athr_dp_sr_1?_encoding=UTF8&field-author=Sam%20Vaknin&search-alias=digital-text&sort=relevancerank

# CONTENTS

Throughout this book click on blue-lettered text to navigate to
different chapters
or to access online resources

<u>Author Bio</u>

<u>Author Bio</u>

# Scams

# Scandals

# And

# Scoundrels

16.

<u>Having kids</u> is a seriously bad idea. Here's why (click on the links in the description of the video).


<u>Return</u>

# Men,
# Women,
# Gender Wars

105.

<u>Intimate relationships and love</u> ("catching feelings") are now perceived by the majority of people under 35 as a double whammy: a massive disruption to one's career and a surefire path to being abused and "played" (exploited).

This unprecedented view of interpersonal liaisons led to a mounting "loneliness gap" pandemic and resulted in four coping strategies:

1. The sociosexually unrestricted (about 20%) remain lifelong singles and play the field in bouts of stranger casual sex and group sex;

2. About 20% avoid all meaningful human contact, sex included. They become schizoid and celibate;

3. Growing numbers turn to same sex dyads. A whopping 1 in 6 women are now lesbian. "Safe" friendships and even intimate relationships between straight and gay are all the rage;

4. Even when in serial relationships, most young people are distrustful and engage in power plays and mind games intended to secure the upper hand. It is all about avoiding being played and not ending up being a loser.

Infidelity is rife and weaponized and is now virtually universal: every year, one in six cheat on their partner (cumulatively, about 60% of both men and women do the deed throughout the life of the relationship).

Strife and myriad forms of abuse (including emotional absence and sex withdrawal) are the norm in these dystopian unions.

106.

<u>Not everyone is built to be in a relationship</u>. There are different attachment styles and the insecure ones predict recurrent relationship failure.

Across multiple studies, at least 15% of adults state that they are much more comfortable and content being alone. 31% of adults are lifelong singles. The majority of the rest are immured in abusive, dead, or ephemeral pseudo-relationships.

Intimacy and love are lost arts and outliers, not the norm.

The problem is that some people feel threatened or constrained by love and intimacy in longer committed relationships.

They anticipate failure, hurt, misery, and discord - so, preemptively, as an anxiolytic strategy, they bring about these very outcomes by repeatedly adopting dysfunctional behaviors ("let the other shoe drop").

These relationship misfits subvert and undermine their relationships and gain "intimacy" and acceptance and faux warmth via sex with strangers, even groups of strangers. They feel "liked", even "loved" in a "connection" when in casual, drunk encounters with anonymous partners.

Typically, they experience dissonance with their choices and they resolve it by dissociating, numbing their emotions, abusing substances, and reduced affect display. Some convert their ego dystony into a narrative ideology of empowerment.

People who dread intimacy feel a lot more unencumbered with strangers. They use fantasy to compensate for the low level of intimacy in these seedy and unsatisfactory exploitative and predatory encounters.

Many of them finally give up on the chase and settle into a career-centered life of celibacy and self-sufficiency.

Dynamic-maturational model of attachment and adaptation teaches us that the majority of attachment strategies lead to relationship failures.

107.

Studies in dozens of countries show that men are loth to form long-term relationships with promiscuous women whose "body count" exceeds 9 sex partners (fewer in some countries). Why is that?

For three excellent and rational reasons:

1. Men are competitive and seek high relative positioning among their peers. A woman who had been summarily used and discarded by multiple guys is an embarrassment ("that's the best you can do? I and all my friends had her for free any time we wanted!").

Such a woman is "cheap" and "easy" and investing in her renders the man a gullible sucker and a "simp": why be the only one to pay for what she had been giving away gratis to everyone?

2. Promiscuity had been linked to subclinical psychopathy, time and again. It is a strong indicator of a lack of boundaries, a weakness of character (people pleasing), or of reckless defiance. Not good qualities to have in a partner.

3. Past behavior is an unfailing prognosticator of future conduct. Promiscuity is strongly linked to serial cheating.

Nonautonomus sexual self-trashing driven by the wish to be accepted and the need to buttress self-esteem by garnering attention are addictive, lifelong behaviors.

## 108.

<u>Pareto, dating, and mating</u>: women prefer "beta" males even for one night stands, definitely for long-term relationships. This is why Friends with Benefits (FwB) is the dominant model for casual sex – not hookups.

Sex among people younger than 25 is on the decline: the number of sexual partners and the frequency of sex is lower than among previous generations.

Not hypergamy, but hypogamy: women more educated and earn as much as men.

Women consume more pornography than men – but text-based, not visual.

## 109.

<u>Advice online and in self-help books</u> is often wrong and counterproductive.

Example:

There is no such thing as "<u>wrong partner</u>". Your mate selection is always on point and on target.

If you are a self-loathing and self-trashing masochist - an abusive narcissist is the right partner for you, for one night or for decades.

If you dread intimacy, being vulnerable, and heartbreak - an avoidant-dismissive mate is a match made in heaven. Having a true intimate partner would only enhance your anxiety and amplify your insecurities to the point of paranoia.

If you are thrill-seeking, reckless, and defiant - you gravitate towards psychopaths.

Your attachment style is lifelong (though life goals, choices, and behaviors in relationships can be modified). It makes sure that whoever you may end up with is always the right partner for you.

110.

<u>Attachment style is stable over the lifespan</u>, but attachment behaviors and internal relationship models change in 30% of people.

Behaviors can be modified to counter effects of attachment style.

Intensity of attachment orientation changes.

The changes are mediated via:

Quality of relationships, type of partner

Traumas

Therapy

Personality Disorders

Life Crises

REFERENCES

Chopik, W. J., Edelstein, R. S., & Grimm, K. J. (2019). Longitudinal changes in attachment orientation over a 59-year period. Journal of

Personality and Social Psychology, 116(4), 598–611.
https://doi.org/10.1037/pspp0000167

Attachment styles and close relationships: A four-year prospective study,
Lee A. Kirkpatrick, Cindy Hazan
Personal Relationships: Journal of the International Association for
Relationship Research, June 1994, https://doi.org/10.1111/j.1475-
6811.1994.tb00058.x

Australian Journal of Educational & Developmental Psychology. Vol 11,
2011, pp. 60- 77
Attachment across the life span: Factors that contribute to stability and
change
Megan McConnell, McGill University and Ellen Moss, Université du
Québec a Montréal

Why does attachment style change? J Davila 1, D Burge, C Hammen
Journal of Personality and Social Psychology, J Pers Soc Psychol. 1997
Oct;73(4):826-38

Personality and Social Psychology Review
Revising Working Models Across Time: Relationship Situations That
Enhance Attachment Security
Ximena B. Arriaga, Madoka Kumashiro, Jeffry A. Simpson, et al.
First Published June 2, 2017

Bartholomew, K., & Horowitz, L. M. (1991). Attachment styles among
young adults: A test of a four-category model. Journal of Personality and
Social Psychology, 61(2), 226–244. https://doi.org/10.1037/0022-
3514.61.2.226

John B. Separation, anxiety and anger. In: In Attachment and Loss:
Volume II. The Hogarth press and the institute of psycho-analysis; 1973:1-
429.

Bretherton I. Updating the 'internal working model' construct: Some
reflections. Attachment & Human Development. Published online
December 1999:343-357. doi:10.1080/14616739900134191

Pietromonaco PR, Barrett LF. The Internal Working Models Concept: What do we Really know about the Self in Relation to Others? Review of General Psychology. Published online June 2000:155-175. doi:10.1037/1089-2680.4.2.155

Bartholomew K, Horowitz LM. Attachment styles among young adults: A test of a four-category model. Journal of Personality and Social Psychology. 1991;61(2):226-244.

Macfie J, Mcelwain NL, Houts RM, Cox MJ. Intergenerational transmission of role reversal between parent and child: Dyadic and family systems internal working models. Attachment & Human Development. Published online March 2005:51-65. doi:10.1080/14616730500039663

111.

The <u>dating scene</u> is infested with autoerotic narcissists. Boundaries are the solution.

112.

<u>Jane Austen</u> would have felt at home nowadays: one third of the population are lifelong singles (spinsters and bachelors); marriages and other committed relationships are driven strictly by economic and financial considerations; intimacy, love, and sex within dyads are dead and are outsourced. Extramarital dalliances and sexlessness in couples are both skyrocketing.

She would have been pleased to note that women give as good as they get. But she would have been shocked and saddened by their choice of role models: rogue cads, promiscuous and psychopathic-chauvinistic bullies.

Women have always traded sex for financial security for themselves and for their children. But many contemporary women do not want children - yet are still looking for a partner who could augment and sustain their lifestyle.

This form of lifestyle prostitution is crystal clear in studies: the number one reason women give for choosing a mate is "he has a stable income".

Men have jubilantly adapted to this shift. Career women give casual sex away for free and men gobble it up.

By the time these "empowered" women wish to settle down with a sponsor, a sugar daddy, or a partner whose income augments their own, they have little left to offer in return: faded looks and their reproductive years behind them. Idiotically, they squander their greatest assets and their best years, doling them out to total strangers in return for bad sex.

Most men nowadays aggressively insist on no strings attached sex or move on to the next gaping anatomy, fueled by porn fantasies.

Few men are willing to commit or to invest anymore. Women are all on their own as some feminists had always wished for.

113.

Gender roles are a subset of social roles and both are crumbling in our anomic societies.

Both men and women had felt enslaved by the previous world order (public domain patriarchy coupled with private domain matriarchy).

Men were wage slaves and women - glorified domestic help.

When women started to contest and undermine their traditionally allocated roles, men jumped at the opportunity and bailed out of theirs.

En masse, men now refuse to commit, invest, get educated, establish families, or work in steady jobs.

This rebellion of the men left women with no choice but to assume these erstwhile masculine functions and become men in their careers, sexual scripts (promiscuity), and relationships.

We are stranded in a unigender world: there are only men now, albeit with two differing sets of genitalia.

114.

The "stalled revolution" means that when it comes to sexual mores, marriage, relationships, and family, men remain stuck in a Victorian England mindset while women have progressed into a feminist 21st century.

Confronted with this abyss, women face a stark choice:

1. They can give up on men altogether and go it alone while assuming masculine traits and roles; or

2. They can regress and subject themselves to male dominance and objectification in raunch culture and in supposedly "intimate" relationships.

There is no other alternative. Men won't budge. Men are fighting back (MGTOW, incels, one third of all men are celibate or lifelong singles).

As things stand now, most men are merely taking advantage of women's newfangled sex positivity and then walk away from casual sex, unscathed.

Women are paying the price of this male sexual opportunism in terms of heartbreak, bad sex, childlessness, loneliness, and career or financial damage.

It's a war that men seem to be winning big time. Even as they make strides in the real world, when it comes to intimate relationships, women are more abused and disempowered than ever. And men just joyfully roam around, humping dozens of throwaway women in the promiscuous Disneyland of post-modernity.

Painting by @bdeaihe_art

115.

Men are saying: Women! You are too independent! I am terrified that you will no longer tolerate my abuse and my infantilism, you will decline to serve me, you abandon me and I will lose you.

You are too well-educated. I feel inferior, inadequate, and outcompeted in the workplace.

You sleep around with strangers and friends alike. It makes me feel like a statistic, a number, a mere conquest, objectified, not special, insecure, and unsafe.

In short: you are too much like the men of yore!

Ask any man: <u>women went too far</u>. Too far not in terms of rights or equal pay (US Soccer Federation).

But in terms of militancy (zero sum game, men as the enemy);

aggressiveness (reactance, defiance, in your face);

usurpation of masculine traits, behaviors, norms, and roles;

and raunch culture (gratuitous, "empowering" promiscuity).

Men are hitting back:

Domestic violence laws repealed in Russia

Women confined to home under a male guardian in Afghanistan

Roe vs. Wade right to abortion repealed in the USA

Toxic masculinity (MGTOW, incels, redpillers, dating coaches).

116.

<u>ROCD (Relationship Obsessive-compulsive Disorder)</u> includes two common presentations: relationship-centered and partner-focused obsessive compulsive symptoms.

People with relationship-centered obsessions often feel overwhelmed by doubts and worries focused on their feelings towards their partner, their partner's feelings towards them, and the "rightness" of the relationship experience. They may repeatedly find themselves thinking "Is this the right relationship for me?", "This is not real love!", "Do I feel 'right'?", and "Does my partner really love me?"

People who present with partner-focused obsessions may focus on their partner's physical features (e.g., "Her nose is too big."), social qualities (e.g., "He is not social enough"; "She does not have what it takes to succeed in life."), or personality attributes, such as morality, intelligence, or emotional stability (e.g., "She is not intelligent enough", "He is not emotionally stable")."

LITERATURE

1. Relationship OCD By Guy Doron, PhD, and Danny Derby, PhD
This article was initially published in the Fall 2014 edition of the OCD
Newsletter.

2. Doron, G., Derby, D., & Szepsenwol. O. (2014). Relationship obsessive-
compulsive disorder (ROCD): A conceptual framework. Journal of
Obsessive-Compulsive and Related Disorders, 3, 169-180.

117.

The three solutions to the Gender Wars offered by third and fourth wave
feminism are:

Standardization: women should retain traditional gender role, one standard
should apply to all

Emasculation: men should become more feminine even as women become
more masculine (stalled revolution)

Masculinization: women should emulate men and outman them (raunch
culture, slut walks).

Consequence:

Marriage, cohabitation, childbirth rates, and even sex fell off a cliff. About
one third of women and men are lifelong singles. Another third are
involved in ephemeral pseudo-relationships, including dead marriages.
40% are raised in single parent poverty-stricken households, most of them
headed by women.

Men and women walked away.

How did we get here?

Until 17th century enlightenment, men and women shared work and home
alike. Muscles provided men with an advantage, so patriarchy was formed.

French revolution and revolutions of 1848 emancipated women for a while
and rendered them revolutionaries: they entered the public sphere

As the home was hollowed out, its functions outsourced, work and home became two distinct spheres.

Work for men was Darwinian jungle and survival of the fittest. Home was the sanctuary. Women's role was to comfort men and socialize boys and girls with traditional gender roles.

Women extended this domesticity to the public sphere, adopting social causes and entering caring professions, like nursing and teaching which used to be male enclaves.

The two world wars pushed women even further into male roles.

The first two waves of feminism were concerned with equity and equality: the franchise; property ownership; access to education, healthcare and the workplace; equal wages; anti-porn and anti-prostitution.

The third wave was about empowerment: women should do whatever made them feel empowered even if it meant conforming to male chauvinistic stereotypes, sex work, and self-objectification via sex and porn, including self-porn and group sex.

Problem is: women want to have the cake and eat it. They want to lead an emancipated, career-centred, and promiscuous lifestyle followed by a reversion to traditional gender roles.

But traditional gender roles depends crucially on purity, especially sexual purity - and on dedication to the domestic sphere. Women gave up the first and, having spent decades as singles, they lack the skillset for domestic, committed, long-term intimacy. Dating is extinct replaced with rare and disappointing hookups, replete with bad sex for women (the orgasm gap).

118.

Profile of the life of a modern woman:

She spends most of her time working, sometimes trapped in jobs she hates or with people she detests (it is called her career);

She is burdened with a mountain of crippling debt;

She deliberately acts and dresses as a "slut" to attract men (it is called sex positivity or raunch culture);

She has one night stands with total strangers (hookups) and near strangers ("dates");

Irregularly and infrequently, she has sex with friends with benefits or a reluctant temporary "intimate" partner;

One in ten offer sex on camera even to random men: that's how desperate they are;

One in 12 participate in degrading group sex and kink when they don't want to. A shocking one third are sexually assaulted;

She fleets and flees from one pseudo-relationship to another. Most of these liaisons end up being sexless, abusive, and last a few months only;

She has 90% fewer best friends than in the 1980s;

She is far more likely to drink heavily regularly and to suffer from mental health disorders: mood, anxiety, and substance abuse;

She is 31% likely to remain a lifelong single and 60% likely to divorce more than once or be a single mother;

She is 20% likely to be childless. Increasingly, she gets pregnant via donor sperm in an IVF procedure.

Well done, third wave feminism. Women have arrived for sure: they have become men and are "empowered".

## 119.

Excerpts from a 4(!) hours interview with a <u>ferocious third wave feminist</u>.

The language used to describe sex is male-centric: penetration, not engulfment. No difference of importance or involvement between key and lock, protein and receptor, or substrate and reagent.

Couples are sexless because sex decoupled from intimacy and associated with risk and novelty (sex positivity).

Casual sex is nothing new, but today it is the dominant/exclusive practice and sexual script, not optional. And casual sex is in lieu of relationships, intended to delay commitment owing, perhaps to fear of divorce (intergenerational trauma).

120.

In a NEW BOOK BY A WOMAN, the world would be a far better place if all men were to perish overnight ("The Men" by Sandra Newman).

If a man were to write a similar novel about women - he would have been arrested by the FBI for <u>hate crimes</u>.

Feminism is fast becoming a death cult and it is ruining men and women alike.

Time to reverse and criminalize its sicker manifestations such as misandry and "sex positivity". Toxic femininity is illegitimate.

There is a male-led backlash around the world. Alas, it is as reactionary and dark as some second wave and all third wave feminism: banning abortions (USA), legalizing domestic violence (Russia), and preventing girls from attending school (Afghanistan) come to mind.

Add to this patriarchal whiplash rabid misogyny in the form of toxic masculinity online (MGTOW, incels, piller red and black, "dating" coaches) and the inter-gender scene of growing belligerence becomes menacing.

Men have been subjugating and abusing women for millennia. Now, driven by a patriarchal hangover of guilt and shame, most males refuse to set clear boundaries to female misconduct. But leaving the rules fuzzy helps sustain a double standard - another form of egregious abuse.

121.

<u>Gaslighting</u> is far more effective when coupled with trauma because trauma is disorienting and induces self-doubt and self-recrimination.

Of course, gaslighting itself induces trauma and so a self-reinforcing vicious cycle ensues.

122.

There is an odd <u>dichotomy in men</u>. On the one hand, most men are predatory. One third of them admit that they would rape a woman if they could get away with it.

Men have sex with unconscious intoxicated women, underage terrified girls, mentally ill and intellectually challenged lasses. Anything goes.

In most casual sexual encounters, men force women to engage in degrading and painful sex acts.

About one quarter of first dates end in sexual assault: men become aggressive when denied sex.

But men also confess in studies to loneliness, seeking a long-term committed relationships, wanting to meet hookup partners more than once.

Men complain that women are now the ones who rebuff their advances, ghost and block them after a one night stand, refuse to date, and, in general, are heartless and emotionless sexual users. Men also use sex for nonautonomus reasons such as to boost their self-esteem or be accepted and accoladed by peers.

It is difficult to reconcile these two conflicting sets of data.

123.

<u>Women always held the ultimate power</u>, even at the height of the patriarchy. All a woman had to do to destroy her family, clan, or tribe was act promiscuously. In societies based on shame or reputation this was a nuclear weapon.

124.

<u>Loving the wrong person</u> can be bad for your health. There are 3 ways to overcome such unhealthy obsession:

1. Meet them frequently. The mundane and the pedestrian will erode the

idealized and mythologized image and bad memories will supplant counterfactual nostalgia;

2. To wait. Time heals. Memories and introjects fade. Perspective and proportion regained help to weaken the sick bond;

3. Let someone else enter your life. New intense emotions often displace old ones. Recent memories crowd out older ones.

125.

Women and men adopted the same type of toxic masculinity and became a unigender. Capitalism and technology encourage consumers to be atomized, narcissistic, and self-sufficient in order to secure sempiternal economic growth.

126.

To him, a woman was an intoxicating swirl of scents and tastes and textures;

her face a topography of his desire;

its smooth elevations and depressions, the delectable vicissitudes of hope and ineluctable despair;

her eyes a drowning invitation, a shimmering freedom, a matching pair of wishing wells.

127.

Men suffer from sexual overperception: they misinterpret feminine kindness as an invitation to copulate.

Histrionics suffer from intimacy overperception: they misinterpret attention as an invitation to fall in love.

128.

Contradictory expectations from one's intimate partner are unrealistic. No single person can be a passionate, exciting lover; an empathic, patient friend; a stalwart companion; a good father/mother, cook, and handyperson; an intellectual equal; an adventurer; a stable breadwinner; and myriad other functions besides.

Hence the need to outsource and the recurrence of emotional and sexual affairs, the disruptive outcomes of overwhelming, all-pervasive ennui.

Continued here: http://www.narcissistic-abuse.com/marriage.html

Return

# Narcissists, Psychopaths, And Other Predators

732.

In my work with <u>alcoholics</u>, I found these three simple steps to be very potent (they are elements of aversive therapy):

1. Wrap every bottle of alcohol in a white sheet of paper. Make finger width marks on the paper. As you pour out of the bottle, scissor out the part of the paper which represents the consumed alcohol.

2. Start a drinking diary. Note down every single drink: the hour of the day, type of alcohol, the precise quantity, the aftermath (how did it make you feel psychologically and physiologically).

Start your day every day by reading ALL the previous entries in your journal.

3. Aim to reduce your drinking by 10% of the residual quantity a day. In other words: 10% of the total on the first day, 10% of the remaining 90% on the second day, 10% of the remaining 81% on the third day, etc.

Good luck. Try these steps. They take little time and are surprisingly efficient at modifying drinking habits.

733.

The elements of the <u>Dark Triad</u> personality include Machiavellianism, subclinical narcissism, and subclinical psychopathy. The Dark Tetrad added everyday sadism. I propose a new construct: the Dark Pentagram Personality which will incorporate borderline personality and covert narcissism, but not everyday sadism (which overlaps psychopathy).

734.

The <u>cerebral narcissist</u> may be celibate, but he is not asexual.

He is not interested in sex per se, only as a way to:

1. Prove to himself his uniqueness and irresistibility (which is why he avoids casual sex with promiscuous women); or

2. Get a woman to fall in love with him and them reject her offhand and push her to cheat on him in her desperation and pain; or

3. Establish a new shared fantasy for the provision of 2 out of 3 Ss: services and narcissistic or sadistic supply- but not sex.

In long term shared fantasies, cerebral narcissists often develop ED (erectile dysfunction) or PE (premature ejaculation) as well as disinterest in or even aversion to sex.

The cerebral's callous misconduct is often misinterpreted as misogyny, but actually it is a compulsive reenactment of earlier childhood conflicts with a parental figure or caregiver.

735.

Fraternities are associations of mostly white, affluent, privileged, straight male students, ensconced in their own housing, and granted a monopoly on serving alcohol and throwing all night parties on campus. Sororities are denied these concessions. So much for gender studies and women's lib lip service in higher education.

Since their inception, fraternities have been cesspools and incubators of toxic masculinity and misogyny: gang rapes and sexual assaults are par for the course - as is hazing.

The only reason these miasmas are left to fester is money, capitalism's sole divinity.

Fraternities save colleges the need to invest in dormitories. They serve to promote and reify the "fun" aspect of collegiate life and thus constitute a selling point in student recruitment. Their alumni donate four to five times more money to their alma maters that non-frats.

When education is considered just another business, money talks and the patriarchy is on full display, as virulently alive as ever.

736.

In 1997, I coined the phrase: "narcissism epidemic". It is now endemic: the new normal and bon ton. We are all suffering from its aftereffects one way or another. Like so many lemmings, we are headed off a cliff. Is there hope? A solution?

Interview with Saralee Cassidy on the FlowGrow Experience Podcast/Empower Hour, Limerick City Community Radio:

https://www.lccr.ie/podcasts.php

737.

Narcissists convert children into sources of narcissistic supply and parentify them. They treat them as extensions of themselves and weaponize them in their attempts to destroy you and get back at you.

738.

Richard Grannon summarizes my insights perfectly: "The narcissist, be they male or female, becomes your mother and they are inviting you to become their mother and now you are in this symbiosis of feeding each other narcissistic supply".

The full convo is available on both our channels.

739.

In relationships with borderlines, the narcissist offers unconditional love and parentifies himself: the borderline stands in for his dead mother and affords him a second chance to fix/heal/rescue/save her and, by extension, himself.

In relationships with non-borderlines, narcissist and intimate partners both are good enough maternal figures in a shared fantasy ("fake family").

740.

Borderline twin anxieties: abandonment and engulfment. Both put borderline in touch with her schizoid core (emptiness), negates her existence

Approach-avoidance repetition compulsion

Sudden change in behavior:

At the beginning of the relationship, she feels focus of attention and in control (internal locus)

Then, daily life gives rise to the twin anxieties (external locus) and she reacts with acting out (psychopathic self-state).

Dual mothering

In relationships with non-borderlines, narcissist and intimate partners are good enough maternal figures in a shared fantasy ("fake family").

In relationships with borderlines, the narcissist offers unconditional love and parentifies himself: the borderline is a dead mother and affords him a second chance to fix/heal/rescue/save her and, by extension, himself.

## 741.

Psychopaths are hypersexual and use sex as a form of control within a power play (e.g., in prisons, corporate settings). But Both cerebral and somatic narcissists are asexual.

The cerebral prides himself on his superior ability to resist sex. He renders his dysfunction an ideology and encrusts it with his grandiosity.

The somatic weaponizes and instrumentalizes sex as a form of instant narcissistic supply. Its sole purpose is to reaffirm his irresistibility through an endless stream of conquests and his pyrotechnic sexual prowess.

Both types are predatory and use sex as a form of "false advertising" intended to acquire partners for their shared fantasies. Mission accomplished, both go sexless within the dyad: the cerebral becomes abstinent and the somatic cheats profusely.

## 742.

Narcissism is glorified and glamorized. The narcissist is a predator who masquerades as a good enough mother and makes you fall in love with your idealized self through his gaze.

## 743.

Narcissist's introject muted, yours active and vociferous.

<u>Narcissist theatre play</u>: he scripts and directs, you act and prop (external locus of control)

Current advice wrong, freezes emergent roles and, therefore, locus.

Reverse the roles: you script and direct, he acts and is a prop, whether he is physically present or not (introject).

Own the narcissist by appropriating his roles and then constellate/integrate the parts

Separation-individuation on the road to recovery and healing.

744.

<u>Narcissist Makes You Dissociate the Abuse</u> (Grannon-Vaknin Convo EXCERPT).

745.

I am putting the finishing touches to a cycle of clinical lectures on <u>addiction</u>, incorporating my new theory of addictions as neurological baseline states.

The 4 lectures are a cycle:

**1. Is Addiction a Disease? (1 lecture)**

Is addiction a biological disease or is it a socially-conditioned response? Is there such a thing as "addictive personality"?

**2-3. Personality Disorders and Addiction (two lectures)**

Addictive behaviors such as substance abuse are much more common in certain personality disorders. Why is that? What are the aetiological and psychodynamic connection and pathways between the two clinical entities?

**4. Emerging addictions: DSM 5 and Beyond (1 lecture)**

New addictions are added every day: to caffeine, to pornography, to the

Internet (social media), prescription drugs (opioids). Is this proliferation of diagnoses justified? The DSM revised the definitions of alcohol abuse vs. social and binge drinking. Has it gone too far?

746.

The narcissist is an actor in a monodrama, yet he is forced to remain behind the scenes.

The scenes take centre stage, instead.

The Narcissist does not cater at all to his own needs. Contrary to his reputation, the Narcissist does not "love" himself in any true sense of this loaded word.

The narcissist feeds off other people who hurl back at him an image that he projects to them. This is their sole function in his world : to reflect his False Self, to admire him, to applaud his actions, even to detest and fear him - in a word, to assure him that he exists by giving him constant attention.

Otherwise, the narcissist feels that they have no right to tax his time, energy, or emotions.

In the essay, I survey the main body of research about Narcissism.

The Frequently Asked Questions deal with various aspects of narcissistic (often abusive) behavior, traits, personality, and style - and there is much more in the journal entries and in the hundreds of excerpts from the Narcissistic Abuse Study List.

747.

In 1995, I coined the phrase "narcissistic abuse" to describe a subtype of abusive behavior that was all-pervasive (across multiple areas of life) and involved a plethora of behaviors and manipulative or coercive techniques.

The narcissist's superego is comprised of infantile, harsh, sadistic introjects. It is frozen in time, in an early stage of personal development, devoid of reflective self-awareness. It is much closer to the Id and leverages its aggression against the self.

The True Self in the unconstellated (unintegrated) precursor to the Self. It includes introjected object-representation (voices and inner objects – "avatars" – which represent caregivers, such as parental figures).

Full interview on the News Intervention website.

748.

Charles Bowes-Taylor (http://www.narcissism.co.za) and Sam Vaknin discuss narcissistic abuse from the narcissist's point of view.

749.

Developed by Sam Vaknin, Cold Therapy is based on two premises: (1) That narcissistic disorders are actually forms of complex post-traumatic conditions; and (2) That narcissists are the outcomes of arrested development and attachment dysfunctions. Consequently, Cold Therapy borrows techniques from child psychology and from treatment modalities used to deal with PTSD.

Cold Therapy consists of the re-traumatization of the narcissistic client in a hostile, non-holding environment which resembles the ambience of the original trauma. The adult patient successfully tackles this second round of hurt and thus resolves early childhood conflicts and achieves closure rendering his now maladaptive narcissistic defenses redundant, unnecessary, and obsolete.

Cold Therapy makes use of proprietary techniques such as erasure (suppressing the client's speech and free expression and gaining clinical information and insights from his reactions to being so stifled). Other techniques include: grandiosity reframing, guided imagery, negative iteration, other-scoring, happiness map, mirroring, escalation, role play, assimilative confabulation, hypervigilant referencing, and re-parenting. It is proving to be an effective treatment for major depressive episodes (see this article about the link between pathological narcissism and depression and this article about depression and regulatory narcissistic supply in narcissism).

750.

Drag your narcissist to attend therapy, of you must. But will it work or be of any use?

Interview with News Intervention.

751.

<u>Codependency is a form of displacement</u>.

The codependent is no longer emotionally invested (cathected) in her partner.

In fact, in many cases, she is averse to him and can't stand him.

But, she displaces her emotional investment (cathexis) onto the the shared fantasy of the relationship ("the dream of us that we had together").

The codependent gives up on her partner but is still strongly emotionally attached to the VISION that he had proposed and, therefore can't let go, becoming unboundaried, dysregulated, stalkish, dramatic, emotionally extortionate, and clinging within the rapidly deteriorating relationship.

752.

The narcissist induces in you a <u>dream state</u> by entraining you, takes over your unconscious, mirrors you as loving mother would, inserts himself as introject in your mind.

The guy in the thumbnail is Jacques Lacan - not Sam Vaknin.

753.

Richard Grannon (@richard.grannon) and Sam Vaknin (@narcissismwithvaknin ) event in Prague, on February 15, 2022.

Join us for free. RSVP assistant4film@gmail.com (write to this email address to present questions and participate in the event).

Part of the forthcoming documentary on narcissistic abuse (a phrase I coined in 1995) by Mark Vicente (@markvicente) and Scott Altomare (@saltosea).

754.

Counterintuitively, <u>aggressive or passive-aggressive defiance is often mistaken for codependency</u>.

The defiant mate has an avoidant-dismissive attachment style.

When confronted with demands for intimacy and commitment, he pushes his partner away and tolerates even her most egregious misbehaviors (for example: ostentatious infidelity) as long as she lets him be. He just wants her out of his hair.

This profound indifference to his partner's whereabouts and wrongdoing is often misinterpreted as abject codependency.

But it is actually a bid for agentic freedom and self-efficacious autonomy.

The perfect partner for such a person is someone who is transactional and equally averse to intimacy.

They both lead parallel lives, happily cocooned in their private worlds, and engage in occasional sex or a shared fantasy (future faking in the case of psychopaths) with each other and with extradyadic partners. Such pseudo-relationships are very durable and can last a lifetime.

## 755.

Ironically, the <u>comorbidity of depression with Borderline Personality Disorder (BPD)</u> reduces the incidence of reckless acting out and improves impulse control.

Depressed Borderlines have been mistakenly dubbed "introverts" or "shy, quiet borderlines".

Outwardly, like every other dysphoric, anhedonic, and dysthymic person, the depressed borderline is mostly homebound and listless.

But when the veil of depression lifts, her true character emerges: she becomes gregarious, promiscuous, a novelty-seeker, and a defiant risk-taker.

## 756.

The narcissist is incapable of attachment, bonding, and positive emotionality

He is possessive of his women only in two situations:

GRANDIOSITY/UNIQUENESS

1. When he is acquiring a woman and she chooses another man over him for sex only or for more, thus disrupting the process of co-idealization;

UTILITARIAN/INSTRUMENTAL/TRANSACTIONAL

2. When in a shared fantasy and he risks losing the 3 Ss that she provides him with (sex, services, narcissistic or sadistic supply).

Similarly, he is <u>interested in sex only in two situations</u>:

GRANDIOSITY/UNIQUENESS

1. As a somatic "player" in short term conquests (but not in casual sex with promiscuous non-discriminating women and not with the conquered women);

UTILITARIAN/TRANSACTIONAL/INSTRUMENTAL

2. As a cerebral in the lovebombing phase which precedes the shared fantasy (but not later).

757.

Dissociation (pay heed: do not use the wrong word disassociation!) and objectification are at the core of <u>separation-individuation</u> around the ages of 18-24 months.

Prior to the separation phase, the child is in a symbiotic state. He regards his mother as a part of himself. To separate from her, he needs to cut off this part and objectify it (render it an external object). He also develops transient grandiosity to be able to take on the world, all by its little self.

Narcissism is a failure of separation-individuation owing to a lack of boundaries between the child and his mother.

So, when the narcissist comes across a mother substitute (an "intimate partner"), he tries to recreate the ancient dynamic by forcing her to merge with him (absorbing her in order to eliminate her object status, her individuality).

He aggressively and grandiosely converts his partner into a self-object or an object representation thus eliminating her ability to separate from him - at least in his mind. He violates all her boundaries to negate her agentic autonomy.

I coined the phrase "narcissistic abuse" to describe this inexorable process.

758.

Men are using the Replika AI chatbot to create virtual girlfriends and then abuse them in public.

This is proof positive that the victim's role in an abusive relationship is largely incidental. Abuse revolves mostly around the psychological dynamics of the abuser.

In narcissistic abuse, the narcissist acts as a ventriloquist: he animates the internal object that represents the victim and misattributes to it his own voice (self-gaslighting via attribution error).

The external object (the actual partner) is erased and supplanted by an introject which acts as a self-object or object representation.

The narcissist also usurps the roles of harsh inner critic, sadistic superego, and rigid conscience in his victim.

Using entraining, the narcissist takes over the victim's ego boundary functions and becomes her external locus of control. He assigns to her the role of victim in his script.

The entire relationship is intended to recreate the dynamics of the conflict with the narcissist's mother during his formative years - but this time around with a different outcome: successful separation-individuation via the twin acts of devaluation and discard.

759.

The entire <u>relationship with the narcissist</u> is intended to recreate the dynamics of the conflict with the narcissist's mother during his formative years - but this time around with a different outcome and different power matrix: successful separation-individuation via the twin acts of devaluation and discard from an empowered position.

How does the narcissist attempt to bring these outcomes about?

In narcissistic abuse, the narcissist acts as a ventriloquist: he animates the internal object that represents the victim and misattributes to it his own voice (self-gaslighting via attribution error).

The external object (the actual partner) is erased and supplanted by an introject which acts as a self-object or object representation.

The narcissist also usurps the roles of harsh inner critic, sadistic superego, and rigid conscience in his victim.

Using entraining, the narcissist takes over the victim's ego boundary functions and becomes her external locus of control. He assigns to her the roles of victim and mother in his script.

760.

These 4 videos are an introduction to this <u>dialog with Richard Grannon</u>.

<u>Part 2 of this dialog</u> on my YouTube channel.

<u>Narcissism is a failure to exit the symbiosis with mother</u>, to separate and individuate. With @richard.grannon

Also watch "Deprogram the Narcissist in Your Mind".

Narcissistic Abuse Recovery: First Separate, Individuate.

SECRET Reason Narcissist Devalues, Discards YOU.

How Narcissist Steals Your Unconscious, Lures YOU into His Nightmare World.

761.

The <u>Borderline hooks up with potential partners</u> using two <u>self-defeating mating strategies</u>: she either offers the full gamut of sex immediately - or she reveals her mental illness by disclosing her personal history, decompensating, and acting out in a dysregulated and unboundaried manner.

The first strategy appeals to predators and players. They use the Borderline sexually, usually only once, and then move on leaving her hurt and dumbfounded, having succumbed to all their kinky and even lurid fantasies on a first encounter.

The second strategy attracts masochistic or savior, fixer, and rescuer types (watch my video on the Karpman drama triangle). But, exposed to her trenchant aggression, approach-avoidance and promiscuity, even they ultimately give up on her.

762.

<u>Healthy aggression</u> is externalized and sublimated: directed outward at people, institutions, and causes in socially accepted ways.

When aggression is internalized, it induces mental illness such as boredom, anhedonia, dysphoria, depression, and even suicidal ideation or suicide.

Infants internalize aggression when frustrated: it feels unsafe to aggress against mommy. When they separate-individuate, they also learn to externalize aggression appropriately and self-efficaciously (regulate their anger).

A failure in separation-individuation engenders fixated grandiosity and, in some cases, narcissism or codependency.

In these mental health disorders, aggression is both externalized inappropriately and internalized self-destructively.

This ambivalent duality is at the source of approach-avoidant behaviors and decompensatory acting out.

Cluster B patients first need to practice externalizing aggression with the aid of a transitory object (such as a punching bag) in a holding or containing environment (like therapy).

Gradually, they can move on to sublimating aggression, for example by becoming social justice activists, moral crusaders, soldiers, cops, surgeons, entrepreneurs, or other similar professionals.

763.

Counterintuitively, anxiety leads to either of two diametrically opposite reactions: avoidance/withdrawal or recklessness.

Psychopaths are prone to the latter behavior (yes, many psychopaths are anxious). It is a counterdependent reaction to the anxiety.

People with anxiety disorders also abuse substances to mitigate their anxiety.

By impairing cognitive-executive functions, substance abuse feeds into reactance and exacerbates defiance, risk-taking, and novelty-seeking.

764.

Interview with Joan Lachkar. She is the pioneering author of the groundbreaking, seminal books The Narcissistic/Borderline Couple, How to Talk to a Narcissist, How to Talk to a Borderline, The V-Spot, The Disappearing Male, New Approaches to Marital Therapy, and Common Complaints in Couple Therapy and How to Talk to an Obsessive-Compulsive (2022).

765.

Andre Green coined the phrase "dead mother" in 1978 to describe maternal figures who are emotionally absent, depressive, or self-centred, unable to provide the child with a safe or secure base.

Of course the dead - often narcissistic - mother does not perceive herself as lacking or inadequate.

She does not let the child separate from her and individuate because, as she vehemently believes, she is protecting him and guaranteeing his wellbeing and safety in a hostile world.

In Karpman's drama triangle, a mother who is not "good enough" (Winnicott) vacillates between the roles of abuser and rescuer/healer/savior/fixer.

Photos: me in different ages. Article title: "Everyone had studied the genius, Sam Vaknin, but no one asked his mother: How to raise a genius?"

766.

Rebecca Ray was 16-17 when she authored her masterpiece, "Pure" (aka "A Certain Age"). It is the best ever insight into the mind of a 13-14 years old girl with emerging <u>Borderline Personality Disorder (BPD)</u>.

767.

The narcissist implants his <u>introjects (voices)</u> in your mind, using abusive entraining. His voices, in turn, trigger your voices.

Here is a map of the narcissist's voices in your mind (D=Death, L=Life, G=God). First letter is his voice in your mind - second letter is your voice triggered by his voice in your mind:

D L (his narcissistic abuse-your survival instincts)
G G (his and your narcissistic defenses)
L D (his narcissistic abuse in order to separate-individuate, your self-sacrifice)

Death voice: You are not lovable, unworthy, inadequate, failure, better off dead.

Can be loved and deserving of life only if perfect (impossible)

Terrified of failure (performance anxiety), the narcissist rejects, disowns, sabotages, and avoids all aspects of life, rendering himself invulnerable by being dead within and without as a form of rigid, proud, defiant, sadistically self-punitive and self-denying ideology. S/he acts entitled and contemptuous (e.g., celibate).

He gives up on and denies his body, health, sex, romance, intimacy, all positive emotions, relationships, family, academic degrees, career, country, language, success, reputation, business, social life, fans, and friends.

With nothing left to take, death voice is appeased and ameliorated by my proximity to actual death, its mission accomplished and it is placated, content to let me decay and decompose inertly.

God voice: Grandiose, magical thinking, my mental illness (cruel false self) eroded by reality (injuries, mortifications).

Life voice: Creativity and cooperation are intermittent, haphazard, corroded by aging and is often too late, failing the narcissist amid cognitive decline.

768.

Communicate your anger honestly, firmly, but not aggressively (never bottle up or internalize your anger, never act passive-aggressively)

Describe your state of mind, don't blame, guilt-trip, or shame

Ask for change: new actions or behaviors or speech acts. Offer change in return, if need be. Be assertive, not submissive.

If change is not possible, acknowledge your anger (honestly point to your state of mind), identify its exact cause, and embrace your helplessness to affect the situation.

Narcissistic rage has two forms:

I. Explosive – The narcissist flares up, attacks everyone in his immediate vicinity, causes damage to objects or people, and is verbally and psychologically abusive.

II. Pernicious or Passive-Aggressive (P/A) – The narcissist sulks, gives the silent treatment, and is plotting how to punish the transgressor and put her in her proper place. These narcissists are vindictive and often become stalkers. They harass and haunt the objects of their frustration. They sabotage and damage the work and possessions of people whom they regard to be the sources of their mounting wrath.

In 1939, American psychologist John Dollard and four of his colleagues put forth their famous "frustration-aggression hypothesis." With minor modifications, it fits well the phenomenon of narcissistic rage:

(i) The narcissists is frustrated in his pursuit of narcissistic supply (he is ignored, ridiculed, doubted, criticized);

(ii) Frustration causes narcissistic injury;

(iii) The narcissist projects the "bad object" onto the source of his frustration: he devalues her/it or attributes to her/it malice and other negative traits and behaviours;

(iv) This causes the narcissist to rage against the perceived "evil entity" that had so injured and frustrated him.

769.


To participate in the seminar, write to: Barbara Gyura narciszcoach@gmail.com @narciszcoach


<u>Narcissist's Relationship Cycle</u> Decoded and What To Do About It

• Lovebombing, grooming, and honeymoon (Dual Mothering)
• Idealization and Introjection (snapshooting)
• Devaluation, Discard, and Separation-Individuation
• Replacement and Repetition-Compulsion


Narcissist regards himself as dream come true, god's gift to you, perfection reified, the ideal intimate partner.

How can he be so sure? Because he first idealizes you. If you are ideal and you had chosen him, then HE must be ideal, too (co-idealization).

When you deviate from the snapshot (the introjected internal object that represents you in his mind and with which he interacts), he has to devalue you to explain your discontent, betrayal, and wish to break up. He is the ideal partner, after all.

Someone must be having a bad influence over you, or you are crazy and stupid (a narcissist, probably), or you are going through a phase or a crisis and you will get back to your senses soon enough.

You, on the other hand, increasingly regard the narcissist as your worst nightmare. You cannot believe that he is so divorced from reality! Yet, he is. Totally so.

You also regard yourself as a victim while he considers you the winner of life's lottery. He resents what he perceives to be your constant carping while you resent his callousness and indifference to your suffering as well as his unwillingness to change.

You react to his nightmarish aspects while he fully expects you to react to him as you would to a dream come true. This mismatch in perceptions and expectations is at the core of narcissistic abuse.

**770.**

It is <u>impossible to love others if you do not love yourself</u>. All love is self-love: regarding yourself through the eyes of your lover allows you to apprehend yourself as an external object and delineate your boundaries, to become, to regulate your sense of self-worth internally, and to take on the world, becoming a better version of yourself.

Narcissism is not self-love: no self to love (Watch this: Ego is Opposite of Narcissism: Ego Functions) and incapacity to love (they fail to generate self-object or object representations). They can cathect, but never love.

Narcissism is self-loathing: the child rejects his helpless self and his lack of self-efficacy and is ashamed of it. He creates the False Self which is everything the narcissist is not. Narcissism is a form of dysphoria, prolonged grief over an internalized bad object.

Watch this: Real Narcissists are Covert, Grandiose Narcissists are Psychopaths.

Ego Dystony

Ego discrepancy (self-discrepancy theory)

Ego incongruency and depletion

Carl Rogers: mismatch between experience and awareness, tension between dreams and reality (grandiosity gap), feelings not aligned with actions

Humans are intentional, aim at goals, are aware that they cause future events, and seek meaning, value, and creativity: they seek to better themselves.

Narcissists are unable to empathize and suffer from severe emotional and cognitive deficits up to the point of failing the reality test. They are, therefore, incapable of love and loving.

Narcissists do not love themselves: they are emotionally invested in a fictitious concoction, the False Self and in the reaction it garners from their sources of narcissistic supply.

771.

How To Love the Narcissist AND Keep Him or Her? Two opposing strategies:

1. Be like his dead mother: cold, rejecting, selfish, absent, unsafe (triangulate, cheat, betray), approach-avoidant, fake. This leads to the narcissist trauma bonding with you in order to reenact early childhood conflicts and results in devaluation, discard, and replacement (separation-individuation) and then hoovering (if no mortification is incurred).

2. Be the opposite of his mother: conform to the snapshot.

Cope with Abuse: Background Noise Technique.

If You Love a Narcissist, This is For You.

Act as "background noise": ask no questions, never criticize or disagree, when addressed confine your response to the issues broached and do not introduce new topics into the conversation. In short: never initiate or be proactive – always react meekly, compliantly, and subserviently.

772.

Negative identity (in contradistinction to others): rejecting – including self-rejection - as MO.

Self-rejection owing to autoplastic defenses and self-loathing.

External locus of control: life out of control

Bad object introjection leads to: estrangement, catastrophizing, OCD rituals, addiction.

Focus on goal rather than process (life) is compensatory and constitutes self-rejection (I am not a bad object).

Some narcissists drop everything, decathect, especially in anomic, narcissistic societies where confusion reigns.

773.

BPD is an extreme form of complex trauma (CPTSD) which involves self-soothing behaviors, repetition compulsions, dysfunctional attachment, dissociative self-states, arrested development and infantile defenses (regressive infantilism and splitting), cognitive distortions, emotional-affective dysregulation, decompensation and acting out. The BPD's secondary psychopathy vs. covert narcissism.

The erroneous foundations of contemporary psychology: self, personality, individual should be replaced with seamlessly fluid self-states. Man is a river, not a lake.

Emotional dysregulation (and inappropriate or reduced affect) result in impaired internal reality testing and empathy deficits. In reappraisal and exposure therapies we use cognition to modify emotions.

774.

Watch parts 2 and 3 of the seminar on my YouTube channel.

Lovebombing, grooming, and honeymoon (Dual Mothering)

Idealization and Introjection (snapshooting)

Devaluation, Discard, and Separation-Individuation

Replacement and Repetition-Compulsion

Coping strategies when in a relationship with a narcissist

The aftermath: ridding yourself of the narcissist's voice (introject)

775.

The codependent needs to be needed (L. Rangelovska @reframingtheself) and the narcissist is needy (an addict). The codependent needs to feel safe by controlling the narcissist's godlike False Self.

The relationships between narcissists, codependents, and borderlines involve splitting, dysregulation, acting out, an external locus of control (no autonomy or agency, no independence or self-efficacy, separation dynamics and insecure attachment), and anxiety reducing behaviors.

The narcissist regards the Borderline as an enigma, a challenge, walking on eggshells makes him feel alive (a form of self-harming). Their mutual intermittent reinforcement (approach-avoidance) is play for power and control. Both externally regulate: a sense of self-worth (narcissist) or moods, affects, and emotions (borderline).

776.

<u>Can pathological narcissism be cured</u>, reversed, or modified? The last of 3 dialogs with @zukowska.daria

Watch 12 Treatments for Narcissists, Other Cluster B Personality Disorders (Borderlines, Psychopaths).

777.

The narcissist regards attending <u>individual or couples therapy</u>, however reluctantly, to be a major concession on his part. He demands reciprocity: you have accede to his demands the way he had catered to yours.

Additionally, the narcissist weaponizes every insight gained in therapy to cast himself as the righteous and hapless victim of a heartless, obtuse, negativistic, or outright malevolent partner.

He attempts to use this newly acquired knowledge and vocabulary to manipulate his intimate partners, past and present and blackmail them emotionally.

778.

Self-splitting: princess/Madonna vs. whore

Freud Father Complex (Oedipus and Electra complexes)

Studies: correlation with promiscuity and sexual recklessness in women. In men: lack of a male role model, feelings of inadequacy such as a lack of self-confidence and self-esteem, and a quest in adulthood to find father substitutes.

What are people with daddy issues looking for?

WOMEN: care, protection, approval, acceptance, understanding, support, validation, adoration, attention, worship, reality testing, unconditional love.

MEN: pampering, safety, regulation of sense of self-worth (grandiosity), unconditional love.

Both genders: "dead" father affects socialization and anxiety regulation, "dead" mother no separation-individuation. Or: extremely close, perhaps even disproportionately close, relationship with their fathers or mothers.

Etiology: Unhealthy Close Bonds , Sexual Abuse , Absentee Dads
Core beliefs about their worth, ability to trust others and feel in control of one's actions.

Repetition compulsions: approach-avoidance, abuse.

Insecure attachment styles and, according to Bianca Rodriguez, impaired intimacy template (intimacy cloud).

Amy Rollo, psychotherapist and owner of Heights Family Counseling in Houston, Texas:

• being anxious when you aren't with your partner
• needing lots of reassurance that the relationship is OK
• seeing any negativity as a sign that the relationship is doomed

Passive or victim position in skewed power matrix

Possessiveness, suspiciousness, jealousy, control

Separation insecurity leads to clinging, coercion, triangulation, emotional blackmail

Drama as way to avoid loneliness, facing oneself, and a kind of self-harming and self-trashing

LITERATURE

DelPriore DJ, Hill SE. The effects of paternal disengagement on women's sexual decision making: An experimental approach. J Pers Soc Psychol. 2013;105(2):234-246.

Inniss D. Emerging from the Daddy Issue: A Phenomenological Study of the Impact of the Lived Experiences of Men Who Experienced Fatherlessness on Their Approach to Fathering Sons. [dissertation]. Philadeliphia: Drexel University, 2013

Yoon S, Bellamy JL, Kim W, Yoon D. Father Involvement and Behavior Problems among Preadolescents at Risk of Maltreatment. J Child Fam Stud. 2018;27(2):494-504.

Find and Buy MOST of my BOOKS and eBOOKS in my Amazon Store: https://www.amazon.com/stores/page/60F8EC8A-5812-4007-9F2C-DFA02EA713B3

779.

Binary narcissism involves an overt structure and a covert one jostling for supremacy. Watch my videos on this much neglected topic.

One outcome of this sempiternal civil war is self-mortification. The binary narcissist maintains an internal "public" or "audience" (the aforementioned structures) and so experiences humiliating and shaming narcissistic injuries as mortifications.

This escalatory mechanism is the main reason for the brittleness of the binary narcissist: his False Self is disabled so often that he is unable to collapse and transition smoothly and seamlessly from one type to another. He remains stuck in a purgatory limbo, as it were.

780.

Don't stay in an abusive relationship just because: you or your family love your partner your in-laws or your mutual friends, emotional blackmail, to avoid failure, thinking you won't find someone better, your partner is apologizing and making promises, you accept that you not worthy of love (gaslighting), because you've been together for a long time (sunk cost fallacy), Because you hate dating or having to move, to maintain stability, your partner is a great catch, for money or the house, for the kids or pets, because you're scared of the future (catastrophizing), have false hope (magical thinking), you are too old, to avoid regretting it, to share the burden or chores, you feel guilty, terrified of being lonely and alone for the rest of your life, because of what other people might think, you are nostalgic for the good old days, or the sex is awesome.

781.

There is jealousy, there is envy, and then there is the Salieri effect.

Jealousy is about wanting to emulate someone and become like them. It motivates the jealous to study, hard work, and investment.

Envy is about eliminating a source of frustration, pulling him down to your level, reducing her to size. It is destructive and sometimes self-defeating.

The Salieri effect combines envy with a grievance, a gnawing sense of injustice. It results in aggression, rumination, or negativistic behaviors.

In the counterfactual movie "Amadeus", Salieri cannot fathom why God had bestowed upon the infantile and undisciplined Mozart the gift of sublime music and denied it to him, hard working, conscientious and diligent as he is.

This sense of injustice drives him to assassinate Mozart and descend into madness.

782.

Gaslighters use deja vu, jamais vu, and entraining via semantic satiation to take over you mind and compromise your reality testing. Here is how to fight back.

783.

Pathological narcissism is an organizing and explanatory principle on multiple levels: the individual, interpersonal relationships, and society. It comprises a post-traumatic condition, an addiction (to narcissistic supply), myriad cognitive distortions (such as grandiosity), and severe deficits in intimacy, self-regulation, and empathy.

But narcissism is also a positive adaptation in today's increasingly more dysfunctional civilization. Narcissistic traits and behaviors are elevated and glamorized, resulting in enhanced self-efficacy.

Narcissism is being normalized. It permeates every institution and discourse, every relationship and interaction, and every attempt to make sense of the world. Increasingly, people conform to expectations, rendering themselves increasingly more narcissistic in order to fit it, prevail, and thrive.

784.

Psychopath: If I pee here, all this will become mine.

Narcissist: If all this becomes mine, I will pee here.

Borderline: If all this becomes mine, I will pee everywhere.

Schizoid: I will never pee again if all this becomes mine.

Paranoid: Someone must have peed here before or else they would not have let all this become mine.

785.

Ironically and counterintuitively, people with anxiety disorders take risks, seek novelty, and act recklessly in desperate attempts to drown their inner tumult.

Self-harming and self-trashing involve these proclivities. They serve a dual function: anxiolytic/antidepressant and stimulant.

When she imperils and hurts herself, the patient feels maximally alive and awakened even as she forgets her woes and painful emotions and memories.

786.

Narcissistic Abuse is not your fault. There is nothing you can do about it. It is the outcome of internal dynamics in the narcissist's psyche.

Read "Hurt People hurt People" By Luke Elijah on Wellness Insider.

787.

Collapsed narcissist fails to secure narcissistic supply or even self-supply and they lose all their Pathological Narcissistic Spaces. Narcissists then switch from one type to another (type inconstancy: cerebral-somatic and overt-covert) as a means to secure supply. When type reversion fails, it leads to narcissistic mortification, grandiosity bubbles, decompensation, and Borderline-like personality.

These hysterical endeavours sometimes result in boom-bust cycles which involve, in the first stage, the formation of a Grandiosity Bubble, replete with self-supply. Long-term, this can lead to Binary Narcissism.

If even these don't restore supply, externally or internally, the narcissist opts for one of these solutions: The Delusional Narrative Solution, The Antisocial Solution, The Paranoid Schizoid Solution, The Paranoid Aggressive (Explosive) Solution, or The Masochistic Avoidant Solution.

788.

Psychopaths and dark triad personalities lie all the time about the FACTS and they are also deliberately deceitful, as a manipulative and goal-oriented strategy.

Narcissists rarely lie about FACTS. They do, however, confabulate: fill in dissociative gaps in memory with plausible or probable scenarios which they then come to believe and defend as factual.

Narcissists break promises because they are delusional: they confuse fantasy with reality and this renders them deceitful, albeit unintentionally so.

Psychopaths break promises callously and intentionally ("future faking").

Self-styled "experts" online often confuse narcissism with psychopathy and dark personalities. They misinform and mislead their audiences egregiously.

789.

There are two types of psychopath.

The "hot" psychopath resembles the Borderline in that he is impulsive, reckless, and anxious. He is aggressive and, sometimes a criminal. His life is chaotic.

Most secondary (factor 2 or F2) psychopaths are hot. Some of them even have empathy and emotions.

The "cold" (factor 1 of F1) psychopath is cunning, scheming, manipulative, goal-oriented, callous, and ruthless. He is devoid of empathy or emotions, but can be obsessive-compulsive and "anal-retentive" (addicted to order and structure).

790.

When the cerebral narcissist collapses, he transitions to a somatic phase. Then, gradually - it could take years! - he reverts to his dominant type (cerebral).

But how to tell when the reversion is occurring? Misogyny and misanthropy are the first signs to re-emerge in the switch back from somatic to cerebral.

The cerebral hates women virulently and despises all humanity as beneath him (expressions of underlying depression and anxiety). In contrast, the somatic is sociable, amiable, flirtatious, and hypersexed.

The cerebral is dour, avoidant, contemptuous, and regards all women as malevolent agents of inexorable degradation and mediocrity. He derives a sense of omnipotence by frustrating women and disrespecting them.

So, even when the cerebral collapses and is forced to become somatic, his hatred of women lurks in the background and manifests in bursts of brutal, demeaning aggression and ambient passive-aggression.

But, as a somatic, the collapsed cerebral's need for sexual conquests overrides his misogyny. So, he suppresses his murderous impulses towards women during his somatic phases. And then, shockingly for all the women in his life, he reverts to form.

791.

Presentation by @zukowska.daria in the National Interdisciplinary Scientific Conference "Faces of Psychopathology".

Brave topic: "Victimhood as a Form of Narcissism".

792.

The narcissist holds in contempt the very people he depends on for narcissistic supply.

He also hates himself for being so dependent on them.

And

He hates the people he so depends on.

793.

I. Loss Induced Dysphoria

This is the narcissist's depressive reaction to the loss of one or more Sources of Narcissistic Supply – or to the disintegration of a Pathological Narcissistic Space (PN Space, his stalking or hunting grounds, the social unit whose members lavish him with attention).

II. Deficiency Induced Dysphoria

Deep and acute depression which follows the aforementioned losses of Supply Sources or a PN Space. Having mourned these losses, the narcissist now grieves their inevitable outcome – the absence or deficiency of Narcissistic Supply. Paradoxically, this dysphoria energises the narcissist and moves him to find new Sources of Supply to replenish his dilapidated stock (thus initiating a Narcissistic Cycle).

III. Self-Worth Dysregulation Dysphoria

The narcissist reacts with depression to criticism or disagreement, especially from a trusted and long-term Source of Narcissistic Supply. He fears the imminent loss of the source and the damage to his own, fragile, mental balance. The narcissist also resents his vulnerability and his extreme dependence on feedback from others. This type of depressive reaction is, therefore, a mutation of self-directed aggression.

794.

As a child, the narcissist constructed an alternative (false) self because he felt that, as he is, his true self, cannot be loved.

Fast forward to adulthood, the narcissist still refuses to believe that he is lovable.

In his mind, intimate partners seek out what he can offer them and nothing else. Or they want to bask in the glow of his celebrity and accomplishments. But they do not - cannot - love who he really is.

When someone tells the narcissist that she loves him as he is, his core, not his false self - he immediately turns paranoid and imputes to her some nefarious agenda and ulterior motives. He becomes aggressive and rejecting.

If she insists and proves herself time and again, the narcissist devalues her: "she is too stupid to truly appreciate my genius or greatness".

This is the dynamic behind the schizoid phase of collapsed narcissism. Devoid of ostentatious narcissistic supply, with his false self shattered, the narcissist feels that there is nothing he can offer to an intimate partner. He withdraws into an avoidant, reclusive, and sexless existence.

795.

Narcissist is mortified when shamed and humiliated in public, in front of sources of supply or people he looks up to.

Narcissist reacts with narcissistic injury to loss of supply.

Borderline reacts with injury or mortification to abandonment or engulfment.

Psychopath reacts with narcissistic injury to frustration (he is goal-oriented, but unable to delay gratification, is impulsive and reckless), "losing" (or not "winning" in a power play or mind game like gaslighting), and being played or conned.

Narcissistic Injury

An occasional or circumstantial threat (real or imagined) to the narcissist's grandiose and fantastic self-perception (False Self) as perfect, omnipotent, omniscient, and entitled to special treatment and recognition, regardless of his actual accomplishments (or lack thereof).

Narcissistic Wound

A repeated or recurrent identical or similar threat (real or imagined) to the narcissist's grandiose and fantastic self-perception (False Self) as perfect, omnipotent, omniscient, and entitled to special treatment and recognition, regardless of his actual accomplishments (or lack thereof).

Narcissistic Scar

A repeated or recurrent psychological defence against a narcissistic wound. Such a narcissistic defence is intended to sustain and preserve the narcissist's grandiose and fantastic self-perception (False Self) as perfect, omnipotent, omniscient, and entitled to special treatment and recognition, regardless of his actual accomplishments (or lack thereof).

Narcissistic rage has two forms:

I. Explosive – The narcissist flares up, attacks everyone in his immediate vicinity, causes damage to objects or people, and is verbally and psychologically abusive.

II. Pernicious or Passive-Aggressive (P/A) – The narcissist sulks, gives the silent treatment, and is plotting how to punish the transgressor and put her in her proper place. These narcissists are vindictive and often become stalkers. They harass and haunt the objects of their frustration. They sabotage and damage the work and possessions of people whom they regard to be the sources of their mounting wrath.

796.

Cerebral narcissist regards himself as misunderstood and unappreciated genius.

Actually, he is depressed. His depression accounts for his sexual abstinence (no libido) around which he constructs a grandiose ideology of superiority.

797.

Borderlines switch between self-states. Self-states naming, Autopilot, "It wasn't (like) me, Can't place myself in the same state of mind or understand it."

Watch Borderline Woman as Dissociative Secondary Psychopath
https://www.youtube.com/watch?v=I01x0o_OISE

Self-states (not the same as Millon's or others's typology or taxonomy)

Classic-dissociative: separation insecurity, engulfment anxiety, Relationship obsessive–compulsive disorder, philophobia, low Self-monitoring, impaired transparency estimation

The shy or quiet borderline internalizes her struggles rather than externalize them. She becomes the exclusive target of her own turmoil. She "acts in".

Psychopathic Borderline/Dark Personality: violent/aggressive

Antisocial (secondary psychopath) Borderline: sociosexually unrestricted, compulsive sexting, transactional sex, promiscuous

Both the classic and covert borderline (many of the latter are men) act out.

LITERATURE

1. Front. Psychiatry, 10 December 2020 |
https://doi.org/10.3389/fpsyt.2020.514905

Executive Dysfunction Associated With the Primary Psychopathic Features of Borderline Personality Disorder

José M. López-Villatoro,  Marina Diaz-Marsá,  Blanca Mellor-Marsá, Irene De la Vega and  José L. Carrasco

2. APA PsycArticles: Journal Article

Borderline personality disorder as a female phenotypic expression of psychopathy?

Sprague, J., Javdani, S., Sadeh, N., Newman, J. P., & Verona, E. (2012). Borderline personality disorder as a female phenotypic expression of psychopathy?

Personality Disorders: Theory, Research, and Treatment, 3(2), 127–139. https://doi.org/10.1037/a0024134

3. Psychopathy and associated personality disorders: searching for a particular effect of the borderline personality disorder?

Nioche A., Pham TH, Ducro C, de Beaurepaire C, Chudzik L, Courtois R,

Réveillère C

Encephale 2010 Jun;36(3):253-9. doi: 10.1016/j.encep.2009.07.004. Epub 2009 Sep 26

4. The Journal of Forensic Psychiatry & Psychology, Volume 25, 2014 - Issue 6

Antisocial personality disorder comorbid with borderline pathology and psychopathy is associated with severe violence in a forensic sample

Richard C. Howard, Najat Khalifa, & Conor Duggan

5. Personality and Individual Differences, Volume 107, 1 March 2017, Pages 72-77

Students, sex, and psychopathy: Borderline and psychopathy personality traits are differently related to women and men's use of sexual coercion, partner poaching, and promiscuity

Roxanne Khan, PhD, Gayle Brewer PhD, Sonia Kim BSc, Luna C. Muñoz Centifanti PhD

6. Personality and Individual Differences, Volume 57, January 2014, Pages 14-19

Emotional dysregulation and Borderline Personality Disorder: Explaining the link between secondary psychopathy and alexithymia

Leigh E. Ridings, Catherine J. Lutz-Zois

7. Personality Disorders, 2022 May;13(3):288-299.

 doi: 10.1037/per0000504. Epub 2021 Oct 21.

Do my emotions show or not? Problems with transparency estimation in women with borderline personality disorder features

Celine De Meulemeester, Benedicte Lowyck, Bart Boets, Stephanie Van der Donck, Patrick Luyten

798.

I propose a new clinical entity in abnormal psychology: <u>Precocious Adulthood Syndrome (PrAS) or adultification</u> in people who were forced into adult roles in their childhood or adolescence.

It is brought on (etiology) via three vectors: chronic illness (including mental illness) of either the parent or the child; sexual abuse; and parentifying or instrumentalizing the child.

Later in life, PrAs leads to compensatory infantilism ("Peter Pan Syndrome") coupled with an impostor syndrome.

Adultified children grow up feeling responsible for everyone around them. They are incapable of having fun, never have had a childhood.

Adultified children become control freaks, are self-reliant, trust no one, and always get involved in conflicts as arbiters or peacemakers.

They feel the need to be "good, worthy, trustworthy, and reliable" even at the expense of their own needs (they are self-sacrificial).

They always feel either that their efforts are not appreciated – or that they should do more.

Consequently, some of them end up being passive-aggressive (negativistic) or even covert narcissists and "empaths".

<u>Adultified children resemble Borderlines</u> in that they engage in compensatory behaviors that are not calibrated and proportionate: reckless promiscuity and substance abuse, for examples.

Some of them end up being codependent, people-pleasers, and highly sensitive people (HSPs).

799.

The narcissist captivates you by infecting you with his/her narcissism.

Watch: Narcissism Virus Vaccine NOW: It Evades Your Immunity! Real Pandemic Is Here! https://www.youtube.com/watch?v=uczI-m4Zb9o

800.

<u>Predators</u> home in on your strengths as well as on your weaknesses and vulnerabilities.

They leverage your perfectionism, kindness, commitment, and love.

Both your shortcomings and your positive traits are chinks in your armor. Predators scan you with their cold empathy and then they penetrate your defenses and intrude on your mind, to the point of hijacking it.

801.

<u>Psychopaths and narcissists have moral cognition (moral judgement)</u> but, exactly like children, they make no distinction between moral transgressions and breaches of social mores and conventions.

802.

Full Interview <u>Resist Narcissism, Grassroots Up!</u> (Interview with Dr. Lisa Alastuey) <u>@lisaalastuey</u>

803.

Types of <u>identity disturbance or diffusion in Borderline and Narcissistic patients</u>: Cyclical, Allotropic, Object-related.

Autobiographical memory (narrative), dissociation, and core identity.

Splitting and other primitive defenses and their role in identity disturbance.

**LITERATURE**

1. Deutsch H. Some forms of emotional disturbance and their relationship to schizophrenia. Psychoanal Q. 1942;11:301–321.

2. Autobiographical memories, identity disturbance and brain functioning in patients with borderline personality disorder: An fMRI study
Paola Bozzatello, Rosalba Morese, Maria Consuelo, Valentin Paola Roccae, Francesca Boscob, Silvio Bellinoa Heliyon, Volume 5, Issue 3, March 2019

3. Psychiatry Research, Volume 271, January 2019, Pages 76-82
Facets of identity disturbance reported by patients with borderline personality disorder and personality-disordered comparison subjects over 20 years of prospective follow-up
Mohammad A.Gada, Hannah E.Pucker, Katherine E.Hein, Christina M.Temes, Frances R.Frankenburg, Garrett M.Fitzmaurice, Mary C.Zanariniac

4. Identity Disturbance, Feelings of Emptiness, and the Boundaries of the Schizophrenia Spectrum
Maja Zandersen, Josef Parnas
Schizophrenia Bulletin, Volume 45, Issue 1, January 2019, Pages 106–113, https://doi.org/10.1093/schbul/sbx183

5. Journal of Personality DisordersVol. 35, No. Supplement B
At the Junction of Clinical and Developmental Science: Associations of Borderline Identity Disturbance Symptoms With Identity Formation Processes in Adolescence
Shawna Mastro Campbell, Melanie Zimmer-Gembeck and Amanda Duffy
Published Online:June 2021 https://doi.org/10.1521/pedi_2020_34_484

804.

Reaction formation is when you behave in ways which defy who you really are and how you truly feel: a homophobic latent homosexual, an over-solicitous hating daughter, and overprotective resentful mother, an pacifist who is violent at heart, a Black Lives Matter activist who is a racist.

LITERATURE

Juni, S. (1981). Theoretical foundations of reaction formation as a defense mechanism. Genetic Psychology Monographs, 104(1), 107–135.

Journal of Personality
Freudian Defense Mechanisms and Empirical Findings in Modern Social Psychology: Reaction Formation, Projection, Displacement, Undoing, Isolation, Sublimation, and Denial
Roy F. Baumeister, Karen Dale, Kristin L. Sommer
First published: 04 January 2002
https://doi.org/10.1111/1467-6494.00043

805.

How does the Borderline lure and captivate you?

Drama (boredom, anxiety)
Approach-avoidance (Intermittent Reinforcement)
Suicide threats
Neediness and clinging, helplessness (gratifies grandiosity)
Idealization
Unboundaried Sex
Fantasy and Lies
Triangulation

806.

Cold therapy has come a long way in the past 6 years and is now a treatment modality for major depression as well as Narcissistic Personality Disorder (NPD). More about it: http://www.narcissistic-abuse.com/faq...

You are invited to attend a FREE 5-days seminar on Cold Therapy in Drobeta-Turnu Severin, the fairytale city in Romania.

To reserve your place, write to: samvaknin@gmail.com

Healing Narcissism: Cold Therapy Seminar (Part 1 of 11 - Link in Description), Vienna, May 2017 (watch the video on my YouTube channel).

807.

There is an <u>affinity between low functioning autism and borderline personality disorder</u>.

In both cases, the sufferer is overwhelmed by stimuli, external (autism) or internal (the borderline's dysregulated affects).

In both cases, self-harm serves to fulfill three self-soothing functions:

1. Reassert control over the dynamic of irritation and aggravation (via the elective act of self-mutilation);

2. Drown out sources of frustration and pain with even greater agony; and

3. Reawaken and feel alive as the self-inflicted hurt negates the erstwhile numbing.

808.

<u>Emotional blackmail</u>
Guilt-tripping ("I sacrificed my life for you…"), dependence-driven ("I need you, I cannot cope without you…"), goal-driven ("We have a common goal which we must achieve") and explicit ("If you do not adhere to my principles, beliefs, ideology, religion or any other set of values, or if you don't obey my instructions – I will impose sanctions on you").

Learned Helplessness

Learned or Acquired Parenting

External Locus of Control

Alloplastic Defenses

Grandiosity

Dysfunctional Responsibility

809.

The narcissist experiences periods of <u>collapse</u>: failure to obtain narcissistic supply.

The collapse can be subclinical (protracted and incremental as barely sufficient maintenance levels of supply are at hand) or traumatic (when he loses all his sources of supply simultaneously).

As long as the supply keeps coming, the narcissist is ego-syntonic. The collapse results in severe ego-dystony and dysphoria (often, depression). It resembles decompensation in borderlines (BPD) but, with the narcissist, there is no emotional dysregulation.

The narcissist then transitions from one type to another: cerebral to somatic or overt to covert. This is akin to the borderline switching between self-states when she is abandoned, rejected, humiliated, or stressed.

In the cerebral type, sexual abstinence is a form of self-supply: it makes him feel superior. It is the collapse-induced depression that drives him to become sexually voracious in a somatic phase.

So, contrary to the rest of humanity, in narcissists depression leads to enhanced libido (sex drive).

The types are highly dissociative self-states, almost distinct personalities.

For example: the somatic mourns the years of cerebral sexlessness while the cerebral grieves over the time wasted by the somatic in the relentless pursuit of sexual conquests.

Both of these types fail to recall the bliss they had experienced during the time spent as the other type, regardless of the "sacrifices" made. They misattribute the depression brought on by imminent or actual collapse to the compulsive behavioral constriction of the other type ("I was depressed as a cerebral because I didn't have sex" or "I didn't have sex because I was depressed").

Finally, both borderlines and narcissists experience separation insecurity (abandonment anxiety) owing to object inconstancy. Both also merge and fuse with an intimate partner in a symbiotic phase (the shared fantasy).

But the borderline distances herself from her partner owing to an overwhelming engulfment anxiety while the narcissist devalues and discards his partner owing to his need to separate from a maternal figure.

810.

The <u>diagnosis</u> matters - not the gender! Intra-diagnostic variation higher than inter-diagnostic variation. In other words: narcissistic women and narcissistic men are behaviorally different, but psychodynamically the same. Borderline women are very different to narcissistic women.

The diagnoses are gender neutral. Feminists criticize psychology and psychiatry as instruments of social control, a part of the patriarchy.

Find and Buy MOST of my BOOKS and eBOOKS in my Amazon Store.

LITERATURE

Gender differences in the structure of narcissism: a multi-sample analysis of the narcissistic personality inventory - Brian T. Tschanz, Carolyn C. Morf, Charles W. Turner - Sex Roles: A Journal of Research - Issue: May, 1998

Eagly, A. H., Makhijani, M. G., & Klonsky, B. G. (1992). Gender and the evaluation of leaders: A meta-analysis. Psychological Bulletin, 111, 3-22

Butler, D., & Gels, F. L. (1990). Nonverbal affect responses to male and female leaders: Implications for leadership evaluations. Journal of Personality and Social Psychology, 58, 48-59.

Carli, L. L., Lafleur, S. J., & Loeber, C. C. (1995). Nonverbal behavior, gender, and influence. Journal of Personality and Social Psychology, 68, 1030-1041.

811.

<u>NEW Comorbidities and Differential Diagnoses YouTube playlist</u> on my channel.

812.

Some <u>borderline women</u> (secondary or subclinical psychopaths and emotionally dysregulated), with or without a prior history of promiscuity (sociosexually unrestricted) embark on a spree of sexual self-trashing after they have been discarded abruptly and cruelly by a long-term intimate partner to whom they had been scrupulously faithful and who was the centre and pivot of their world.

Such self-harming can last for years or decades and deteriorate into full-fledged sex work.

By letting men - individuals and in groups - do with and to her body as they please, the brutally abandoned borderline is attempting to accomplish three goals:

1. Secure male attention and acceptance, compassion and affection, however fake and even if only for a few minutes;

2. Reaffirm her self-perception as bad, worthless, unworthy, whorish, and incorrigible;

3. Punish her erstwhile partner by cheapening and prostituting his "property".

Sexual self-trashing is non-autonomous, non-agentic, and self-objectifying. It involves copious and ubiquitous dissociation as well as self-incapacitating and disinhibiting substance abuse intended to help legitimize the self-harm ("I was drunk") and resolve cognitive and other dissonances.

Self-trashing borderlines, especially those who end up in sex work, create a counterfactual narrative of choice and empowerment. But in reality, such behaviors are lifelong addictions. Studies show that such women are unable to commit in relationships and they break up and cheat much more often than the average.

813.

Cerebral narcissists rarely have sex. By definition, any narcissist who is sexually active is somatic.

In the binary system of somatic-cerebral which often characterizes the period of switching, the narcissist cycles rapidly between abstinence and hypersexuality, a part of his approach-avoidance cycle (binary systems are dissonant and dysregulated and so resemble the borderline personality).

The cerebral's narcissistic supply is a sublimation of his sex drive (eros or libido). Consequently, a collapse and the ensuing dysphoria - his incapacity to sublimate - render the cerebral sexual again and facilitates the switching to a somatic phase.

There are <u>two variants of somatic</u>:

1. The shared fantasy, single partner one; and

2. The promiscuous subtype.

What determines which sub-species of somatic the cerebral turns into is his sociosexuality.

But subtypes can also collapse (fail), leading the somatic to switch from one subtype to another.

Finally, when all subtypes have failed, the newfangled somatic narcissist switches back to cerebral.

814.

The inimitable Grannon @richard.grannon and the sui generis Vaknin banter, howl, and generally have a good time as they <u>upset everything you think you know about yourselves</u> - and about the pseudoscience of psychology.

815.

The <u>narcissist requires 4 Ss from his intimate partners</u>: sex, supply (sadistic or narcissistic), services, and safety. Supply is a sine qua non and the others are optional on condition that at least one of them is fulfilled at any given time.

I have expounded on the first 3 Ss in many videos. But the new element of safety requires some elaboration.

The narcissist's intimate partner is a substitutive maternal figure. She assuages his separation insecurity (abandonment anxiety) by providing him with a constant presence, reliable support, and unwavering honesty, at least as far as facts go.

He interprets these as "unconditional love" and it makes him feel safe and in control of the situation.

Still, safety is not as constitutive as supply. It is just one of three options. Sex and supply are fine and so are services and supply or safety and supply.

816.

Even non-narcissists idealize potential intimate partners during the limerence and infatuation phases.

As time passes, they form a more realistic, integrated, and nuanced view of the other and this leads to one of three outcomes:

1. A long-term committed dyad;

2. Friendzoning; or

3. A breakup with no contact or communication thereafter.

817.

Narcissism is about YOU - not about HIM/HER. With @richard.grannon

818.

A relationship with a narcissist is a surrealistic experience, part fantasy dreamscape, part nightmare. What is real and what is imagined? How are you being transformed against your will?

Luke Elijah's YouTube https://www.youtube.com/c/LukeElijah/

Read "Hurt People hurt People" By Luke Elijah.

819.

The typical mass shooter is white, male, and young

The shooting spree is a spectacle, showmanship, movie intended to make sense of life and render them meaningful by imbuing it with purpose and a mission

Grandiosity is compensatory and connected to a general rise in narcissism and relative positioning (social media)

It is about immortality, not suicidality, about a legacy

It is a form of exerting control, empowerment, and anxiolysis

Shooters have no social skills: feel rejected, bullied, persecuted, humiliated, and a failure – real or perceived/imagined

The acting out follows a collapse and transition to a factor 2 psychopathic self-state

The role of echo chambers and confirmation bias

Aggression and the path to violence

Negative affectivity (hatred, envy)

Intimate grievances and strangers

820.

The new text revision (TR) of the DSM 5 includes several important changes:

1. Covert narcissism as well as malignant narcissism finally made it into the text;

2. The DSM 5-TR recognizes the parity between women and men in terms of NPD diagnoses;

3. Pathological narcissism is reframed as compensatory in nature, intended to offset deep feelings of inferiority, shame, failure, and inadequacy;

4. NPD is associated with depression, reactive to self-perception of failure.

But, unlike the ICD-11, the DSM 5-TR fails to transition fully from the categorical to the dimensional model of personality disorders and fails to embrace the emerging realization that all personality disorders are mere facets of one underlying condition, a single clinical entity.

Watch my <u>video on DSM vs. ICD</u>.

821.

<u>Trauma is contagious</u>. You can develop PTSD just being exposed to a victim's story (according to the DSM 5-TR). This is known as vicarious or secondary trauma. The risk is especially high if you had experienced a primary trauma. Reactions fall into two camps: avoidance or hyperarousal.

How to cope? Community and happiness (or wellbeing) are the answers. Seek help if the symptoms get worse.

822.

Narcissist is in a state of prolonged grief and misery seeks company.

<u>Exposure to prolonged grief is traumatizing</u>: transmission vector.

Endogenous vs. Exogenous dysregulation.

Driven to re-enact loss and resolve trauma with a maternal stand-in by recreating the trauma space (ideal Mom-ideal Kid in a shared fantasy engendered by secondary trauma).

Vicarious trauma fosters role reversal from Mom to Kid (infantile regression);

Narcissist as Mom can now abuse the Kid and disarm it (narcissistic abuse);

Once power and hurt asymmetries are righted, narcissist reverts to Kid and his partner is restored to a much less threatening Mom.

Narcissist now attempts to complete the separation-individuation phase from his Mom partner without fear of retribution from an enfeebled, shattered Mom.

He separates from her (discarding her or pushing her to abandon him) thus reasserting control, even at the cost of elevated anxiety (which he resolves by replacing).

Hoovering is outcome of unresolved conflict (introject permanence leads to attempts at restoring object permanence).

Watch Narcissist as Grieving Infant: It Affects YOU

Watch When Your Pain Traumatizes Others: Vicarious (Secondary) Trauma

Watch Why Narcissist Hoovers, Replaces YOU.

823.

: How a narcissist REALLY sees you: Doctor of psychology (who's also narcissistic!) reveals your emotions make them feel weak, you mean 'nothing' to them and they discard you to get back at their mother.

824.

Psychosis is the natural state in childhood: hyperreflexivity and internal objects=external ones.

If the external is terrifying (abuse, trauma), the child transitions to BPD where internal objects are external (psychoticism) and with a False Self which starts as external (special friend) and ends as internal.

This Self fragment or figment prevents full-fledged psychosis (a state of no self).

If the BPD False Self is attacked and disabled by abuse and trauma, the child attempts to transition to NPD.

NPD is mirror image of BPD:

External objects are internal (fantasy and delusionality) and False Self which starts as internal (grandiosity) and ends as external (true self vanishes).

This solution fails when reality intrudes and cannot be reframed and the False Self remains internal.

The child then transitions to psychopathy where only external objects exist and there is no false self or any self (unimpaired reality testing).

Decompensation reverses this sequence. Therapy can leverage decompensation to affect regression and fix the failures (second chance).

825.

Signs of imminent <u>devaluation and discard by the narcissist</u>:

Emotional absence, indifference, and coldness

Affected "civility"

Constant criticism and denigration

Passive-aggression

Unfavorable comparisons

Setting you up for failure and misconduct

Paranoid ideation and pathological jealousy

Sudden secret actions (financial or romantic)

Public disparagement and humiliation, also with common children

Sex withholding or degradation

Cessation of all joint activities, especially of a social nature

Pervasive distrust and micromanagement

Discard reenacts unresolved separation phase.

Individuation depends on devaluation (in order to preserve grandiosity and exit the shared fantasy) and externalization-projection (reversal of internalization-introjection). When either of these two processes fails, hoovering results.

So, emotionally, discard precedes devaluation. The narcissist hangs on to his partner only in order to complete the devaluation.

Devaluation resembles also the separation phase in adolescence: reactance (defiance), contempt, distancing, negative identity formation, approach-avoidance.

826.

<u>Discard reenacts unresolved separation</u> phase.

Individuation depends on devaluation (in order to preserve grandiosity and exit the shared fantasy) and externalization-projection (reversal of internalization-introjection). When either of these two processes fails, hoovering results.

So, emotionally, discard precedes devaluation. The narcissist hangs on to his partner only in order to complete the devaluation.

Devaluation resembles also the separation phase in adolescence: reactance (defiance), contempt, distancing, negative identity formation, approach-avoidance.

827.

Watch this first: <u>Narcissist First Discards You in His Mind, Then in Reality</u>.

<u>Why Narcissist Hoovers, Replaces YOU</u>.

During the devaluation and discard phases, the narcissist's attempts to hand over to you the introject (snapshot) that represents you in his mind, imbuing it with negativity (devaluation). It never works owing to the narcissist's introject constancy (intended to allay his abandonment anxiety/separation insecurity) and to his repetition compulsion.

828.

Narcissistic supply and perceived success (self-supply) are <u>aphrodisiacs</u>. When they are deficient or absent in the collapse phase, the narcissist becomes dysphoric (watch my video titled "The Narcissist's 3 depressions").

Depression is closely correlated with hyposexuality or even sexlessness (a transient subtype of asexuality). In this sense, all narcissists have gray sexuality and are on the a-spectrum (though, of course, not all asexuals are narcissists).

Normally, cerebral narcissists switch to somatic in order to restart the interrupted flow of supply. But when they have body image problems, this may take longer than normal.

829.

Narcissists attaches to objects (books, human bodies) and functions (the 4 Ss: sex, supply, services, and safety); borderline attaches to her regulated states.

Different but complementary functions of their shared fantasies: engulfing (narcissist) vs. being engulfed (borderline).

Dual mothership in operation in both types of shared fantasy.

Approach-avoidance (borderline) vs. narcissist's attempted separation (devaluation and discard)

Hoovering for different reasons (introject constancy vs. object constancy).

830.

This is a summary of my shared fantasy-dual mothership framework for the narcissist's intimate interpersonal relationships.

7 Stages of shared fantasy:

1. Co-Idealization (lovebombing, introject and narcissist all good because he owns object)

2. Dual mothership in a shared fantasy (recreation of childhood)

3. Need to reenact separation leads to mental discard which results in narcissistic injury (narcissist not omniscient, his judgment was wrong)

4. Devaluation of external object to restore grandiosity (make ego-congruent sense of the discard of an hitherto idealized object).

5. Devaluation of introject via splitting defense (introject now all-bad, narcissist grandiosely all-good)

6. Real life discard: projection of introject to you in an attempt to integrate it with external object. Projection-integration fails owing to abandonment anxiety triggered by introject inconstancy and your refusal to own split, all-bad introject. Devalued, split, all-bad introject remains as internal object, in narcissist's mind. This creates anxiety (bad object internalization-introjection)

7. The only way to reintegrate this internal object and reduce anxiety is by re-idealizing the external object and the corresponding introject. This is impossible if the narcissist has been mortified. He then departs from his previous version and reinvents himself which allows for self-idealization (grandiosity restored).

831.

SCIENCE, 31 Jul 2022
Dr. Sam Vaknin - the global narcissist database
From Sunday Morning, 11:36 am on 31 July 2022

Dr Sam Vaknin is the author of one of the first in depth books about narcissism and has a large database on narcissists which is now used globally. Not only is he an expert on the disorder, he's a clinically diagnosed narcissist himself, so he's got some good insights to share, and to beware of. He's now a visiting professor of psychology as well, and the author of the book Malignant Self Love: Narcissism Revisited. Dr Vaknin speaks to Jim.

832.

The narcissist invests emotional energy (cathexis) only in internal objects (introjects), never in external objects like you. This is because he feels safe only with internal objects: they never abandon or reject him. The introjects and internal objects are not constellated (integrated), so the narcissist has no ego or self. Some of the internal objects constitute self-states.

In clinical terms: the narcissist has only introject (diffuse narcissistic) libido, never object libido. He identifies with and cathects only his introjects, never a love object. He can never lose a love object.

If you challenge the narcissist's introjects or undermine them, you are threatening to take away his libido (his life force), thereby becoming his enemy (a persecutory internal object).

833.

All narcissists interact with introjects (internal objects), never with the external objects which they represent. They all seek introject constancy.

Depending on the island of stability, some narcissists maintain long-term constancy of the introject related to the intimate partner.

These are the "rocks" or the "special friends" in the borderline's world.

The Borderline senses this long-term commitment to and investment in the introject and it is a source of object constancy to her, assuaging her separation insecurity (abandonment anxiety). It is also a fount of engulfment anxiety. This duality causes her to approach the narcissist and then avoid him.

She reactivates the narcissist's introject from time to time in her approach-avoidance repetition compulsion.

834.

My new proposed diagnosis - covert borderline - combines elements of pathological narcissism with classical borderline's.

Consequently, the covert borderline is subject to a greater range of anxieties than either of its constituents.

The covert borderline is capable of narcissistic injury and mortification and experiences the borderline's push and pull (abandonment vs. engulfment).

The covert borderline's narcissistic defenses serve him well, though. They fend off these tremors. They allow him to put on a facade of stability and imperturbability.

835.

Narcissism is a surrealistic landscape. It is so removed from daily experience and what it is to be a human that it defies comprehension.

Convo with Trisha Goddard of TalkTV.

836.

For a while, I call him Theo (his brother's name) to force him to adopt the perspective of a loving outsider. It also provokes him and riles him up and this reduces the efficacy of his defenses and resistances. "Estrangement" is a technique I use in Cold Therapy.

Vincent van Gogh has Borderline Personality Disorder (BPD):

Itinerancy, instability (professions, locations)
Grandiosity
Self-harm
Violent outbursts
OCD (painting)
Parasitic lifestyle
Dysfunctional relationships

837.

Richard Grannon @richard.grannon leverages Sam Vaknin's synthesis the concepts of shared fantasy, dual mothership, entraining, self-states, and introjection to come up with the beginnings of a fix for narcissistic abuse.

Richard Grannon's @richard.grannon amazing new course based partly on my new framework for understanding narcissism, narcissistic abuse, and borderline personality disorders:

https://www.richardgrannon.com/unplug-from-the-matrix-of-narcissism

838.

DAILY MAIL: "I'd rather be a narcissist than one of today's pathetic, self-pitying young women: Her ego knows no bounds but at least, says JULIE BURCHILL, she's proud of what she's achieved".

839.

Both narcissists and borderlines alternate between fantasy and reality - but their fantasies are very different. The borderline's is object (person)-

centred, the narcissist's is process (narrative)-centred. Moreover: the fantasies cater to the narcissist's and borderline's deepest psychological needs.

Richard Grannon's @richard.grannon YouTube channel.

840.

Questions I have never been asked before on narcissists, psychopaths, empaths, victimhood, fantasies, singles, and love. With the British journalist Eve Tawfik.

841.

Passive-aggressives are people pleasers who express negative affectivity (anger, sadness, resentment, annoyance, envy) dysfunctionally (by frustrating and obstructing others). Covert narcissists are focused on sustaining a grandiose, fantastic view of themselves - not on their negative affects (emotions).

842.

Narcissism is a critical phase in healthy development. However, if it persists into adulthood in its infantile form, it becomes a pathology and a dysfunction.

Full interview here: https://www.youtube.com/watch?v=ZM13rJpigjM

843.

External regulation by the intimate partner: of emotions and moods (borderline), of needs (codependent), or of narcissistic supply (inverted narcissist, a subtype of covert narcissist).

Inverted narcissism may be the outcome of arrested narcissistic development: the formation of the False Self is disrupted and incomplete and the inverted narcissist is forced to resort to and depend upon the False Self of another narcissist (her partner) in order to regulate her sense of self-worth.

The Inverted Narcissist is a co-dependent who depends exclusively on narcissists (narcissist-co-dependent). If you are living with a narcissist,

have a relationship with one, if you are married to one, if you are working
with a narcissist, etc. – it does NOT mean that you are an inverted
narcissist.

To "qualify" as an inverted narcissist, you must CRAVE to be in a
relationship with a narcissist, regardless of any abuse inflicted on you by
him/her. You must ACTIVELY seek relationships with narcissists and
ONLY with narcissists, no matter what your (bitter and traumatic) past
experience has been. You must feel EMPTY and UNHAPPY in
relationships with ANY OTHER kind of person. Only then, and if you
satisfy the other diagnostic criteria of a Dependent Personality Disorder,
can you be safely labelled an "inverted narcissist".

844.


Psychopathic (malignant or antisocial) narcissists are far less adept at
acting and pretending. They are too grandiosely contemptuous of everyone
to bother to fake empathy, compassion, and modesty (which run of the mill
narcissists often do).

Their reactance (defiance) prevents them from fitting in, team work, or
accommodating others. Even the need to secure narcissistic supply is not
compelling enough to motivate them to act prosocially. They are never
nice.

Consequently, they are far more likely to suffer disruptions in the flow of
narcissistic supply and the ensuing dysphorias (depressions) that
accompany such impediments.

Whenever the narcissist is depressed, he becomes asexual. He loses his sex
drive altogether. Depression has an antilibidinal effect on the narcissist.

Inevitably, psychopathic narcissists end up spending a much bigger portion
of their adult life sexless than any other type of narcissist.

845.

Here is one of the most narcissistic texts ever (from the "Little Prince" by
Antoine de Saint-Exupéry):

"(To other roses) You're beautiful, but you're empty...One couldn't die for
you. Of course, an ordinary passerby would think my rose looked just like

you. But my rose, all on her own, is more important than all of you together, since she's the one I've watered. Since she's the one I put under glass, since she's the one I sheltered behind the screen. Since she's the one for whom I killed the caterpillars (except the two or three butterflies). Since she's the one I listened to when she complained, or when she boasted, or even sometimes when she said nothing at all. Since she's my rose."

The rose ("MY rose") is merely an inert object in a fantasy. The Little "Prince" doesn't give a shit about the rose. He is attached to his INVESTMENT in the rose, to HIS memories of the rose. HIS, HIS, HIS. It is all about HIM. The rose is made special (idealized) BECAUSE OF HIM!

A typical narcissistic shared fantasy.

846.

<u>Narcissism is a critical phase in healthy development</u>. However, if it persists into adulthood in its infantile form, it becomes a pathology and a dysfunction.

Full interview with @richard.grannon on my channel.

Richard Grannon's YouTube channel
https://www.youtube.com/c/RICHARDGRANON

847.

Donald W. Winnicott, the famous paediatrician turned psychoanalyst, suggested that <u>abused and traumatized children</u> dare not hope for love. To protect themselves against disappointment, they hate others ostentatiously and desire to be hated in return. It is their way of testing the waters: can these people or institutions hate the child without resorting to maltreatment and rejection?

Epictetus: Men are disturbed not by events, but by the views which they take of them.

Albert Ellis, founder of REBT, precursors to CBT: experience causes no specific emotional reaction, the individual's belief system produces the reaction.

Harry Stack Sullivan: people are products of their environment.

Boris Cyrulnik: trauma consists of the injury and the representation of the injury. Adult interpretations of events are the most damaging post-traumatic experience for children. Labels can be more damaging and damning than the experience.

Dorothy Rowe: when we are wrong, we self-blame and feel guilt, shame, helplessness.

Georg Hegel: consciousness of self depends on presence of the Other

Jean Paul Sartre: perception of the world, including of others, changes when another person appears, we absorb their concept of the Other into our own.

Jacques Lacan: the unconscious is the discourse of the Other.

Charles Horton Cooley's looking glass self (way we view ourselves based on how we imagine that other people view us).

Heinz Kohut: when child's needs are not met, a fragmented self emerges, consisting of the narcissistic self and the grandiose self.

Eric Berne: lifelong child, adult, parental ego states.

Fritz Perls, founder of Gestalt therapy: sense of reality created through perception, the ways we view our experiences, not the events themselves.

848.

The narcissist is focused on YOU - not on himself. He makes you fall in love with YOUR idealized image through his relentless, invasive gaze. With @richard.grannon

849.

The Borderline outsources to her intimate partner the regulation of her affects (emotions) and moods - even her cognitions (thoughts) and ego functions (such as reality testing and sense of self-worth).

This helps her to sustain the fantasy that she is perfect (buttress her grandiose False Self): stable, regulated, happy, functional.

With @richard.grannon

850.

All autosexuals (Erotic Target Identity Inversions) are autoerotic, but only a minority of autoerotics are autosexual. Autoerotism more frequently finds expression via activities such as same-sex partnerships (homosexuality), or incest (which is sex with the living expression of one's own genetic makeup). Gender dysphoria, transvestism, autogynephilia, autopedophilia, and similar paraphilias are all autoerotic.

REFERENCES

1. Erotic Target Identity Inversions Among Men and Women in an Internet Sample
Ashley Brown , Edward D Barker , Qazi Rahman

J Sex Med. 2020 Jan;17(1):99-110.

DOI: 10.1016/j.jsxm.2019.10.018

2. Autogynephilia: an underappreciated paraphilia
Anne A Lawrence

Adv Psychosom Med 2011;31:135-48.
doi: 10.1159/000328921

3. Erotic target location errors: an underappreciated paraphilic dimension
Anne A Lawrence

J Sex Res, 2009 Mar-Jun;46(2-3):194-215.
doi: 10.1080/00224490902747727.

4. Clinical observations and systematic studies of autogynephilia
R Blanchard

J Sex Marital Ther, 1991 Winter;17(4):235-51.
doi: 10.1080/00926239108404348.

5. Early history of the concept of autogynephilia
Ray Blanchard

Arch Sex Behav, 2005 Aug;34(4):439-46.
doi: 10.1007/s10508-005-4343-8.

6. Autopedophilia
Kevin J Hsu , J Michael Bailey

Psychological Science, November 29, 2016
DOI: 10.1177/0956797616677082

7. Autoerotism
The Freud Encyclopedia: Theory, Therapy, and Culture 1st Edition
by Edward Erwin (Editor), Routledge, 2001

## 851.

Never heard before tips on how to break up with a toxic partner (especially a narcissist) - from the horse's mouth!

Interview for Heartbreak to Happiness Podcast with host Sara Davison @saradavisondivorcecoach and Guest Sam Vaknin.

If you would like support for coping with any of the issues raised do visit www.sara davison.com for our online support groups and coaching.

## 852.

You are invited to attend a FREE 7-days seminar on Cold Therapy between September 19-25, 2022 in Drobeta-Turnu Severin, the fairytale city in Romania, including 2 days for Questions and Answers and additional material.

Cold therapy has come a long way in the past 6 years and is now a treatment modality for major depression as well as Narcissistic Personality Disorder (NPD). More about it: http://www.narcissistic-abuse.com/faq77.html

First day of 7 days of the FREE Cold Therapy seminar in Drobeta Turnu Severin, Romania lasted 4 hours rather than 2 because people had so many questions and I couldn't resist the narcissistic supply

Sam and the Introjects: <u>Group photo with some of the participants of the seminar</u>, the loveliest, liveliest audience I have ever had.

<u>Snippets from the Cold Therapy seminar</u>. Courtesy @steckerl_fisch

<u>Another angle</u>

<u>Back from the seminar in Romania</u> and on to Budapest (October 20-23) via Vienna (October 10).

Available for personal, face to face counselling in both locations on these dates.

So what does any of this have to do with the playful canines in Drobeta Turnu Severin?

Nothing whatsoever.

## 853.

Some <u>victims of narcissistic abuse</u> don't want your help, resent you for offering it, the shared fantasy is their refuge, too. They dread loneliness.

BPD God fantasy: I am the perfect intimate partner, beautiful, irresistible, fascinating.

There are six common fallacies of victims of abuse:

1. His abuse is actually a sign of love and commitment

2. HE DEFINES WHO I AM (HE MADE ME)

3. I AM LUCKY

I am worthless, damaged goods. I am lucky to have found even my abuser. If I leave the relationship, who else would want me and where will I find another partner?

4. THE BEST OF ALL WORLDS

Life is harsh and it doesn't get much better than this. The grass is always greener on the other side of the fence, but that is merely as an optical illusion. This is as good as it gets.

## 5. MY PARTNER IS NOT WORSE THAN OTHERS

Every other partner I may find will have flaws and quirks that I will have to get used to and accommodate all over again. Better stick with what I know. No one guarantees that my next partner will not be even worse than this.

## 6. HAPPINESS? BAH!

Life is a serious business. It is not about the selfish pursuit of elusive "happiness". It is about meeting your obligations and getting on with it. At best one can expect companionship and mutual support in old age. Anything more than that is self-defeating and destructive wishful thinking.

## 854.

The borderline has difficulties to maintain stable introjects (inconstancy) and so when the object (e.g., the intimate partner) is gone, s/he is out of sight out of mind.

The narcissist has difficulties to maintain object constancy (recognizing the separate existence of an external object) and so when the object (e.g., the intimate partner) is gone, s/he is out of sight out of mind.

## 855.

In Borderline Personality Disorder (BPD), self-mutilation and behavioral reckless self-harm fulfill four functions:

1. To numb dysregulated emotions and the hurt of real or perceived rejection or abandonment that threaten to overwhelm;

2. To allow the borderline to feel alive through pain;

3. To punish, defeat, and self-destroy the borderline as a self-loathed and self-hated bad object;

4. To punish other people for having failed to cater to the borderline's needs and succumb to her whims.

856.

New effective treatments for BPD as the disorder is being redefined.
Correction: 1:04:31 "This difference was NOT statistically significant".

LITERATURE

1. The hidden borderline patient: patients with borderline personality
disorder who do not engage in recurrent suicidal or self-injurious behavior
Published online by Cambridge University Press: 29 July 2022
Mark Zimmerman and Lena Becker
Psychological Medicine , First View , pp. 1 - 8
DOI: https://doi.org/10.1017/S003329172200...

2. Effectiveness of Predominantly Group Schema Therapy and Combined
Individual and Group Schema Therapy for Borderline Personality
Disorder: A Randomized Clinical Trial
Arnoud Arntz, PhD; Gitta A. Jacob, PhD; Christopher W. Lee, PhD; et
alOdette Manon Brand-de Wilde, PhD; Eva Fassbinder, MD; R. Patrick
Harper, MSc; Anna Lavender, DClinPsy; George Lockwood, PhD; Ioannis
A. Malogiannis, DrMed; Florian A. Ruths, DrMed; Ulrich Schweiger,
DrMed; Ida A. Shaw, MA; Gerhard Zarbock, PhD; Joan M. Farrell, PhD
JAMA Psychiatry. 2022;79(4):287-299.
doi:10.1001/jamapsychiatry.2022.0010

3. Effect of 3 Forms of Early Intervention for Young People With
Borderline Personality Disorder: The MOBY Randomized Clinical Trial
Andrew M. Chanen, MBBS(Hons), PhD; Jennifer K. Betts, DPsych(Clin);
Henry Jackson, PhD; et alSue M. Cotton, MAppSc(Statistics), PhD; John
Gleeson, PhD4; Christopher G. Davey, MBBS(Hons), PhD; Katherine
Thompson, PhD; Sharnel Perera, PhD; Victoria Rayner, BBSci(Hons);
Holly Andrewes, PhD; Louise McCutcheon, DPsych(Clin)
JAMA Psychiatry. 2022;79(2):109-119.
doi:10.1001/jamapsychiatry.2021.3637

4. Borderline Personality Disorder: 6 Studies of Psychosocial Interventions
Sy Atezaz Saeed, MD, MS; Angela C. Kallis, MD
Curr Psychiatr. 2022;21(2):18-26.

857.

Both try to dissolve you and eliminate your separateness, agency, personal autonomy, and independence

Either by rendering you inanimate and penalizing you for any deviation and divergence

Or by merging and fusing with you while outsourcing to you critical psychological needs and functions.

Both need to devalue and discard you:

The narcissist in order to reenact separation-individuation from a mother figure

The borderline in order to ameliorate engulfment anxiety.

Both of them become avoidant and schizoid at some stage.

The narcissist either because of deficient or negative supply (narcissistic injury or mortification) or to process a corrupted introject

The borderline in order to lick her wounds and develop abandonment anxiety sufficient to trigger another round of approach-avoidance repetition compulsion.

Should not be confused with Avoidant Personality Disorder which is an anxiety reaction to perceived or anticipated rejection – rather than a psychopathic reaction (like the Borderline's).

AvPD is connected to people pleasing, indecisiveness, schizoid states, and to risk and conflict aversion, hesitancy, and extreme self-doubt.

WATCH Hypervigilance and Intuition as Forms of Anxiety.

858.

Covert narcissist is a narcissist who develops Avoidant Personality Disorder in order to cope with a permanent state of collapse.

Major difference between Borderline and Avoidant: ACTING OUT (not the same as ACTING IN or ENACTMENT).

Bowlby's monotropy.

859.

Tele2 TV reporting about the Cold Therapy seminar in Drobeta Turnu
Severin. Reporter @andreealasculescu

https://m.facebook.com/Tele2drobeta2021/videos/667440637722165/?refsr
c=deprecated&_rdr


860.

Cats are psychopaths, a new study finds. But, if we were to apply some of
the same questions to our pet dogs or even ourselves, by the study's
standards, we may all be psychopaths!

861.

Available for personal, face to face counselling in Budapest on October 12-
13 and 19-22.
Write to: samvaknin@gmail.com if you would like to schedule an
appointment.

862.

Interview on the Heartbreak to Happiness Podcast with Sara Davison is
live.

Apple Podcasts: https://podcasts.apple.com/gb/podcast/interview-with-a-
narcissist-what-really-goes-on-in/id1542659968?i=1000581683232

Excerpt https://m.youtube.com/watch?v=tC_XXX94jac

Full interview https://m.youtube.com/watch?v=HyuLhMKWE0o

Instagram & Facebook - @saradavisondivorcecoach

Twitter SDDivorceCoach

LinkedIn https://www.linkedin.com/in/sara-davison-742b453/

863.

I am super excited to be back with Sam Vaknin and Richard Grannon for this one day live event where we will be discussing….

What is going on in the mind of a Narcissist?

How do you get into a relationship with a Narcissist?

Why do you stay?

How do you divorce a Narcissist?

How to coparent with a Narcissist

How to take your power back after your toxic relationship

How to rebuild your life and feel happy again

And much more…

Join us in person or virtually on 4th February 2023 tickets are limited and going fast!

Link to buy tickets in bio & below

https://www.saradavison.com/coaching/one-day-live-with-special-guests/

864.

The borderline patient requires an intimate partner who would partake in her approach-avoidance dance. Only the narcissist fits the bill.

When the borderline is in the throes of her abandonment anxiety (separation insecurity), the narcissist regulates her emotions and stabilizes her labile moods with his lovebombing and idealization.

When the borderline experiences engulfment (enmeshment) anxiety, he obliges by devaluing and discarding her, pushing her away.

The twin cycles are compatible and feed on and off each other.

865.

I talk to Andras Lacfi of Bronson Men about narcissistic abuse as distinct from all other types of abuse owing to its underlying psychological dynamics and why victim identity leads to aggression.

I talk to Andras Lacfi of Bronson Men about toxic romanticism and how it ruined intimacy and relationships.

866.

When the Borderline's intimate partner is enmeshed and immersed in her shared fantasy as the external regulator of her dysregulated emotions and labile moods, he is likely to internalize her inner turmoil, thereby ending up amplifying it.

Once he gets disenchanted with her, she is likely to mirror image his newly gained unperturbed equilibrium by reacting with dysregulation to his perceived indifference and rejection.

Finally, the dyad settles into a transactional regulatory valley when the Borderline re-idealizes her partner within a new halcyon fantasy or withdraws into a nostalgic state coupled with desperate attempts to hoover erstwhile partners or descends into a promiscuous whirl.

867.

The narcissist uses on you entraining, a kind of trance. Hypnosis may be a form of extreme empathy, a suggestible state of mind or a people-pleasing experience.

LITERATURE

Best evidence yet that hypnotised people aren't faking it

https://www.newscientist.com/article/2125645-best-evidence-yet-that-hypnotised-people-arent-faking-it/

868.

<u>Mate selection and attachment style</u> are two separate things.

For relationships to work, attachment styles need to match.

Impaired mate selection (choosing the wrong partners and then going on to have horrible relationships) is the core problem. It is typically the outcome of bad parental programming.

In our most modern approach to attachment, we divide all attachment styles to secure and insecure (avoidant).

Even someone with an anxious-ambivalent attachment style would be avoiding relationships and intimacy or destroying them because of anxieties and doubts.

My contribution is to suggest the additions of a flat attachment style.

Everyone has an attachment style. But some people have "flat attachment": they are incapable of any kind of bonding or relatedness at all.

Flat attachers regard other people as utterly interchangeable, replaceable, and dispensable objects or functions.

When a relationship is over, people go through a period of "latency": mourning the defunct bond and processing the grief and withdrawal symptoms associated with a breakup.

Not so the flat attacher: he or she transition instantaneously, smoothly, abruptly, and seamlessly from one (in)significant other to the next "target" and fully substitutes a newly found beau, lover, mate, or "intimate" partner for the discarded one whose usefulness has expired for whatever reason.

Many narcissists and almost all psychopaths are flat attachers. Borderlines, on the other hand, tend to sexualize attachment (sex is proof of attachment and assuages abandonment anxiety).

869.

1. I will treat myself with <u>dignity</u> and demand respect from others. I will not allow anyone to disrespect me.

2. I will set clear boundaries and make known to others what I regard as permissible and acceptable behavior and what is out of bounds.

3. I will not tolerate <u>abuse</u> and aggression in any form or guise. I will seek to terminate such misconduct instantly and unequivocally.

4. I will be assertive and unambiguous about my needs, wishes, and expectations from others. I will not be arrogant - but I will be confident. I will not be selfish and narcissistic - but I will love and care for myself.

5. I will get to know myself better.

6. I will treat others as I want them to treat me. I will try to lead by way of self-example.

7. If I am habitually disrespected, abused, or if my boundaries are ignored and breached I will terminate the relationship with the abuser forthwith. Zero tolerance and no second chance will be my maxims of self-preservation.

(From the book "Malignant Self-love: Narcissism Revisited" by Sam Vaknin).

870.

<u>Mate poaching</u> is mating strategy in societies or periods when there is gender imbalance or asymmetrical eligibility criteria in mate selection ("hypergamy").

Examples: active flirting and courting, sexting and camming (cybersex), trying to stop the couple from spending time together, and pointing out negative qualities of the romantic rival.

References

Davies, A. P., & Shackelford, T. K. (2017). Don't you wish your partner was hot like me?: The effectiveness of mate poaching across relationship types considering the relative mate-values of the poacher and the partner of the poached. Personality and Individual Differences, 106, 32-35.

Lemay Jr, E. P., & Wolf, N. R. (2016). Human mate poaching tactics are effective: Evidence from a dyadic prospective study on opposite-sex "friendships". Social Psychological and Personality Science, 7(4), 374-380.

Schmitt, D. P., & Buss, D. M. (2001). Human mate poaching: Tactics and temptations for infiltrating existing mateships. Journal of Personality and Social Psychology, 80, 894–917.

Belu CF, O'Sullivan LF. Once a Poacher Always a Poacher? Mate Poaching History and its Association with Relationship Quality. J Sex Res. 2020 May;57(4):508-521. doi: 10.1080/00224499.2019.1610150. Epub 2019 May 20. PMID: 31106590.

Davies, A. P. C., Shackelford, T. K., & Hass, G. R. (2007) 'When a "poach" is not a poach: Re-defining human mate poaching and re-estimating its frequency' Archives of Sexual Behavior, 36, 702-716.

Mogilski, J. K. & Wade, T. J. (2023) 'Friendship as a Relationship Infiltration Tactic during Human Mate Poaching' Evolutionary Psychology, 11 (4), 926-943.

Schmitt, D. P., International Sexuality Description Project (2004) 'Patterns and Universals of Mate Poaching Across 53 Nations: The Effects of Sex, Culture, and Personality on Romantically Attracting Another Person's Partner.' Journal of Personality and Social Psychology, 86(4), 560-584.

Schmitt, D. P., & Shackelford, T. K. (2003) 'Nifty ways to leave your lover: The tactics people use to entice and disguise the process of human mate poaching' Personality and Social Psychology Bulletin, 29, 1018-1035.

871.

Intermittent reinforcement creates ambivalence and dissonance. The abuser is perceived as TWO separate people.

Ambivalence and dissonance yield intolerable anxiety.

To ameliorate anxiety, you might fantasize about the abuser being dead.

<u>Killing the hated external object</u> preserves the loved internal object.

Another mechanism is to preserve both the external and the internal objects by redirecting your hate at yourself.

872.

Cerebral narcissism is a relatively stable construct across the lifespan. It involves early life sublimation so massive and all-pervasive that it renders the cerebral asexual, all but eradicating his sex drive (arrested sexual development).

Sensing his abnormality, potential sex partners shun the often creepy and robotic cerebral. In return, he conjures up a defensive ideology: celibacy is evidence of superior strength and women are contemptible.

Cerebrals become somatic following a collapse: when they can no longer garner supply by placing their intellect on public display or when offered an extremely rare opportunity to obtain quick fixes of narcissistic supply via sex.

As somatics, erstwhile cerebrals resemble sex addicts: from zero to hero.

But there is another reason for such a startling transformation: age and looming death.

The cerebral narcissist attempts to deny his age and fend off his ineluctable demise by having sex, preferably with much younger partners.

The cerebral being a narcissist, the sex is compulsive and autoerotic (masturbatory). The partners are mostly fungible and forgettable except when they are mentally ill (borderlines, for example) and cater to the narcissist's grandiosity as a "healer" or "fixer".

The shared fantasies then offered to these partners often incorporate a fresh start typical of younger ages: relocation, marriage, children, incessant travel, or a long-term relationship.

The cerebral turned somatic frantically thrashes about, trying to make up for lost time and missed sexual and romantic opportunities.

But as he inexorably declines, it becomes harder and harder to maintain the delusional self-deception and the cerebral ends up, often alone, in a degenerative schizoid state.

873.

The Borderline's <u>engulfment or enmeshment anxiety</u> has to do with her internalized bad object: the lifelong introjects that keep informing her how unworthy, unloveable, and inadequate she is.

Exposure to messages that countermand the bad object creates dissonance and the aforementioned anxiety. This leads to withdrawal, aggression, and avoidant behaviors.

874.

People pleasers, borderlines, and codependents have a <u>constricted life</u>: they subsist only through others and for others, vicariously, by proxy. Their identity is determined externally and is consequently sometimes disturbed.

If you suffer from this <u>syndrome</u>, to get better:

1. Establish a people-free time and zone. Banish all people from this space and from your thoughts for at least 1 hour a day;

2. Introduce structure into your life by embarking on a consuming task or assignment or by adopting a hobby;

3. Stop being emotionally invested in the past or in the future. Focus exclusively on the present. Use techniques like mindfulness, if need be.

875.

When faced with the Borderline incessant and injurious <u>approach-avoidance</u>, <u>tell her this</u>:

I am always here for you.

You are and always will be dear to me.

If I place boundaries it is not only for my self-protection but also in order to be strong for both of us

I will accept and respect any decision you make.

876.

<u>Narcissist's POV (point of view)</u> is the outcome of his internal dynamics,
especially the compulsive need to devalue and discard you.
Here is how he sees you:
You have changed
You blame-shift
I am the victim
You guilt-trip
You are not self-aware
You are self-destructive and you want to drag me with you
You are disloyal
You are looking for alternatives
You are out to get me
You are after my money
You lie, deceive, and cheat
You entrapped me
You never mean what you say
You gaslight me
You hate me while I love you self-sacrificially
You humiliate me and shame me, you are malicious

877.


Narcissists cheat on their spouses, commit adultery and have extramarital
affairs and liaisons for a variety of reasons which reflect disparate
psychodynamic processes:

1. In the quest for narcissistic supply, the somatic narcissist resorts to serial
sexual conquests.

2. Narcissists are easily bored (they have a low boredom threshold) and
they have a low tolerance for boredom. Sexual dalliances alleviate this
nagging and frustrating ennui. The quest for novelty, diversions, and thrills
– a vacation from his own life - is combined with a journey of self-
exploration and discovery that involves "filling in the gaps" in the
narcissist's biography: a missed adolescence, an old flame, a new aspect of
his personality.

3. Narcissists maintain an island and focus of stability in their life, but all the other dimensions of their existence are chaotic, unstable, and unpredictable. This "twister" formation serves many emotional needs which I expound upon elsewhere. Thus, a narcissist may be a model employee and pursue a career path over decades even as he cheats on his wife and fritters their savings away.

4. Narcissists feel superior and important and so entitled to be above the law and to engage in behaviors that are frowned upon and considered socially unacceptable in others. They reject and vehemently resent all limitations and conditions placed upon them by their partners. They act on their impulses and desires unencumbered by social conventions and strictures.

5. Marriage, monogamy, and child-bearing and rearing are common activities that characterize the average person. The narcissist feels robbed of his uniqueness by these pursuits and coerced into the relationship and into roles - such as a husband and a father - that reduce him to the lowest of common denominators. This narcissistic injury leads him to rebel and reassert his superiority and specialness by maintaining extramarital affairs.

6. Narcissists are control freaks. Having a relationship implies a give-and-take and a train of compromises which the narcissist acutely interprets to mean a loss of control over his life. To reassert control, the narcissist initiates other relationships in which he dictates the terms of engagement (love affairs).

7. Narcissists are terrified of intimacy. Their behavior is best characterized as an approach-avoidance repetition compulsion. Adultery is an excellent tool in the attempt to retard intimacy and resort to a less threatening mode of interaction.

There are two types of triangulation (using a third party to manage the emotional, intimacy, and transactional aspects of a relationship): breakup and restorative.

Breakup triangulation involves overt and ostentatious cheating with a third party in conjunction with other egregious misbehavior. Its aim is to irrevocably break up with a current partner.

Why triangulate rather than simply terminate? A myriad reasons: revenge, rage, community property, inability to let go (codependency), restoring the cheater's self-esteem, feeling desirable and alive again, obtaining succor and ersatz intimacy, or uncertainty about one's true wishes.

But usually, it is simply the desire to cast one's mate as the villain who ended it all because of he is insanely jealous and not magnanimous or empathic enough to forgive and understand.

Restorative triangulation has the exact opposite goal: to revive the relationship by provoking an emotional response from the jilted partner. Such triangulation involves the mere favorable mention of another person, hints at possible misconduct or compromising circumstances, or, at a maximum, aggressive flirting and non-penetrative sex acts, such as kissing, petting (making out), or hugging.

878.

Video Presentation in the 38th International Conference on Psychiatry and Mental Health, Paris, February 2023

Narcissistic families present a facade of either harmony (pseudomutuality) or disharmony (constant bickering, pseudohostility). In both cases, the members of the dysfunctional family are not allowed to separate and individuate and are subjected to a cultlike power asymmetry.

879.

Children are loved by mothers, as I was not. They are bundled emotions, and happiness and hope.

I am jealous of them, I am infuriated by my deprivation, I am fearful of the sadness and hopelessness that they provoke in me. Like music, they reify a threat to the precariously balanced emotional black hole that is myself.

They are my past, my dilapidated and petrified True Self, my wasted potentials, my self-loathing and my defences. They are my pathology projected.

I revel in my Orwellian narcissistic newspeak. Love is weakness, happiness is a psychosis, hope is malignant optimism. Children defy all this. They are proof positive of how different it could all have been.

But what I consciously experience is disbelief. I cannot understand how anyone can love these thuggish brats, their dripping noses, gelatinous fat bodies, whitish sweat, and bad breath.

How can anyone stand their cruelty and vanity, their sadistic insistence and blackmail, their prevarication and deceit? In truth, no one except their parents can.

Children are always derided by everyone bar their parents. There is something sick and sickening in a mother's affections. There is a maddening blindness involved, an addiction, a psychotic episode, it's pathological, this bond, it's nauseous. I hate children. I hate them for being me.

880.

Enablers are often mistaken for friends when, in reality, they are your worst enemies.

Enablers encourage your self-destructive behaviors. They aid and abet your suffering. They amplify self-harm.

A true friend would never hand you a loaded gun knowing that you may be suicidal. An enabler would do it.

An enabler would have sex with your girlfriend at your request, aware that this will cause you excruciating pain.

An enabler would ply their alcoholic or junkie friend with drinks or drugs, would encourage a workaholic to work even more, would go on retail therapy sprees with a shopaholic, would induct you into bad company.

Beware the enabler: charming and smiling and solicitous, he is a snake in your grass.

881.

What Makes Us Tick: Intrapsychic Activation Model (IPAM) and No More Grannon

Watch Why Narcissists Can't Think Straight (Constructs, Introjects, Memories, Defenses) https://www.youtube.com/watch?v=3u_1GoFA3Ig

Why People-pleasers Can't Think Straight (Self-states, Constructs, Introjects) https://www.youtube.com/watch?v=O1Dp4KMyreA

882.

Intermittent reinforcement is the core mechanism behind trauma bonding. It covers disparate phenomena such as giving false hopes and approach-avoidance repetition compulsion in Borderline Personality Disorder.

There are 4 types of intermittent reinforcement:

Fixed interval schedule(FI)

Variable Interval schedule (VI)

Fixed ratio schedule (FR)

Variable Ratio Schedule (VR)

883.

Predators make their victims feel loved and accepted. They create an instant mini cult with the victim at the center. They tell their victims what they eagerly want to hear. They badmouth and devalue other people to garner the victim's gratitude and allegiance.

This is why predatory behavior should be determined objectively. The victims are likely to defend the predator and consider him kind, benevolent, loving, or just fun. Confronted with a cognitive dissonance, victims often resolve it by renouncing reality.

Predation is any abusive breach of boundaries and morals by someone in a position of formal or informal power.

If you end up having sex with someone who is clearly heartbroken, if you groom someone much younger than you, if you get someone drunk or drugged, if you abuse a position of authority or trust - these are instances of predatory behavior, regardless of how the victim feels about the whole incident.

884.

<u>Being victimized</u> is a dissonant, anxiety-inducing experience. Some of the abused resolve the cognitive dissonance by claiming to have orchestrated or provoked the perpetrator, thus regaining a sense of agency and appearance of control:

"I wanted the sex and initiated it, so it is all my fault"

"What happened felt good and empowering"

"I was dressed scantily, acted sluttishly, was wasted, had it coming"

"I provoked him to mistreat me, I keep pushing all his buttons"

"I should have known better than to walk this rough hood at night"

These are all counterfactual statements, of course. The passive voice often disguises a deep discomfort.

Recognizing and accepting that you have been victimized is the first step on the road to healing.

Still, one should refrain from adopting victimhood as an identity. Being victimized is not the same as being a victim.

885.

<u>Borderline's POV (point of view)</u> is the outcome of her internal dynamics, especially the compulsive need to approach and then avoid you.

Here is how she sees you:

APPROACH

You are my world and life
You will save me from myself and from others
Everything is meaningless without you
You are a stable rock
You stabilize my moods and regulate my emotions, with you I feel safe and whole (completed)

I will give my life for you (self-sacrificial)
I am bad and evil (bad object) but with you I feel good and worthy because
you accept and love me as I am

AVOIDANCE

I am overwhelmed by pain owing to your rejection and abandonment
(often projected and anticipated): you are not protective, you don't care,
you found someone else to take my place, You are disloyal, You are
looking for alternatives
Dissociation (amnesia, auto-pilot depersonalization, derealization)
I have to do something, anything to hurt you and then regain your love
You want me dead, shackled, only yours, to disappear into you
You have changed, You blame-shift, I am the victim
You guilt-trip
You are not self-aware: You are self-destructive and you want to drag me
with you
You are just after my sex, looks
Paranoid ideation, persecutory object: You lie, deceive, and cheat, You are
out to get me, You entrapped me, You never mean what you say, You
gaslight me, You hate me while I love you self-sacrificially, You humiliate
me and shame me, you are malicious

886.

The more grounded the shared fantasy - the more elements of reality it
incorporates - the more pernicious and insidious it is.

Love is the polar opposite of a shared fantasy. It is always embedded only
in reality and it is never about converting the partner into a figment or a
character in a fantastic narrative.

Shared fantasies are not limited to the intimate sphere. Many friendships
are shared fantasies as well. Your "friend" backstabs, badmouthes, and
betrays you in every possible way for years - and yet it is difficult to let go
of the fantasy because the alternative is a lonely, barren reality.

887.

Borderlines and Narcissists engage in a danse macabre with highly
idiosyncratic dynamics. This is how they see each other.

888.

Narcissists regard mentally ill people with utter contempt because they deplore any weakness and vulnerability.

Reaction formation is a defense mechanism: we vehemently and aggressively reject in others the very traits and qualities that we find unacceptable in ourselves.

Narcissists are dependent on others (for narcissistic supply) and brittle. Hence their sadistic glee in harming people with the same mental constitution.

Narcissists are also hypervigilant and paranoid. They suspect that others are merely faking fragility and neediness in order to manipulate the environment. They convert any interaction into a power play, replete with defiance (reactance).

889.

Alloplastic defenses

Blaming others for the predictable consequences and outcomes of your own choices and decisions.

A feature of cluster B disorders.

Autoplastic defenses

Blaming oneself for the consequences and outcomes of one's own choices and decisions as well as for the outcomes of the choices that others make and even for circumstances beyond one's control.

A common type of defense in neuroses.

890.

What is common to NPD, BPD, dependent personality disorder (codependents), people pleasers, parentified children? Bad object internalization.

Early on in life, some <u>children internalize a bad object</u> whose main message is "you are not lovable". They learn to associate love with rejection and hurt.

Later in life, as adults, the bad object affects mate selection with a preference for rejecting, abandoning, dysregulated, and withholding intimate partners.

The introjects in such people compel them to either avoid reciprocated love (insecure attachment style) or to deny love as a form of sadistic abuse by weaponizing frustration.

Another coping strategy involves projective identification: manipulating and baiting lovers, spouses, and friends to the point of betrayal, thus affirming the bad object and fulfilling narrative expectations (comfort zone).

Bad object adults have both alloplastic defenses (feel victimized) and autoplastic defenses (they deserve to be hated and betrayed).

They regard themselves as innocent babes: everyone else it tasked with safeguarding and promoting their wellbeing and interests, protecting their emotions, and catering to their needs, totally disregarding their soul-destroying and egregious abuse.

Regardless of their chronological age, they are never the adults in the room.

Being unlovable in one's mind causes a lot of anxiety and paranoid ideation: you can trust no one to love you and to have your best interests in mind. You anticipate the worst and preemptively act to bring it about ("let the other shoe drop").

You cannot trust your judgment of people owing to the cognitive distortion field of the bad object.

Example: many narcissists, in a shared fantasy, grandiosely trust that they are so special that regardless of their abuse, no one will cheat on them, retaliate, or betray them.

Such people mislabel and misinterpret their "anxiety artifacts" as emotions:

heartbreak, love, dysregulation, somatization are all actually transformations of anxiety.

891.

<u>Suggested topics for future research</u>:

Narcissism in collectivist-traditional societies vs. individualistic ones

Narcissism and feminism

Rise in narcissism owing to the disintegration of the family

The role of narcissism in religion

Narcissism in cities vs. villages

Artificial intelligence and narcissism

892.

Watch Victim in Drama Triangle with Abuser, Savior: Karpman's Drama Triangle https://www.youtube.com/watch?v=ujw-jbjOOpg

Karpman's triangle, shifting roles

Based on a guy I used to hang out with and broke up with recently after an incredible incident of egregious badmouthing and backstabbing. So, a lot of what I say in this video is based on this rotten character.

Perfidious fake friends, who always claim to be the helpless and defenseless victims of manipulation and abuse and so, oh so in need of love. Women lap it up, of course.

<u>Saviors, healers, fixers, rescuers are grandiose, covert (fake), and predatory.</u>

Wingman or backdrop for contrast as empathic, compassionate, altruistic, loving, caring, saintly.

Can't see them coming, like a snake in the grass. Masquerade as good people but engage in perfidy and betrayal.

Actually rabidly misogynistic (closet gays), narcissistic, and psychopathic in dating (players).

Pick up line: self-appointed savior of damsels in distress from bad, mentally ill, dangerous, damaging so called abusers. "I am the alternative to the horrors of your relationship".

But often savior is the abuser, not the "abuser" (Karpman: roles not fixed, playacting)

Select heartbroken, sad, damaged, crying, devastated, anxious, depressed women as targets. They need to talk and end up being preyed on.The "abuser" could be a friend or a colleague. They are fake friends, seething with envy and resentment owing to inferiority complex. Saving is omnipotence.

Badmouth and betray confidences for hours, not realizing that their words are reported back to the "abuser" (example: this guy and me, I gad info from multiple sources about his badmouthing and egregious backstabbing, but I refused to believe it, he is that good at faking).

Savior/rescuer attempts to create alliance/coalition with victim against abuser.

Predatory 3 Ss: save you, sex you, scram ("not another fantasy", "not ready for a relationship")

May believe their own lies about saving or rescuing as their "job" (abuser all bad, they all good splitting): caters to grandiosity, unboundaried sexual needs

893.

Borderlines often feel that the only things they have to offer are <u>sex and drama</u>. Their dysregulation is their only asset. They are but a spectacle.

894.

Narcissists lack empathy so they never feel remorse or regret for their actions or inaction. They deny responsibility and shift the blame and guilt to others. Possessed of magical thinking, the narcissist feels immune to the consequences of his actions for four reasons:
(1) The narcissist's False Self; (2) his dissociation; (3) his sense of entitlement; and (4) his past successes at evading justice.

Gdansk seminar https://www.youtube.com/watch?v=WnfstvImfvg

Citations of my work:

https://samvak.tripod.com/mediakit.html

https://samvak.tripod.com/academia695.png
https://samvak.tripod.com/academiareversename.png
https://samvak.tripod.com/academiaabbrev.png
https://samvak.tripod.com/academiareverse2.png

895.

Narcissistic supply, even sex are anxiolytic. So is betrayal. Narcissist has been betrayed by his mother in early childhood. He seeks to recreate this betrayal throughout life. He chooses fake friends who badmouth him, steal from him, poach his mates, and betray him. He behaves obnoxiously to make people hate him and hurt him. And he pushes his intimate partners to betray him in a variety of ways, including by cheating on him.

Narcissists convert intimate partner to a substitute mother in order to accomplish separation-individuation.

One way to make this happen is by insistently and persistently pushing the partner to betray the narcissist for example by being with another man. This way, separation is coupled with debilitating pain to guarantee its irreversibility and finality. The narcissist always mourns the mother fantasy, not the actual departed intimate partner.

The narcissist is not a masochistic cuckold. He does not get sexually aroused by the betrayal. On the contrary, his subsequent suffering causes depression and a decrease in libido.

Mate poaching is not met with mate guarding or sexual gatekeeping but with projective identification with the partner and mate sharing with the man she would cheat with (often chosen by the narcissist himself).

Having idealized his partner, the narcissist's self-idealization (grandiosity) depends on his ownership of her. Relinquishing her to another man, handing her over to another man undermines the narcissist's sense of self-worth and results in self-devaluation so extreme that the bad object takes over and its dual messages are amplified: you are not lovable and you do not deserve happiness.

The narcissist is also extremely envious of the other man who now comes to possess the good, idealized object. He feels like a self-destructive fool for having handed her over to a man who envied him for possessing her, desired her, and will now replace him in her heart and mind, likely badmouthing the narcissist as a predator or a monster. He feels that his repetition compulsion renders him defenseless, disrespected by everyone involved, weak, and pathetic. He consoles himself by clinging to the fact that he made it all happen, he was in control, the others being merely puppets.

The narcissist perceives the man the partner cheats with as superior to him in some ways. The narcissist is a child and mother is cheating on him with a real man, a grown up. These are the preconditions for separation: a devalued mother and a painful breakup in a reenacted childhood. It involved splitting as a precondition for individuation: child all good, mother all bad.

The narcissist engineers the whole situation of betrayal. He is fully in control of it. He selects mates who are more likely to collaborate in realizing it: promiscuous, unboundaried, and mentally ill. Such women are anyhow prone to fantasy and they collude with the narcissist to the point of complying with his wishes even when his demands of them are ego dystonic (for example: that they cheat on him).

The narcissist then abuses them, prompts them to betray him, and sets the stage even to the point of choosing the other man.

But his fantasy is that of having fallen victim to an evil partner (reminiscent of his real mother). His fantasy is mostly counterfactual and delusional (persecutory), but he defends it fiercely in order to accomplish separation-individuation from both a bad mother and her sadistic, tormenting introject. But this attempt is doomed to failure owing to its inherent contradictions.

The narcissist distorts and reframes reality, deceives himself into accepting a version of the events which is largely untrue but excruciatingly agonizing and, therefore, conducive to separation-individuation: a confabulated fable of rejection and humiliation. But such a confabulation only buttresses and magnifies the twin messages of the bad object (you are no good and therefore deserve no happiness and you are not lovable).  So, the cycle has to be restarted with a new partner.

Narcissist's self-harming is a form of emotional disinvestment (decathexis). Separation requires it. Watch Narcissist's Emotional Involvement Preventive Measures (EIPMs)

Why do I break up with women by pushing them to cheat on me? In order to avoid future stalking (they feel guilty and vanish) and so as to not feel guilty for having abandoned my partner and let her down.

Some of the women I broke up with without cheating became demented stalkers or just bitter and hateful. The cheating causes me excruciating pain for a few weeks, but it still far preferrable to stalking and charges of unfulfilled promises.

I am not seeking pain when I push women (dates, girlfriends, intimate partners) to be with other men, often orchestrating the betrayal. I merely wish to get rid of them altogether or minimize their footprint in my life.

Unconsciously, this strategy is intended to control inevitable abandonment, rejection, cheating, betrayal, and humiliation and to satisfy the need to sadistically punish my partners with withdrawal or absence coupled with coerced self-trashing, sexual or axiological (betraying one's values).

I couldn't care less that the woman is with another man. I feel relieved that she is gone and will not make any further demands or stalk me.

I am actually angry at those who resist the manipulation and survive in the relationship because they are perceived as either clingy or threatening with ineluctable pain.

But this strategy does cause me excruciating pain all the same. How come?

The pain I experience is narcissistic injury or narcissistic mortification, not romantic jealousy or possessiveness.

It is solely about being disrespected and humiliated by other men as a doormat, cuckold, or coward (for not protecting my woman) and being rejected and humiliated by my women as inadequate and mentally ill (less than perfect).

In a way, I internalize their point of view and come to regard myself as inefficacious, helpless, unlovable, obsequious, unworthy, ugly, and craven. It feeds into my harsh inner critic (sadistic superego or bad object) and amplifies the shame to life-threatening proportions.

So, why not change strategy?

Because the shared fantasy is highly addictive and generates stalking and virulent hatred in spurned women.

Once they cheat at my behest, however, they are disadvantaged: I can always point to the cheating, emotionally blackmail them, silence their vocal complaints, and get rid of them for good.

This is, therefore, not about masochism. It is just that the effective dissolution of the shared fantasy requires narcissistic injury or mortification by posing as a cuckolded partner in full view.

Ultimately, such posture benefits me as I am able to retain the high moral ground as a victim even as I devalue and discard my partners callously and cruelly.

So, the short-term cost is outweighed by the long-term benefits of a victimhood narrative.

I use a variant of strategy in all intimate settings (such as friendship) and interpersonal relations (e.g., with colleagues or collaborators).

Once I deem someone undesirable (for instance: having mistreated me), I entrap or tempt them and cause them to betray me once more spectacularly and ostentatiously.

I accomplish that by playing on their weaknesses and vulnerabilities. Then, having been mortified and morally indignant and righteous, I am compelled to get rid of them.

896.

<u>Narcissists are hypervigilant</u>. They see slights everywhere, even in the most innocuous speech.

897.

They are grotesque caricatures of masculinity: buff, deformed veined musculature, like tightly packed meat; slicked, gel oozing hair; ostentatious tattoos; and pants too tight so as to emphasize the crotch.

The internet gave rise to a new breed of <u>gurus, coaches, and self-styled experts</u> who spend more time in gyms and nightclubs than in libraries and museums. They are covert and somatic narcissists who often pose as empathic or codependent victims, saviors and healers – all this intended to lure women to engage in sex and then cruelly dispatch them on their way.

But sexual conquests are not enough for these delusional and vainglorious megalomaniacs. They also posture as sages and visionaries. These cerebral wannabes pontificate and spew half-baked and ill-informed conspiracy theories, analyses, observations, and opinions in fields as diverse as philosophy and science.

They get most info disastrously wrong or just make it up as they go along as they self-importantly aspire to pretend that brain and brawn are interchangeable.

They are somatic covert narcissist whose dream it is to be cerebral. They often team up with intellectually superior cerebrals, appropriate and plagiarize their work, and bask in the purloined glory. But they stumble when on their own because they are incapable of generating a single original idea or truly comprehending those that they steal.

Some of them are smooth talkers and disguise their vacuity and nonsense effectively with resounding verbiage, pronouncing words like dissociation wrongly and awash in malapropisms.

Others merely engage in displays of aggression or nauseating eroticism.

Creepy to the last, most of them are covert narcissists and psychopaths cloaking themselves in a mantle of saviors and healers.

898.

Fawning and people pleasing are often excuses for psychopathic, immoral, antisocial, and narcissistic acts and misconduct:

"Poor me, I couldn't help myself, I had to say 'yes', I am actually the victim of my own proclivities and character flaws! People are leveraging and taking advantage of my weaknesses! I never do wrong!"

The need to believe in the essential goodness of people - especially gurus posing as saviors and healers - and the need to not feel like a victim result in cognitive dissonance when these role models misbehave.

Resolution: "My savior and healer is flawed, weak, human, means well, and so in need of love!" coupled with autoplastic defenses (if he acted morally wrong, it was all my fault, I made him do it).

899.

Borderlines (women and men alike) pendulate between two anxieties: abandonment (separation insecurity) and engulfment (enmeshment). This creates an approach-avoidance repetition compulsion ("I hate you, don't leave me").

During the avoidance phase, the borderline seeks futilely to become more grounded in reality, often through the agency of a sexual partner or friends.

But then she reverts to the approach phase of the cycle and re-enters a fantasy world, a simulation in which her intimate partner provides external regulation: stabilizes her moods and affects (emotions).

She merges with her significant other, fuses into a single organism by outsourcing her mind to him.

900.

Five misconceptions about cluster B personality disorders:

1. The codependent controls from the bottom. She uses her neediness and

clinginess to rule and to extort her intimate partner. The Borderline surrenders to her intimate partner: he is tasked by her with stabilizing her moods and regulating her emotions.

2. Abuse is the glue that holds dysfunctional relationships together: it is proof of love and identified with it. Healthy people walk away when they are victimized - the mentally ill bond and get attached.

3. The mentally ill prefer objects to people and attempt to objectify others. Objects are more predictable and controllable.

4. Approach avoidance repetition compulsion should not be confused or conflated with intermittent reinforcement. The first is a reactive pattern to the twin anxieties: abandonment vs. engulfment. The second is the coercive control technique that results in trauma bonding.

5. The empty schizoid core at the heart of disorders of the self (such as narcissism and borderline) is habituated: gradually it becomes a choice. Absence of being guarantees invulnerability and impermeability.

## 901.

Invulnerability signaling is at the core of the grandiosity of the psychopathic narcissist: a defiant "see if I care" attitude, no one and nothing have the slightest power over me, I never get attached, emotions are weaknesses, I am a free spirit, a law unto my own.

This attitude leads to some counterintuitive behavioral outcomes.

The psychopathic narcissist never engages in mate guarding. His message to other men: "The women in my life mean so little to me that you can have them, if you wish. They are dispensable, fungible, and interchangeable. They have no power over me, nothing they do matters or has the capacity to hurt me."

Another example: "Go ahead and plagiarize my work and my ideas. They mean little to me. I can generate revolutionary breakthroughs faster than you can steal them!"

Harvey Cleckley, the author of "Mask of Sanity", was repeatedly stunned by what he called the psychopathic narcissist's "rejection of life".

The ultimate in <u>invulnerability signaling</u> is all-pervasive ostentatious apathy: the profound neglect and abandonment of all personal goals and plans and behaving in ways which are in your face self-destructive - as if one couldn't care less about one's wasted life and looming devastation or demise.

902.

<u>Masochists, the self-destructive, psychopathic narcissists, and people pleasers</u> are different breeds even though sometimes they behave in the same ways.

Masochists crave hurt and pain and engineer or orchestrate incremental situations whose outcomes are agonizing, mortifying, and humiliating - but never life threatening.

Self-defeating and self-loathing folks act out recklessly, petulantly, and defiantly in order to sabotage their best interests and wellbeing in a decisive, self-harming, self-trashing, and almost suicidal manner.

Psychopathic narcissists puppeteer others and co-opt them into goal-oriented scenarios that appear superficially to be masochistic but are, in reality, either sadistic or self-efficacious, as far as the psychopathic narcissist is concerned.

Finally: people pleasers are conflict-averse and need to be needed. They are self-sacrificial but often enjoy their role and find it gratifying.

Example:

The masochist will push his girlfriend to cheat on him in order to endure exquisite torment;

The self-destructive sort will act the same way but will then proceed to break up with her or divorce;

The psychopathic narcissist will make sure that he is cucked but really in order to get rid of an unwanted and burdensome intimate partner;

Finally, the people pleaser will permit his intimate partner to sleep with others just so as to make her happy.

903.

Interpellation - a process first described in socioeconomic settings by Louis Althusser - is when one reacts to other people's wishes, desires, urges, and expectations as if they were one's own and then acts accordingly.

People pleasers are the reification of interpellation, but it makes an appearance in other mental health disorders such as dependent and borderline personality disorders, psychotic disorders, and anxiety disorders, among others.

904.

Never say good morning to a narcissist.

905.

Victims of narcissistic abuse? Two minutes to exonerate you from any guilt, purge you of any shame, and rinse you of any blame!

Prof. Sam Vaknin odgovara na pitanje šta možete uraditi ukoliko ste u vezi sa narcisoidnom osobom. Ukoliko ste zainteresovani za knjigu prof.Sama Vaknina "Malignant Self-Love", kao i njegova predavanja i seminare u Srbiji možete poslati upit na mejl: marketing.bgonline@gmail.com

Video editing: Zoran Jelenković/ VU Covers

906.

The narcissist is capable of having pseudointimate relationships that do not involve a shared fantasy. In such liaisons, he is indifferent and dismissive, but not abusive.

Within a shared fantasy, the narcissist snapshots (introjects) his partner and then idealizes the resultant internal object.

Henceforth, the narcissist abusively coerces his partner into conforming to this inner representation of her (avatar) in his mind.

This course of action guarantees the ultimate dissolution of the bond via devaluation and discard and the long sought after separation from a maternal figure.

The narcissist's partners end up abandoning him, triangulating or mortifying him with infidelity or other forms of betrayal in a desperate attempt to jump start the moribund relationship (a cry for help, having been exposed to the narcissist's inexorable betrayal fantasy), or succumbing and becoming a figment in his fantasy.

When his partner consents to suspend her autonomy and agency and give in to the shared fantasy, separation-individuation fails.

Resentful and frustrated, the narcissist defeminizes and maternalizes the obsequious partner: the relationship becomes sexless and transactional.

She becomes a full-fledged mother figure, free to have sex and romance with others, but always at the beck and call of the permanently infantilized narcissist.

907.

Is the covert BPD "typically" more toxic than the classic BPD or covert narcissism?

Is the covert BPD in a shared fantasy of 1 or for 2?

Does the covert BPD experience dual mothership?

Is intermittent reinforcement the same as devalue and discard cycles?

Is the covert BPD in a state of prolonged grief like the narcissist?

When the covert BPD feels slighted, disappointed and hurt by interpersonal communication , circumstances or partner behavior – because the covert is a hybrid does it cause Narcissistic injury? When the covert BPD then goes into a fight/flight attack mode is that Narcissistic rage or symptom of classic BPD?

Interpersonal communication was a huge platform for disagreement, arguments. If a person is chronically feeling slighted, disappointed, hurt and accusations/ paranoia of lying, withholding using this to justify for the verbal abuse. Is this the chronic victimhood of Covert Narcissism or these traits BPD.

What specific behaviors in the covert BPD are under the category of psychopathy?

Any research to show that some people with covert BPD might traits of both classic and covert elements? If yes, what elements are borrowed from each?

908.

Pathological narcissism, borderline personality, and anxious psychopathy involve the only partly successful suppression of cognitions (thoughts) via ironic processes. Similarly entrained abuse involves ironic processes in the victim's mind.

909.

The following techniques are used in CBT and psychodrama, especially for cluster B personality disorders.

Doubling: The therapist or counsellor acts and emulates the client's emotions and behaviors. The therapist verbalize what the client may be thinking or what they seem to be withholding as well as the client's disavowed and defended against behaviors.

Doubling connects the client's internal reality with external reality (restores reality testing via insight). The client then acknowledges that he sees himself in his double.

Mirroring: The client observes others as they act out scenes, events, and conversations for his benefit. This way, he gains perspective and some emotional distance and better understands his emotions.

Role-playing: The client assumes the role of a particular person or object, that is a source of stress or conflict in their life.

Role reversal: The client acts the role of another person in their life (could be the therapist or counsellor) while someone else (usually the therapist or counsellor) plays the part of the client. This can help improve empathy and understanding of other people's perspective and separateness.

Soliloquy: The client describes his inner thoughts and feelings to an audience (e.g., the therapist or counsellor). This way he gains greater insight into his inner feelings and thoughts and experiences catharsis.

LITERATURE

Roleplay in Psychotherapy:General effects of roleplay techniques in psychotherapy by Roger Schaller, 25th June 2021 https://psychodrama.world/method/roleplay-in-psychotherapy-general-effects-of-roleplay-techniques-in-psychotherapy/

Blatner, A. & Cukier, R. (2007).  Moreno's basic concepts. In: Baim, C., Burmeister, J. & Maciel, M. (Editors). Psychodrama – Advances in Theory and Practice. London: Routledge

Castonguay, L.G., & Beutler, L.E. (2006). Principles of therapeutic change: A task force on participants, relationships, and techniques factors. Journal of Clinical Psychology, 62, 631–638.

Gallese, V., Migone, P. & Eagle, M. (2006). La simulazione incarnata: i neuroni specchio, le basi neurofisiologiche dell'intersoggettivita ed alcune implicazioni per la psicoanalisi. Psicoterapia e Scienze Umane XL,3: 543-580. www.psicoterapiascienzeumane.it

Hammond, B. (2014). Cognitive Behavioural Therapy and Psychodrama. In: Holmes, P, Farrall M. & Kirk, K. (Editors): Empowering Therapeutic Practice. Integrating Psychodrama into other Therapies. London: Jessica Kingsley Publishers

Hayes, S. C., Follette, V. M., & Linehan, M. M. (Eds.). (2004). Mindfulness and acceptance: Expanding the cognitive-behavioral tradition. New York: Guilford Press.

Malloch, S. & Trevarthen, C. (2009). Communicative Musicality: Exploring the Basis of Human Companionship. Oxford: Oxford University Press.

Orlinsky,D.E., Grawe, K. & Parks, B.K. (1994). Process and Outcome in Psychotherapy. In: Allen E. Bergin, Sol L. Garfield: Handbook of Psychotherapy and Behaviour Change. 4th Edition. 1994, 270–376.

Schaller, R. (2016, 2.Aufl.). Stellen Sie sich vor, Sie sind…- Das Ein-Personen-Rollenspiel in Beratung, Coaching und Therapie. Bern: Hogrefe

Schaller, R. (2017). Regiegespräch – die zentrale Technik für das Psychodrama im Einzelsetting. Zeitschrift für Psychodrama und Soziometrie, 2, https://doi.org/10.1007/s11620-017-0393-x

Tschacher, W. Junghan, U.N. & Pfammatter, M.(2014). Towards a Taxonomy of Common Factors in Psychotherapy – Results of an Expert Survey. Clinical Psychology and Psychotherapy, 21, 82-96. Published online 6 November 2012 in Wiley Online Library (wileyonlinelibrary.com). DOI: 10.1002/cpp.1822

Tschacher, W. & Pfammatter, M. (2016). Embodiment in Psychotherapy – A Necessary Complement to the Canon of Common Factors? European Psychotherapy, 2016/2017, pp. 5-21. CIPMedien https://boris.unibe.ch/id/eprint/93002

910.

Abuse is never love and true love is enough to sustain a relationship.

911.

Autoplastic defenses

Blaming oneself for the consequences and outcomes of one's own choices and decisions as well as for the outcomes of the choices that others make and even for circumstances beyond one's control.

A common type of defense in neuroses.

Alloplastic defenses

Blaming others for the predictable consequences and outcomes of your own choices and decisions.

A feature of cluster B disorders.

Examples of alloplastic defenses: "It is their fault, they made me do it", "They should have been more careful or less gullible".

Even characters flaws which are rarely associated with psychopathy and narcissism – actually are.

Example:

There are many people who people pleasers and other people who are emotionally dysregulated or delusional or paranoid or narcissistic or passive aggressive or depressive or anxious or …

But all these psychopathologies are often excuses or covers for psychopathic, immoral, antisocial, and narcissistic acts and misconduct. It is a unique combination of both alloplastic and autoplastic defenses.

"Poor me, I am actually the victim of my own proclivities, weaknesses, mental illnesses, and character flaws! People are leveraging and taking advantage of my frailties! I never do wrong! I am never to blame! I am never responsible for my actions! There are higher internal forces at work!"

The need to believe in the essential goodness of people, that the world is essentially just and structured is a bit naïve, of course. Another need is to not feel like a victim: we don't want to feel stupid, that our judgment is wrong, to suspect that we misapprehend people, that we can and do fall in the hands of predators.

These needs result in a cognitive dissonance when people we have trusted and role models misbehave or betray us: a great unease, a sense of discomfort, an inner conflict.

To allay this, we deceive ourselves in order to mitigate, ameliorate, and overcome this internal upset when we are confronted with the truth. We lie to ourselves, reframe.

So we say: "She is flawed, weak, human, means well, mentally ill, and so in need of love!" or "She is a people pleaser, emotionally dysregulated, depressed, anxious, delusional, or labile".

Dissonance gone. In reality though, she did victimize you, damage you, prey on you. But she did not mean to, it is not her fault. It was stronger than her, you see.

This is coupled with grandiose autoplastic defenses, the tendency to blame yourself for anything that goes wrong because you need to feel in control: if she acted immorally, it was all my fault, I made her do it, I caused it to happen, I am not the victim, I am the victimizer and the abuser. So, everything is fine: I am the one who talk advantage of the character flaws and mental illness of others, reducing any hero to a common zero. I am still safe and in charge.

912.

Some borderlines switch imperceptibly, glacially, and incrementally. They maintain continuity, memory, and a semblance of identity across the various self-states.

LITERATURE

American Psychiatric Association. (2022). Diagnostic and statistical manual of mental disorders (5th ed., text rev.). https://doi.org/10.1176/appi.books.97...

European Journal of Trauma & Dissociation
Volume 1, Issue 1, January–March 2017, Pages 63-71
Complex trauma, dissociation and Borderline Personality Disorder: Working with integration failures; By Dolores Mosquera and Kathy Steele

Borderline Personal Disorder and Emotion Dysregulation. 2014; 1: 13.
Published online 2014 Oct 14. doi: 10.1186/2051-6673-1-13
Chronic complex dissociative disorders and borderline personality disorder: disorders of emotion dysregulation? By Bethany L Brand and Ruth A Lanius

Is Dissociation an Integral Aspect of Borderline Personality Disorder, Or Is It a Comorbid Disorder? By Marilyn I. Korzekwa, Paul F. Dell
Book: Dissociation and the Dissociative Disorders, 2nd Edition, 2022, Routledge

913.

This is a compilation of older videos that summarize the narcissist's dual fantasies: shared and betrayal.

914.

<u>Parents</u> (Primary Objects) and, more specifically, mothers are the first agents of socialisation. It is through his mother that the child explores the answers to the most important existential questions, which shape his entire life. How loved one is, how loveable, how independent one becomes, how guilty one should feel for wanting to become autonomous, how predictable is the world, how much abuse should one expect in life and so on.

To the infant, the mother is not only an object of dependence (as his survival is at stake), love and adoration. It is a representation of the "universe" itself. It is through her that the child first exercises his senses: the tactile, the olfactory, and the visual.

Later on, she becomes the subject of his nascent sexual cravings (if a male) – a diffuse sense of wanting to merge, physically, as well as spiritually. This object of love is idealised and internalised and becomes part of his conscience (Superego). For better or for worse, she is the yardstick, the benchmark against which everything in his future is measured. One forever compares oneself, one's identity, one's actions and omissions, one's achievements, one's fears and hopes and aspirations to this mythical figure.

Growing up entails the gradual separation from one's mother. At first, the child begins to shape a more realistic view of her and incorporates the mother's shortcomings and disadvantages in this modified version. The more ideal, less realistic and earlier picture of the mother is stored and becomes part of the child's psyche. The later, less cheerful, more realistic view enables the infant to define his own identity and gender identity and to "go out to the world".

From the book "The Developmental Psychology of Psychopathology" by Sam Vaknin.

915.

The <u>twin theories of structural dissociation and betrayal trauma</u> provide a profound insight into the formation of cluster B personality disorders.

916.

The narcissist's entrained voice (introject) controls your mind long after he is gone from your life. Here is how to get rid of it.

Also watch "Deprogram the Narcissist in Your Mind"
https://www.youtube.com/watch?v=bCKm2lywhZg

Narcissistic Abuse Recovery: First Separate, Individuate
https://www.youtube.com/watch?v=95QBUV9CR_4

SECRET Reason Narcissist Devalues, Discards YOU
https://www.youtube.com/watch?v=Hi3PjMeV1xw

How Narcissist Steals Your Unconscious, Lures YOU into His Nightmare
World  https://www.youtube.com/watch?v=EuR2p6VIUec

917.

Cold Empathy evokes the concept of "Uncanny Valley", coined in 1970 by
the Japanese roboticist Masahiro Mori. Mori suggested that people react
positively to androids (humanlike robots) for as long as they differ from
real humans in meaningful and discernible ways. But the minute these
contraptions come to resemble humans uncannily, though imperfectly,
human observers tend to experience repulsion, revulsion, and other
negative emotions, including fear.

The same reactive trajectory and emotional cascade apply to psychopathic
narcissists: they are near-perfect imitations of humans, but, lacking
empathy and emotions, they are not exactly there. Psychopaths and
narcissists strike their interlocutors as being some kind of "alien life-
forms" or "artificial intelligence", in short: akin to humanoid robots, or
androids. When people come across narcissists or psychopaths the
Uncanny Valley reaction kicks in: people feel revolted, scared, and
repelled. They can't put the finger on what it is that provokes these
negative reactions, but, after a few initial encounters, they tend to keep
their distance.

Contrary to widely held views, Narcissists and Psychopaths may actually
possess empathy. They may even be hyper-empathic, attuned to the
minutest signals emitted by their victims and endowed with a penetrating
"X-ray vision". They tend to abuse their empathic skills by employing
them exclusively for personal gain, the extraction of narcissistic supply, or
in the pursuit of antisocial and sadistic goals. They regard their ability to
empathize as another weapon in their arsenal.

I suggest to label the narcissistic psychopath's version of empathy: "cold empathy", akin to the "cold emotions" felt by psychopaths. The cognitive element of empathy is there, but not so its emotional correlate. It is, consequently, a barren, detached, and cerebral kind of intrusive gaze, devoid of compassion and a feeling of affinity with one's fellow humans.

918.

In the wake of narcissistic abuse, support is crucial. But some online groups offer bad advice and a perpetuation of your victim stance.

919.

Alloplastic and autoplastic defenses often intermingle when mental illness is used as an excuse and cover to abuse others.

920.

When you break up with the narcissist, you literally fall apart. To end your grieving is to acknowledge and accept the loss of an object - but that object is YOU. You cannot get over your bereavement because you are mourning yourself.

At first, during the lovebombing and grooming phase, the narcissist offers you unconditional love, as a mother would. Then he idealizes you and causes you to become infatuated with your own idealized image. He invites you into a simulation, a paracosm, a shared fantasy where you merge/fuse into a single selfobject. Then he withdraws all these. He cancels YOU.

921.

Borderlines seek fantasy with an intimate partner and then flee to reality with a rescuer or savior (Karpman drama triangle). This is the avoidance leg of the approach-avoidance repetition compulsion, driven by the twin anxieties: abandonment (separation insecurity) and engulfment (enmeshment).

922.

There are 3 voices whose interplay results in pathological narcissism: the voices of death, of life, and of "god".

923.

Everything you wanted to know about <u>Borderline Personality Disorder (BPD)</u> and didn't dare ask the borderline: from switching between self-states to identity disturbance and intimate relationships.

924.

<u>Shame</u> is a powerful, defining dynamic in vulnerable, fragile, shy, covert narcissism. Not so in the grandiose-overt variant. Time to redefine pathological narcissism and Narcissistic Personality Disorder (NPD)?

**LITERATURE**

1. Shame and its relationship to early narcissistic developments

F Broucek

International journal of psycho-analysis (1982).International Journal of Psychoanalysis ,63():369-378

2. Andrew P. Morrison (1983) Shame, Ideal Self, and Narcissism, Contemporary Psychoanalysis, 19:2, 295-318, DOI: 10.1080/00107530.1983.10746610

3. Wurmser, L. (1987). Shame: The veiled companion of narcissism. In D. L. Nathanson (Ed.), The many faces of shame (pp. 64–92). The Guilford Press.

Morrison, A. P., & Stolorow, R. D. (1997). Shame, narcissism, and intersubjectivity. In M. R. Lansky & A. P. Morrison (Eds.), The widening scope of shame (pp. 63–87). Analytic Press.

4. Gramzow, R., & Tangney, J. P. (1992). Proneness to Shame and the Narcissistic Personality. Personality and Social Psychology Bulletin, 18(3), 369–376. https://doi.org/10.1177/0146167292183014

5. Pincus AL, Ansell EB, Pimentel CA, Cain NM, Wright AGC, Levy KN. Initial construction and validation of the Pathological Narcissism Inventory. Psychol Assess. 2009 Sep;21(3):365-379. doi: 10.1037/a0016530. PMID: 19719348.

6. Cain NM, Pincus AL, Ansell EB. Narcissism at the crossroads: phenotypic description of pathological narcissism across clinical theory, social/personality psychology, and psychiatric diagnosis. Clin Psychol Rev. 2008 Apr;28(4):638-56. doi: 10.1016/j.cpr.2007.09.006. Epub 2007 Oct 2. PMID: 18029072.

7. Kathrin Ritter, Aline Vater, Nicolas Rüsch, Michela Schröder-Abé, Astrid Schütz, Thomas Fydrich, Claas-Hinrich Lammers, Stefan Roepke,

Shame in patients with narcissistic personality disorder,

Psychiatry Research, Volume 215, Issue 2, 2014, Pages 429-437,

https://doi.org/10.1016/j.psychres.2013.11.019

8. Hibbard, S. (1992). Narcissism, shame, masochism, and object relations: An exploratory correlational study. Psychoanalytic Psychology, 9(4), 489–508. https://doi.org/10.1037/h0079392

9. Elena Bilevicius, Darren C. Neufeld, Alanna Single, Melody Foot, Michael Ellery, Matthew T. Keough, Edward A. Johnson,

Vulnerable narcissism and addiction: The mediating role of shame,

Addictive Behaviors, Volume 92, 2019, Pages 115-121,

https://doi.org/10.1016/j.addbeh.2018.12.035

925.

Narcissism is a black hole, a void, there is nobody home. Narcissism is an absence, not a presence.

926.

Both narcissists and borderlines alternate between fantasy and reality - but their fantasies are very different. The borderline's is object (person)-centred, the narcissist's is process (narrative)-centred. Moreover: the fantasies cater to the narcissist's and borderline's deepest psychological needs.

927.

Empathy is comprised of two components:

I. Cold Empathy: an intersubjective agreement as to the mental content (especially emotions) of two or more human subjects;

II. Warm Empathy: the emotional response to Cold Empathy.

Cold Empathy is an act of taxonomy and an attempt to overcome the barriers posed by the inaccessibility of the private languages of the empathee and the empathor. It entails a comparison of the mental states of the subjects, based on introspection and the classification of said mental states within agreed linguistic and cultural frameworks, vocabularies, and contexts.

Warm Empathy is the emotional arousal engendered by Cold Empathy in the empathor and the panoply of emotional responses it evokes.

Both cold and warm empathy assume the commonality and universality of human experience. This is why we tend to empathise with people who resemble us in every way, but this resemblance also provokes strong narcissistic defenses (see this article about the Narcissism of Small Differences.)

Empathy may be an intuitive mode applied to the minds of other people, yielding an intersubjective agreement.

Empathy is the bedrock of morality. Morality can have an external locus (induced by God, social strictures, or upbringing) which is outside the emapthor's control - or an internal locus (reason): the outcome of conscious, fully-controlled, inner processes.

928.

Narcissist - or merely narcissistic? Use these tests to decide (some of these tests should be administered only by a qualified diagnostician).

929.

There is one telltale difference between narcissists and psychopaths in relationships.

930.

The narcissist's voice is in your head. It will coopt and compromise your therapy - and, often, your therapist. Do this BEFORE you attend therapy for narcissistic abuse.

Daria Zukowka's @zukowska.daria (clinical psychologist) YouTube channel.

931.

"Empaths" lack empathy, are often aggressive or even vicious, and many of them are probably covert narcissists. Empaths and dark empaths are nonsensical terms, almost unanimously rejected by the academic community. They are not valid constructs or clinical entities.

932.

Narcissism is the proof that the greater good often comes at the expense of individual welfare.

Narcissists are frequently the engines of human progress - but they are also its fuel, burning out in the process and consuming everyone around them in a self-destructive conflagration, the twilight of these self-imputed gods.

933.

Narcissist: Abuser-savior, death-life, punitive-mother duality

Separation: silencing narcissist's voice in your mind

What about individuation?

Once narcissist's voice silenced, both abuser and savior, mother and child are gone.

Authentic voice is disembodied.

Embodying.

Individuation requires mind-body work: owning your voice also by connecting it to your body.

Reconstituting three lost functions: self-mothering (self-love), self-saving (agency), choosing and affirming life (negating depression, anxiety, catastrophizing, and ANTS)

Watch Take These 4 Steps BEFORE Therapy for Narcissistic Abuse

https://www.youtube.com/watch?v=JAE_z8gD5-8

Watch Love Yourself: Here's How - or, The Four Pillars of Self-love
https://www.youtube.com/watch?v=2vzBf9QvClo

Watch Decode, Heal Your Mind with IPAM (Intrapsychic Activation Model)

https://www.youtube.com/watch?v=YTfpJ3RHf7g

Watch Hijacked by Narcissist's Serpent Voice? Do THIS!

https://www.youtube.com/watch?v=fT7pQ35LYlU

Watch Take Your Life Back, Own It

https://www.youtube.com/watch?v=SUggi8tRTbE

Watch Go to Your Desert, Listen to Your Inner Silence

https://www.youtube.com/watch?v=qOh-iOaWTt8

934.

Healthy narcissism is rendered malignant by trauma and mental illness.

935.

My Dual Mothership concept:

The narcissist becomes your idealizing mother and offers you unconditional love.

<u>You become the narcissist's idealizing mother</u> and offer him unconditional love.

This is the core of your shared fantasy with the narcissist.

When you break up, there is triple mourning: over your idealized self, over the narcissist as your mother, and over the narcissist as your child.

936.


<u>Mirror image of separating-individuating from the narcissist</u> in the wake of narcissistic abuse

Engulfment anxiety and dependency cause the borderline to cast you as an abuser

Admit your contributions as an intimate partner (mate selection, for example, or savior-rescuer complex)

I am not an abuser: your authentic voice, get rid of guilt and shame

Borderlines parentify: Get rid of the maternal function in the shared fantasy

Hand over ownership, regulation

Separation: silence your voice in her mind, enhance her authentic voice

What about individuation?

Once your voice is silenced, both external regulator ("abuser") and savior, mother and child are gone.

Authentic voice is disembodied.

Embodying.

Individuation requires mind-body work: owning your voice also by connecting it to your body.

Reconstituting three lost functions: self-mothering (self-love), self-saving (agency), choosing and affirming life (negating depression, anxiety, catastrophizing, and ANTS)

Watch Take These 4 Steps BEFORE Therapy for Narcissistic Abuse https://www.youtube.com/watch?v=JAE_z8gD5-8

Watch Love Yourself: Here's How - or, The Four Pillars of Self-love https://www.youtube.com/watch?v=2vzBf9QvClo

Watch Decode, Heal Your Mind with IPAM (Intrapsychic Activation Model) https://www.youtube.com/watch?v=YTfpJ3RHf7g

Watch Hijacked by Narcissist's Serpent Voice? Do THIS! https://www.youtube.com/watch?v=fT7pQ35LYlU

Watch Take Your Life Back, Own It https://www.youtube.com/watch?v=SUggi8tRTbE

Watch Go to Your Desert, Listen to Your Inner Silence https://www.youtube.com/watch?v=qOh-iOaWTt8

Watch How to Individuate, Heal from Narcissistic Abuse https://www.youtube.com/watch?v=I3gmcbWsyBM

937.

No point to attempt to communicate with the narcissist or negotiate or compromise with him. From the Vice documentary "How Narcissists Took Over the World".

938.

How to tell if someone is a pathological liar? Watch this video for all the signs and tells!

Is someone lying to you? A lack of detail may give them away https://www.newscientist.com/

There are nine types of lies:

1. Utilitarian: a lie that is intended to accomplish something, a lie that is goal-oriented, a lie whose structure and content are planned to promote or inspire changes conducive to the furtherance of the liar's aims and aspirations;

2. Smokescreen: a lie whose purpose is to obscure, conceal, or remove true information and thus mislead others (common in espionage or military operations) or to avoid facing a humiliating or shameful truth;

3. Compassionate: a lie that is geared towards sparing other people's feelings, catering to their sensitivities and vulnerabilities, and allowing them to save face and avoid shame and embarrassment. Most white lies are compassionate and empathic;

4. Ceremonial: lies and dissimulations whose function is to establish a pecking order by demonstrating reverence and glossing over facts and behaviors that inconveniently contravene the accepted hierarchy. Manners and etiquette are highly-elaborate forms of ceremonial lying;

5. Compensatory: lies that are used to disguise the oft-humiliating fact that we do not know the truth or can't remember it. Lies of this type amount to fiction, but with most of the interlocutors being unaware of it;

6. Confabulatory: intricate lies that weave a fabric of alternate reality which is frequently an exaggerated form of the liar's traits, conduct, and personal history (though it can, of course, be completely unrelated to anything real in the confabulator's life);

7. Inferential: fallacious conclusions or extrapolations based on true assumptions or statements. Most logical fallacies are inferential lies;

8. Hybrid: lies that contain markers of an occult truth or pathways to true information, allowing its recipients to "read between the lines". Hybrid lies are common in authoritarian and totalitarian regimes;

9. Fantastic: wishes and dreams dressed up as facts.

Gaslighting and confabulation involve lies but not lying. There are 9 types of lies and lying.

939.

What is the precise relationship between <u>BPD and CPTSD</u>? Or are they one and the same?

940.

A review of <u>17 treatment modalities (therapies) used to tackle Narcissistic Personality Disorder (NPD)</u> and co-diagnosed (comorbid) mental health conditions.

941.

The narcissist is an inverted human: his <u>unconscious</u> is conscious and parts of his conscious are repressed. Fantasy replaces his missing ego and it is the language mediating between his conscious and unconscious.

942.

<u>Dramatic-erratic behaviors</u> are indications of mental illness: personality, mood, anxiety, psychotic disorders.

Narcissists, paranoids: grandiosity+paranoia

Borderlines: vulnerability+aggression

Psychopaths: invulnerability+coercion/reactance

Histrionics: attention+fantasy

Bipolar: mania (affirming unrealistic projects)

Psychotic: hyperreflexivity (externalizing interior processes)

943.

To preserve one's mental health – one must abandon the narcissist. One must move on.

<u>Moving on</u> is a process, not a decision or an event.

First, one has to acknowledge and accept painful reality.

Such acceptance is a volcanic, shattering, agonising series of nibbling thoughts and strong resistances.

Once the battle is won, and harsh and agonizing realities are assimilated, one can move on to the learning phase.

Continued here: https://samvak.tripod.com/faq80.html

944.

Online, there are many myths and loads of nonsense about narcissism and narcissists. Here are some of them.

945.

The narcissist is a child pretending to be a parent, a toddler usurping adulthood.

946.


Enduring Personality Changes After Catastrophic Events (EPCACE) is the bridge between cPTSD and PTSD. Late onset (adulthood) trauma is far worse than personality disorders that are the outcomes of early childhood abuse.

LITERATURE

1. How Catastrophe Can Change Personality, Sep 26, 2019

Gen Tanaka, MD, Hansen Tang

Psychiatric TimesPsychiatric Times Vol 36, Issue 9

2. Preserve Enduring Personality Change After Catastrophic Experience (EPCACE) as a diagnostic resource, Gen Tanaka, Hansen Tang, Omar Haque, Harold J Bursztajn

Published: May, 2018 DOI:https://doi.org/10.1016/S2215-0366(18)30126-3

3. Diagnosis and classification of disorders specifically associated with stress: proposals for ICD-11.

World Psych. 2013; 12: 198-206, Beltran R, Silove D

4. Expert opinions about the ICD-10 category of enduring personality change after catastrophic experience. Compr Psychiatry. 1999; 40: 396-403 Bursztajn H, The healing power of photographs.

Psychiatr Times. 2017; 34: 8

5. Lasting personality pathology following exposure to severe trauma in adulthood: retrospective cohort study, by Jasna Munjiza, Dolores Britvic & Mike J. Crawford

BMC Psychiatry volume 19, Article number: 3 (2019)

947.

Do not seek closure from your abuser. Do not give them this power.

948.

The narcissist wants and expects 2 out of 4 things from you: sex, supply (narcissistic or sadistic), services, and safety. You are a mere fungible service provider.

949.

Narcissism can be healthy (primary) or pathological (secondary), style (Sperry) or disorder (Kohut).

950.

The narcissist couldn't care less about goals. Anything that yields supply would do (fungibility).

The psychopath is emotionally invested in obtaining his goals, in the process, not the end result: he is cold, calculated, obsessed.

The borderline cathects goals, experiences them as emotional states.

951.

There are two forms of supply: narcissistic and sadistic. They both serve to buttress grandiosity, a cognitive distortion.

In any given environment, the narcissist feeds off either narcissistic supply or sadistic supply - never both.

Where the locus of grandiosity is narcissistic (example: "I am a good father, husband, or boss") or histrionic (attention) - sadistic supply would actually be perceived as negative and result in a narcissistic injury!

Psychopaths who are also sadistic and sadists (people with the now discarded diagnosis of sadistic personality disorder) seek only sadistic supply.

Finally, borderlines alternate between the two types of supply, depending on their self-state. Like narcissists, borderlines are fantasy-prone and grandiose.

952.

The dual mothership concept: the narcissist becomes your idealizing mother and offers you unconditional love.

You, in turn, become the narcissist's idealizing mother and offer him unconditional love.

When you inevitably break up, there is triple mourning: over your idealized self, over the narcissist as your mother and over the narcissist as your child.

953.

Antisocial Personality Disorder (AsPD, psychopathy) is not a clinical entity. It is a societal-relational mental health disorder, exactly like Narcissistic Personality Disorder. What predicts psychopathy and predisposes one to become a lifelong psychopath?

954.

Often the narcissist believes that other people are faking it: leveraging emotional displays to achieve a goal.

He is convinced that their ostensible "feelings" are grounded in ulterior, non-emotional motives.

Faced with other people's genuine emotions, the narcissist becomes suspicious and embarrassed.

He feels compelled to avoid emotion-tinged situations, or worse experiences surges of almost uncontrollable aggression in the presence of expressed sentiments.

They remind him of how imperfect he is and how poorly equipped.

955.

A guided tour of the phantasm that is the narcissist: a dark space, replete with nightmares, imaginary beings, divinities, and extreme mental illness. With Moshe Fabrikant of Israel.

956.

In our narcissistic world:

Make someone feel special - and they will do anything FOR you.

Fail to idealize them - and they will do anything TO you.

957.

Video presentation in the 35th International Conference on Psychiatry and Mental Health, Osaka, October 2023.

Overperception bias:

Sexual (men)

Intimacy (histrionic)

Threats (paranoid ideation)

Slights (hypervigilance and referential ideation)

Narcissistic supply (grandiosity: when bias meets distortion)

Abandonment-Engulfment (borderline personality organization)

LITERATURE

Brady, W.J., McLoughlin, K.L., Torres, M.P. et al. Overperception of
moral outrage in online social networks inflates beliefs about intergroup
hostility. Nat Hum Behav (2023). https://doi.org/10.1038/s41562-023-
01582-0

958.

Alloplastic defenses:
It is all their fault.
Autoplastic defenses:
It is all my fault.
Healthy insight:
I contributed to the situation with my choices, decisions, and behaviors.

959.

Women are way more prone to narcissistic mortification than men. Self-
styled experts confuse narcissistic mortification with narcissistic injury.
With @zukowska.daria

960.

It is by moving on that we defeat our abuser, minimize him and his
importance in our lives.

Remaining obsessed with the past is a perpetuation of your abuse. Getting
on with your life and thriving is the ultimate revenge.

961.

Narcissists commit suicide as a way to re-assert and restore their
grandiosity.

LITERATURE

Narcissistic Personality Disorder: Recognition and Treatment, Elsa Ronningstam, Ph.D., Igor Weinberg, Ph.D., Focus: The Journal of Lifelong Learning in Psychiatry, Spring 2013, Vol. XI, No. 2

962.

My Narcissism

The Toxic
waste of bottled anger
venomized.
A shamed.
Life belly up.
The reeds.
The wind is hissing
death
downstream,
a river holds
its vapour breath
and leaves black lips
of tar and fish
a bloated shore.

Strolling in the boneyard of my life:
bleached dreams,
mementoed ossuary of my insights.

On flaking fenceposts, impaled the child that I had been.

Peering from desiccated sockets, the Plague that's me:
dust-irrigated,
arid tombstones,
a being eclipsed.

963.

Craving attention, teasing men, sexually frigid, tormented by introjects, collapses: Histrionic Personality Disorder (HPD).

964.

The narcissist aims to impress or to provoke - not to communicate or to teach.

965.

Narcissists either merge and fuse with their children - or envy them and seek to destroy them.

966.

Narcissist tries to match internal object with external object. So, he will first communicate with the introject, reach an equilibrium or homeostasis with it and then try to impose this entente on the external object.

Similarly, both idealization and devaluation first occur internally, with the internal object which is rendered either perfect or persecutory. Only then will the narcissist attempt to coerce the external object to match the internal one (for example: via projective identification).

The internal state of the introject is always dominant over the internal state of the external object, simply because the narcissist is aware of the former and has no clue about the latter (he lacks empathy and access to positive emotions). So, the answer is yes. This a form of projection.

No, of course not. The narcissist maintain functional reality testing. Unlike the psychotic, the narcissist and borderline never hallucinate (except during psychotic microepisodes).

But, the narcissist feels that he exerts control and ownership over you. Like leaving your car in a carpark or your phone charging. You are out of sight, but not out of mind (introject constancy). It is a form of magical thinking: you are the narcissist's extension and ambassador, wherever you may be. Wherever you are, he is. The introject is like a rope and he gives you enough of it, or like giving you a line off a fishing reel.

This creates in you the illusions of autonomy and agency – and in him the delusions of possession and control.

Introjects have on/off switches. You can silence them.

When he has sex with someone else, your introject is either deactivated or is left active. Disabling the introject to avoid negative affectivity (shame, guilt, anger) – leaving it on to accomplish some goal and restore grandiosity (e.g., revenge sex).

Internal objects are cathected and reframed (made to fit into a narrative).

BPD example:

When there is a failure to convert idealized object to a persecutory object, this leads to acting out.

Borderline legitimizes forbidden, repressed introjects, resonates with pathological parts, becomes a vector of contagion.

967.

BPD suffer from persecutory delusions, paranoid ideation as an instrument to extricate themselves from engulfment/enmeshment anxiety.

The persecutory dynamic is either autoplastic (I am a bad object abuser) or alloplastic (I am a victim).

When there is a failure of the defense allowing the Borderline to convert an idealized object to a persecutory object, she can't regard herself as a victim, but only as bad object, an abuser. This ego dystony leads to decompensation and acting out.

Borderline legitimizes forbidden, repressed introjects, resonates with pathological parts in her intimate partner, becomes a vector of contagion.

Borderline is the mirror image of the narcissist:

She has introject inconstancy, he has object inconstancy.

She considers herself as a bad object externally but not internally, he considers himself a bad object internally but not externally.

The Borderline encourages the narcissist to interact exclusively with his internal objects because she doesn't want him to realize that she is an external, bad object.

She considers herself bad and flawed: "If he gets too close to me, he will abandon me; if he finds out the truth about me, he will run away. Better that he should live in a fantasy".

She incentivizes and reinforces his pathological fantasy defense. Feeds him with drama and conflicts to keep him busy and distracted as he desperately attempts to realign, reframe, and redefine his internal objects.

Borderline pushes narcissist to become psychotic while narcissist pushes borderline to become a psychopath.

968.

Watch Freud and Jung: Re-integrating the Narcissist's Self
https://www.youtube.com/watch?v=eLV8P_2spuo

"When alarmed, the child seeks proximity to a caregiver. But proximity to a frightening caregiver increases the alarm" (Hazen and McFarland, 2010)


969.
Where others strive to be nice, the narcissist is always contemptuous, coercive, and abusive.

People communicate by sharing - the narcissist lectures and hectors.

And while most people are, indeed, transactional - the narcissist is always exploitative.

970.

When lovebombing is an integral part of coercive control, intermittent reinforcement, and not the behavioral outcome of mental illness - it should be criminalized. But we are treading a thin line: we are beginning to criminalize flirting, courtship, intimacy, and sex.

971.

Narcissist is in a constant state of NDE, inhabits an inner landscape of internal objects, absent from reality. Borderline is in a constant state of NDE, absent from her inner world.

The abused and traumatized child was not allowed to become (separate-individuate) and so remained in a state of suspended mental animation, dead inside (emptiness or empty schizoid core).

Introjects represent significant figures the same way NDE patient meets up with deceased relatives.

Borderline depersonalizes the same way an NDE patient hovers about her body and observes resuscitation attempts.

Both hear voices the same way an NDE patient does. But they do not misidentify or misconstrue the sources of the voices as external (not psychotic).

972.

WATCH Narcissist Entrains Codependent, Borderline: Brainwash, Regulate, Repeat https://www.youtube.com/watch?v=gHAeew65frU

WATCH How to Individuate, Heal from Narcissistic Abuse https://www.youtube.com/watch?v=I3gmcbWsyBM

WATCH Narcissistic Abuse Recovery: First Separate, Individuate https://www.youtube.com/watch?v=95QBUV9CR_4

The shared fantasy results in a mass psychogenic illness affecting both members of the couple as well as in the victim's prolonged grief disorder.

This is because the grooming phase involves the induction of a trans or pseudo-hypnotic dissociative state in the suggestible targets: amnesia, depersonalization, derealization (gaslighting), and fantasy (paracosm).

The abuser entrains ("brainwashes") the abused party's mind and deploys intermittent reinforcement, approach-avoidance, trauma bonding, and abuse in all its forms to effect a transfer of regulatory functions from the victim to himself.

The entrainment of the abuser's intimate partner consists of the reorganization of her mind so that it generates nonautonomous cognitions and emotions ("artefacts") intended to make sense of the shared fantasy. These linger long after it is over.

973.

Abuse is about breaching boundaries and not allowing the child to separate and individuate (become a person). Both BPD and NPD are the sad outcomes of such bad parenting.

974.

Two types of shared fantasy: companionship (with compensatory, cerebral and covert narcissists) or submissive (with overt-grandiose and psychopathic narcissist).

975.

I published this article 23 years ago: "If all else fails, the abuser recruits friends, colleagues, mates, family members, the authorities, institutions, neighbours, the media, teachers – in short, third parties, a kind of "flying monkeys" – to do his bidding.

He uses them to cajole, coerce, threaten, stalk, offer, retreat, tempt, convince, harass, communicate and otherwise manipulate his target. He controls these unaware instruments exactly as he plans to control his ultimate prey. He employs the same mechanisms and devices. And he dumps his props unceremoniously when the job is done.

One form of control by proxy is to engineer situations in which abuse is inflicted upon another person. Such carefully crafted scenarios of embarrassment and humiliation provoke social sanctions (condemnation, opprobrium, or even physical punishment) against the victim. Society, or a social group become the instruments of the abuser.

Abusers often use other people to do their dirty work for them. These - sometimes unwitting - accomplices belong to three groups:"

Continued here: https://samvak.tripod.com/abuse11.html

976.

According to the dual mothership principle, when you break up with the narcissist or are discarded by him, you are orphaned. You need to parent yourself. Here's how:

See yourself: document yourself, revisit yourself, be your friend and mentor, get to know yourself.

Frustrate yourself, push yourself away (give yourself space), allow yourself to separate, individuate, and form proper boundaries, reality testing, get rid of magical thinking.

At the same time, be your own secure base: empathic, attuned, caring, loving, accepting.

Invest in and prepare yourself for physical reality, social reality (socialization), hegemonic culture (acculturation), and skills acquisition: research, skills acquisition, education, training.

Love yourself.

Self-love is a healthy self-regard and the pursuit of one's happiness and favorable outcomes.

It rests on four pillars:

1. Self-awareness: an intimate, detailed and compassionate knowledge of oneself, a SWOT analysis: strengths, weaknesses, others's roles, and threats;

2. Self-acceptance: the unconditional embrace of one's core identity, personality, character, temperament, relationships, experiences, and life circumstances;

3. Self-trust: the conviction that one has one's best interests in mind, is watching one's back, and has agency and autonomy: one is not controlled by or dependent upon others in a compromising fashion;

4. Self-efficacy: the belief, gleaned from and honed by experience, that one is capable of setting rational, realistic, and beneficial goals and possesses the wherewithal to realize outcomes commensurate with one's aims.

Self-love is the only reliable compass in life. Experience usually comes too late, when its lessons can no longer be implemented because of old age, lost opportunities, and changed circumstances. It is also pretty useless: no two people or situations are the same.

But self-love is a rock: a stable, reliable, immovable, and immutable guide and the truest of loyal friends whose only concern in your welfare and contentment.

WATCH Love Yourself: Here's How - or, The Four Pillars of Self-love
https://www.youtube.com/watch?v=2vzBf9QvClo

WATCH Narcissistic Abuse Recovery: First Separate, Individuate
https://www.youtube.com/watch?v=95QBUV9CR_4

WATCH How to Individuate, Heal from Narcissistic Abuse
https://www.youtube.com/watch?v=I3gmcbWsyBM

977.

Psychopathic narcissist would imitate a sensitive, much-wronged victim of narcissistic abuse, or an empathic savior-rescuer. S/he then proceeds to reel you in by offering you everything you ever dreamed of.

How to Recognize a Narcissist or a Psychopath on Your First Date, Before It is Too Late?

https://groups.google.com/g/NARCISSISTIC-PERSONALITY-DISORDER/c/XpBghb0rZL0

How to Spot an Abuser on Your First Date: The Tocsins of Abuse
https://samvak.tripod.com/abuse7.html

How to Recognise a Narcissist? https://samvak.tripod.com/faq58.html

978.

To justify our cognitive bias (the belief in karma, or "just-world hypothesis"), we blame and shame victims: they deserve their suffering, they had it coming.

Psychology attempts to stand out from philosophy and religion as a rigorous, almost exact science. Hence the rejection of morality and value judgments in psychological theories and practices.

But narcissistic abuse shatters our belief in a just cosmos. In this sense, it is a moral calamity.

LITERATURE

Griffin, B.J., Purcell, N., Burkman, K., Litz, B.T., Bryan, C.J., Schmitz, M., Villierme, C., Walsh, J. and Maguen, S. (2019), Moral Injury: An Integrative Review. JOURNAL OF TRAUMATIC STRESS, 32: 350-362.

https://doi.org/10.1002/jts.22362

Shay, J. (2014). Moral injury. Psychoanalytic Psychology, 31(2), 182–191. https://doi.org/10.1037/a0036090

Jinkerson, J. D. (2016). Defining and assessing moral injury: A syndrome perspective. Traumatology, 22(2), 122–130. https://doi.org/10.1037/trm0000069

Shay, Jonathan. "Moral Injury." Intertexts, vol. 16 no. 1, 2012, p. 57-66. Project MUSE, doi:10.1353/itx.2012.0000.

979.

Covert self-supplies and is avoidant. He is his own audience.

Overt depends on external sources and approaches them.

When unable to deceive himself owing to public shaming, the covert endures narcissistic injury and the overt endures mortification.

When unable to deceive others, the covert endures self-efficacy injury and the overt endures narcissistic injury.

Mortification in the covert is the simultaneous occurrence of both injuries: narcissistic and self-efficacy. It is an internal event, independent of any witnessing. It is self-shaming.

Crisis and drama - anxiety - are defenses against depression. Narcissist provokes and engineers crises intentionally and artificially to mask like-threatening emptiness, dysphoria, and anhedonia. Abusive misconduct is one such crisis-inducing dramatic strategy. Abuse is anxiogenic - but also anti-depressant. It is more common when the narcissist is deflated.

Reacts with self-aggrandizing paranoia or mythologizing fantasy.

980.

Watch 7 Phases of Shared Fantasy: Why Narcissist Needs YOU
https://www.youtube.com/watch?v=Kp3YFC0OQfU

Why does narcissistic abuse cease after the shared fantasy is definitely over? What in the shared fantasy triggers abusive misconduct?

The shared fantasy metamorphesizes and mutates. It can become paranoid or anticipatory or courting or nostalgic.

It is terminated only via mortification, successful devaluation (betrayal), or appropriation (introject taken over by a substitute maternal figure).

Once switched off, the abuse stop instantly and thoroughly. Why is that?

The maltreatment within the shared fantasy is reframed by the narcissist as tough love, reactive abuse, a test of loyalty and allegiance, or the outcome of disillusionment with and exposure of the partner (devaluation).

But the abuse is also a form of cathexis. It is a pattern of attempts to coercively align the external object with the idealized internal object in order to maintain the idealization.

The narcissist mislabels idealisation as profound love because it is a reciprocal process (co-idealization) and involves maternal introjects.

But the narcissist associates love with hurt and anxiety. The abuse is a prophylactic: preemptive effort to forestall pain and, possibly, mortification by controlling and manipulating the potentially frustrating objects, both external and internal.

When the internal object is dormant (suspended), discarded, or no longer idealised (cathected), it no longer possesses the power to hurt the narcissist. At that point, there is no longer call for abuse. Any interaction following this phase is civil, even amiable.

Still, the minute the object is re-idealized (recathected in the hoovering phase), the abuse starts all over again.

Abuse and idealisation are inextricably linked because idealisation is a form of abuse: it involves objectification, parentification, and instrumentalization.

981.

There is disagreement as to whether people diagnosed with Borderline Personality Disorder have an IQ which is higher than the average (Carver, 1977), or lower (Swirsky-Sacchetti, 1993). The same debate rages over NPD and psychopathy.

But this may be the wrong question. IQ tests measure types of intelligence that have little to do with life skills and perspicacity (wisdom).

The cluster B personality disordered are pseudo-stupid (covert) or actually stupid (overt, grandiose): their grandiosity (a severe cognitive distortion) impairs their reality testing and self-efficacy and it alienates people, narrowing their opportunities and subjecting them to adversity.

They often lack impulse control, are defiant and contumacious, or decompensate under stress. These drawbacks guarantee frustration or worse.

They are dissociative, so are bad at learning from past experiences.

They are entitled and manic, so never plan thoroughly or execute with attention to detail.

They are immature: the mental equivalents of children. This renders them naive and gullible. They leverage the appearance of infantile haplessness to signal: please don't hurt me!

Most of them suffer from identity disturbance and so unable to maintain continuity and coherence. They depend on others for external regulation of a sense of self-worth (NPD) or of emotions and moods (BPD). This dependency involves alloplastic defenses and a paralyzing external locus of control.

These dark personalities may be Machiavellian but they are so embedded in fantasy, paranoid, and firewalled by defenses that they are not very good at deceiving people or manipulating them in the long run. This is why they resort to entraining and coercion.

Finally, cluster B personalities are post-traumatic and compensatory. Broken and false. They also tend to abuse substances or develop addictions.

Image: page 169 of the manuscript of my autobiography (in Hebrew, written 1996-7 in Israel).

982.

Only the narcissist is the cause of his intimate partner's behaviors. No other causes are ever present during the idealization phase. When the narcissist withdraws (decathects and devalues), he ceases to exist as a cause and only other causes operate. This results in splitting and paranoia (other causes are all bad, narcissist all good).

The narcissist is omnipresent and always present because he interacts only with internal objects. So he is the cause of both the behavior - and its absence!

This dialectic is resolved by having to radically transform the traits and identity of the internal objects - or by denying reality (e.g., by reframing inaction as action).

Narcissists and even moreso psychopaths adhere to a rigid entity theory, cathect it (are proud of their rigidities), and convert it into an ideology, organizing and interpretative principles, and set of rules and values (axiology and deontology).

In cluster B PDs, the motives can be self-defeat, self-handicap, self-harm, self-trashing, and self-destruction. Rational self-love is inhibited. The mirror image of mental health.

Observing the behaviors of people with cluster B PDs leads to wrong inferences. They are compulsive, not free; chaotic not intentional (identity disturbance); always act abnormally and always in a way that brings opprobrium and worse (penalties).

Narcissist confuses external and internal objects and his cognition is distorted (grandiosity).

So, he is incapable of situational attribution, only of the dispositional kind with regards to the positive aspects of himself (grandiosity, hyperreflexivity) - and incapable of dispositional attribution only of the situational kind when it comes to the negative aspects of himself (alloplastic defenses).

He is incapable of any kind of attribution with regards to others. This is especially evident in the shared fantasy.

983.

The Psychology of Border Violations in Mental Abuse

Declarations: The Human Rights Podcast

Centre of Governance and Human Rights, University of Cambridge.

On Apple Podcasts and Spotify:
https://podcasters.spotify.com/pod/show/declarations/episodes/Season-7-Episode-6-The-Psychology-of-Border-Violations-in-Mental-Abuse-e246v1b

In our sixth episode, host Neema Jayasinghe is joined by previous podcast host and panellist, Dr Maryam Tanwir. With special guest, Professor Sam Vaknin, the episode unpacks discourses related to the psychology of personal border violations in mental abuse.

The conversation questions how borders and boundaries are not only demarcated, violated, or transgressed in global politics, but also at the level of the personal. Here, physical or mental abuse is a form of structured aggression, and can be surreptitious, coercive, or disguised in a myriad of ways.

Invariably, it involves the violation of our borders and boundaries - both personal and societal. In this episode, we explore these various levels of abuse and their psychological implications.

984.

Grieving in the wake of narcissistic abuse is a fantasy. We mourn the shared fantasy via a fantasy of grief.

We internalize the narcissist's snapshot of us which started off as a mental representation of reality and then became an idealized, fantastic, constant, internal object. We do it to both please the narcissist and to answer the question: what does he want from me? (Lacan's neurotic fantasy).

Self-contained vs. incorporating fantasy: reality repressed or reframed (cathected fiction, symbols, signifying structure), involves compensatory wish fulfillment (future) or reconstruction (past): erotic, aggressive, self-aggrandising, ego-syntonic, soothing (defensive, to avoid trauma, Lacan), and experimental (testing out scenarios safely).

In a shared fantasy, these roles are outsourced, allowing for passivity and a sense of safety and stability. In this sense, the intimate partner in a shared fantasy is rendered a borderline.

985.

In the wake of narcissistic abuse, attend therapy only once you have eradicated the narcissist's voice in your mind (his introject). Otherwise, it will hijack the process and use it against you.

With clinical psychologist @zukowska.daria

986.

Self-supply is critical in the regulation of the narcissistic personality, especially during the schizoid phases. These are some of the techniques the narcissist uses to self-supply:

Reframes reality
Inflated, counterfactual self-perception (good person victimized or paranoid ideation)
Reassigns weights to sources of supply with you as sole arbiter

Converts negative to positive supply (locus of grandiosity)
Future or past orientation (will be adulated in the future or would have been appreciated in the past)
Self-aggrandising referential ideation
Delusional revenge fantasies
Magical Thinking

987.

Failed hoovering leads to cognitive dissonance and to a delusional devaluation and discard (the narcissist convinces himself that he did not want you in the first place and that he is the one who has discarded you).

WATCH Why Narcissist Hoovers, Replaces YOU
https://www.youtube.com/watch?v=ACdRrnfcQKQ

WATCH "Hoovering": Narcissist Re-idealizes Discarded Sources of Narcissistic Supply https://www.youtube.com/watch?v=Va32SSPWa1w

988.

Two narcissists of the same type (somatic, cerebral, classic, compensatory, covert, inverted, etc.) cannot maintain a stable, long-term full-fledged, and functional relationship. Same goes for two codependents or two coverts.

Soon: video about covert borderline with borderline, covert narcissist, or codependent.

989.

You are out of the shared fantasy with your mentally ill ex.

But now reality itself feels unreal!

990.

Rejection, abandonment trigger separation insecurity and constitute extreme narcissistic injury (trigger grandiosity cognitive distortion).

The cognitive dissonance is resolved via a mix of aggression and passive-aggression.

Drama linked to hyperemotionality, fills the existential void, a simulated and compressed life

Entitlement to be unique and exclusive as measured via currency of attention.

Splitting (I am all good, s/he is all bad).

Projection

Hoovering is the ultimate goal unless mortification sets in (Borderline: unsafe, Narcissist: publicly shaming)

Aggressive techniques (histrionic and psychopathic comorbidities):

Revenge fantasies (rarely translated to action beyond ostentatious demonstrative acts like a smear campaign because the fantasy is perfect and action might fail and exacerbate the narcissistic injury).

Delusional reframing (I rejected him/her).

Actual violence.

Passive-aggressive techniques:

Triangulation (esp. emotionally injurious with best friend, worst enemy, colleagues, stable of exes, and so on)

Setting you up for failure (undermining, sabotaging, defeating, handicapping you):

Unrealistic demands or expectations.

Engineering situations that are bound to trip you up.

Motivating others to withhold help, support, or collaboration or to actively conspire against you.

Fostering an environment that requires talents, skills, or knowledge that you do not possess or do not excel at.

991.

<u>Autistic and dereistic thinking</u> are the only exceptions to enactivism.

Ways of relating to reality, experience, logic, and to other people.

<u>Fantasy-infused thoughts (dereism) or narcissistic and egocentric self-absorption (autistic).</u>

These patients's illogical and idiosyncratic cognitions derive from an overarching and all-pervasive daydreaming or fantasy life. They infuse people and events around them with completely subjective meanings.

They regard the external world as an extension or projection of the internal one.

Such patients often withdraw completely and retreat into his inner, private realm, unavailable to communicate and interact with others.

Examples: autists, narcissists, paranoids, delusional (religious).

Mindful Wealth Mastery AI channel
https://www.youtube.com/@mindfulwealthmastery/videos

The Psychology of Border Violations in Mental Abuse (Declarations: The Human Rights Podcast, Centre of Governance and Human Rights, University of Cambridge)

https://podcasters.spotify.com/pod/show/declarations/episodes/Season-7-Episode-6-The-Psychology-of-Border-Violations-in-Mental-Abuse-e246v1b

Vaknin Musings channel https://www.youtube.com/vakninmusings

Sam Vaknin's work on Academia.edu (top 0.5% of 270,000,000 academics) https://calmu.academia.edu/SamVaknin

Smear campaign debunked http://www.narcissistic-abuse.com/rebuttal.html

Work in psychology: http://www.narcissistic-abuse.com/mediakit.html

992.

If you are nice, kind, and drama-averse, stay away from cluster B dark personalities: they need, seek, and impose drama, even at the personal cost of being abused.

They are unforgiving when their cravings for drama go unmet.

993.

"Dead" mothers are emotionally unavailable, self-absorbed, withholding, frustrating, neglectful, and hurtful. I examine three types: the mother with Borderline Personality Disorder (BPD), with Narcissistic Personality Disorder (NPD), and the psychotic mother. The last 20 minutes are dedicated to a deeper analysis of Andre Green's work.

WATCH How to Be Good Enough Mother
https://www.youtube.com/watch?v=eFTlUGFvQEU

WATCH 13 Signs of Mentally Ill Family (5th World Mental Health Congress) https://www.youtube.com/watch?v=MxKkBkbOeMA

WATCH Are Fathers Needed? Mothers Are, For Sure! (Literature Review)
https://www.youtube.com/watch?v=RQd5jIQbfF0

LITERATURE

Green, André. (2001). The dead mother. In his Life narcissism/death narcissism (Andrew Weller, Trans.). London, New York: Free Associations Books.

The Dead Mother: The Work of Andre Green (New Library of Psychoanalysis), Gregorio Kohon, 1999

994.

Here is the bleeding-edge info about Antisocial Personality Disorder and its extreme form, psychopathy. From heredity and neuroscience to psychopathology and medication.

Just reload/refresh the page after YouTube's warning.

995.

You are victimized through no fault of your own.

But, you choose to be a victim.

Victimhood is a grandiose identity, self-defeating, toxic, and coercive.

996.

The diversity of microorganisms in the gut and the ratios between different phyla of bacteria have a substantial effect on the brain and on mental health and illnesses, including Borderline Personality Disorder, Major Depressive Disorder, Autism Spectrum Disorder, and Anxiety Disorders.

LITERATURE

The gut microbiome and mental health: advances in research and emerging priorities, by Andrew P. Shoubridge, Jocelyn M. Choo, Alyce M. Martin, Damien J. Keating, Ma-Li Wong, Julio Licinio & Geraint B. Rogers, Molecular Psychiatry volume 27, pages1908–1919 (2022)

Gut microbiome-brain axis and inflammation in temperament, personality and psychopathology by Alexander Sumich, Nadja Heym, Sabrina Lenzoni, Kirsty Hunter

Current Opinion in Behavioral Sciences, Volume 44, April 2022, 101101

https://doi.org/10.1016/j.cobeha.2022.101101

Alterations of the gut microbiota in borderline personality disorder by

Hannah Rössler, Vera Flasbeck, Sören Gatermann, Martin Brüne

Journal of Psychosomatic Research, Volume 158, July 2022, 110942

Pathoetiology and pathophysiology of borderline personality: Role of prenatal factors, gut microbiome, mu- and kappa-opioid receptors in amygdala-PFC interactions by George Anderson, Progress in Neuro-Psychopharmacology and Biological Psychiatry, Volume 98, 2 March 2020, 109782

997.

Grandiosity is a diagnostic dimension in NPD, BPD, psychopathy, Bipolar Disorder (the manic phase), paranoid PD, some psychotic disorders, and a host of other mental health problems.

But grandiosity is not the same as pathological narcissism, which includes many more clinical aspects.

Therefore, NPD has to be diagnosed separately in all the above conditions (comorbidity).

If it is not diagnosed - then the patient is not a narcissist, regardless of their grandiosity and haughtiness.

Thus, only a minority of borderlines and psychopaths are narcissists.

998.

Narcissist's insignificant other provides any 2 of the following 4 Ss:

Sex
Services
Supply
(narcissistic or sadistic)
Safety

999.

The narcissist internalizes a "snapshot" of you (introjects you) and continues to interact only with it, never with you out there. Narcissists never interact with external objects, only with internal ones.

The narcissist punishes and devalues you every time you deviate and diverge from the static, idealized snapshot.

Video by @shadowdeangelis

1000.

Watch Child's Defense Against Madness: Personality Disorders (Schizotypy and Neoteny)
https://www.youtube.com/watch?v=Y0az5F9igi8


Psychosis or Schizophrenia?

Schizotypal, Schizoid, Paranoid Personality Disorders are pre-psychotic.

Role play in (erotic, aggressive, self-aggrandizing) fantasy (e.g., hero) about self (others=self)

Self-directed self-efficacy (wish-fulfilment and substitutive action as self-regulation)

Pathetiology: childhood trauma (PTSD)

Internal vs. External (hyperreflexivity)

Paranoia and Paranoid PD

Magical thinking (persecutory: demons or grandiose: hero, tasked by god)

Delusions (cognitive distortions such as grandiosity)

Hallucinations (stress in BPD)

Derealization and depersonalization

Lability and dysregulation (erratic)

Self-perception (e.g., as victim)

Anhedonia

Reduced affect display

Avolition

Asociality

WATCH Narcissist to Schizoid to Psychotic: Progression, Common Roots, Modernity https://www.youtube.com/watch?v=yzYq6HvL9eM

LITERATURE

Psychosis and Schizophrenia-Spectrum Personality Disorders Require Early Detection on Different Symptom Dimensions by Frauke Schultze-Lutter, Igor Nenadic, and  Phillip Grant

Front. Psychiatry, 11 July 2019, Sec. Psychopathology, Volume 10 - 2019 | https://doi.org/10.3389/fpsyt.2019.00476

Psychotic symptoms in borderline personality disorder: developmental aspects by

Marialuisa Cavelti, Katherine Thompson, Andrew M. Chanen, Michael Kaess, Current Opinion in Psychology, Volume 37, February 2021, Pages 26-31

The Concept of Narcissism in Psychosis and in Severe Personality Disorders by Trifu, Simona; Zamfir, Raluca.  Euromentor Journal; Bucharest Vol. 5, Iss. 1,  (Mar 2014): 120-127.

1001.

How Narcissist Breaks Your Spirit: conditioning (both classical and operant), entraining, shared fantasy, coercive control, snapshotting.

1002.

The extent of the narcissist's self-deception defies belief.

He even deceives himself into believing that he is not deceiving himself.

1003.

"Empaths" are self-aggrandising professional victims, most likely covert narcissists. Everyone has empathy, even narcissists and psychopaths.

1004.

<u>My new concepts are now being shamelessly plagiarized and stolen</u> - and not for the first time: "snapshotting" (confusing external and internal or introjected objects), the dual mothership (regression to infancy in intimate relationships), and the shared fantasy space, among others.

I found one exception, a breath of fresh air: this guy @shadowdeangelis (Cyberviking on TikTok).

The covert narcissist steals from you habitually: your ideas, your life's work, your girlfriends and wives, your job, your money, anything he can.

He acts this way for 3 reasons:

Self-aggrandisement

Oneupmanship

Passive-aggression (symbolic destruction of the frustrating object of narcissistic rivalry and malicious envy)

To be able to face himself in the mirror and to allay his justified fear of retribution, the covert narcissist deploys a host of good object infantile primitive defenses:

denial (the things I am stealing do not really belong to him and actually what I am doing is for the greater good);

repression (I don't recall the stolen ideas or goods being someone else's);

splitting (he is a bad person and deserves what I am doing to him, so my acts of pure theft are punitive and morally upright); and

projection (he stole these things from me or I paid for them, so I am just reclaiming them).

1005.

Video presentation at the 40th Global Psychiatry and Mental Health Conference, July 17-18, 2023 London, UK

Is malicious envy a form of sadism? Wish to destroy your betters is. Covert narcissist's pseudo-humility and victimhood stance masks sadistic malicious envy. He compensates with fantasies (good person, superhero against supervillains, behind the scenes power, rescuer/savior/healer, etc.)

Our wellbeing depends on connectivity and narcissists are hurtful because they deny this possibility.

Sadistic component in narcissistic pathological related to power, not only to pain. More precisely: to the power to inflict pain, even if it is not used. Sadism is mediated via sadistic rivalry and malicious envy.

Sadism can be externalized-aggressive (inflicting pain) or passive-aggressive (frustrating, withholding, avoiding).

Wary of possible retribution, narcissists withdraw into a world of fantasy where they are adulated, loved, and shielded from the consequences of their actions (because they are preciously unique or childlike).

LITERATURE

Pathological narcissism and sadistic personality: The role of rivalry and malicious envy by Guyonne Rogier, Alessandro Amo, Beatrice Simmi, Patrizia Velotti, Personality and Individual Differences, Volume 205, April 2023, 112097, https://doi.org/10.1016/j.paid.2023.112097

1006.

The narcissist acts childlike and weaponizes his infantile vibe in order to:

1. Manipulate people to do his bidding
("How can you do this to a toddler, not give them what they want?")

2. Avoid and evade adult responsibilities and culpabilities
(Learned helplessness coerces others to step in, a codependent strategy)

3. Disarm potential intimate partners and adversaries by provoking parental reflexes ("I am just a kid, don't hurt me, I need your love and forgiveness")

4. Garner narcissistic supply ("He is so creative! He sees the world through a child's eyes!")

1007.

You can see overt-grandiose narcissists coming. They are in your face. You can take protective measures. Not so with covert narcissists: they snakes in the grass, slow-acting poison.

1008.

Watch Covert Narcissist's Sadistic Envy Fantasy (conference presentation) https://www.youtube.com/watch?v=beIvpL4Fz4E

WATCH an honest person in the last 6 minutes of this video.

My new concepts are now being shamelessly plagiarized and stolen - and not for the first time: "snapshotting" (confusing external and internal or introjected objects), the dual mothership (regression to infancy in intimate relationships), and the shared fantasy space, among others.

I found one exception, a breath of fresh air: this guy @shadowdeangelis on Instagram (Cyberviking on TikTok).

The covert narcissist steals from you habitually: your ideas, your life's work, your girlfriends and wives, your job, your money, anything he can.

He acts this way for 3 reasons:

Self-aggrandisement

Oneupmanship

Passive-aggression (symbolic hyperreflexive consuming of the frustrating object of narcissistic rivalry and malicious envy)

To be able to face himself in the mirror and to allay his justified fear of retribution, the covert narcissist deploys a host of good object infantile primitive defenses:

denial (the things I am stealing do not really belong to him and actually what I am doing is for the greater good);

repression (I don't recall the stolen ideas or goods being someone else's);

splitting (he is a bad person and deserves what I am doing to him, so my acts of pure theft are punitive and morally upright); and

projection (he stole these things from me or I paid for them, so I am just reclaiming them).

1009.

The art of con artists is their con.

They could have easily become what they falsely claim to be. So, why don't they?

Because they abhor, loathe, and are terrified of intimacy and commitment.

They prefer fantasy where these are not required and they can bail out at any time.

They substitute drama for reality because the former is thrilling and has an expiry date.

They are too easily bored with the world. They need to be bigger than life in order to feel alive at all.

Narcissistic fraudsters are also grandiose. When confronted with the truth about who and what they are, they experience life-threatening shame.

They con and scam in order to ward off depression and suicidal ideation. It is a survival strategy.

1010.

Former cult members are typically gullible, mentally unwell, and unintelligent.

Many of them are virulent covert narcissists.

Driven by malicious envy, humiliation, and narcissistic rivalry, they seek to expose and take down cult leaders in order to engender a cult following for themselves.

They maintain a facade of pseudo-humility and the semblance of a moral crusade, casting their relentless self-promotion as a morality play of good vs. evil (splitting).

1011.

As many of you know, my ideas and work are recently being egregiously plagiarized and monetized. The typical plagiarist is a collapsed (often covert) narcissist.

To be able to face himself in the mirror and to allay his justified fear of retribution, the plagiarist deploys a host of "I am a good object" infantile primitive defenses:

denial (the ideas and work I am stealing do not really belong to their current originator and actually what I am doing is for the greater good);

repression (I don't recall the stolen ideas or work being someone else's);

splitting (he is a bad person and deserves what I am doing to him, so my acts of pure theft are punitive and morally upright); and

projection (he pilfered these ideas and work from me or I paid for them, so I am just reclaiming them).

Return

# Sex
# And
# Intimacy:
# Forgotten Arts

234.

<u>Transactional sex</u> is any exchange of sexual services for goods, services, and benefits, however minimal - or for the promise of such in the future, within a relationship, a perceived liaison (fantasy), or extradyadically.

A multitude of studies had demonstrated the strong connection between unrestricted sociosexuality, dark triad traits (subclinical psychopathy, Machiavellianism), self-focused sexual motivation, and the Ludic (game-playing, manipulative) love style.

A transactional attitude to sex was also correlated with a borderline personality organization: impulsivity, dysregulation, compulsivity, anxiety, a history of trauma or victimization, unstable interpersonal relationships, and low self-esteem.

Unexpectedly, multiple studies have shown that subclinical narcissism is not correlated with a propensity for transactional sex.

People who are into transactional sex often mistake their involvement (emotional investment in the goal or the project) as "love" or "intimacy".

235.

<u>Sex is an act of love. Love is not merely a sex act.</u>

When sex is confused for or conflated with love, there is no love and no (good) sex.

Psychopaths often mistake the two (unrestricted sociosexuality is associated with dark triad personalities).

236.

The New York Times published yesterday an opinion piece against marriage, calling on people to remain single. It is titled: "What Does Marriage Ask Us to Give Up?" And the answer: "Our hard won independence as singles".

What this odious op-ed wants you to think is that all marriages are bad and that the ONLY alternative to marriage is to be single. Both assumptions are of course totally FALSE.

To resolve the onerous cognitive dissonance of loneliness, singlehood had become an ideology.

Everyone - men and women - are expected to be career-oriented, cherish money above all else, and act unrestricted sociosexually (be casual about sex). This is the new unigender role and its attendant social and sexual scripts.

According to Pew Center, maintaining one's career is 2.2 times more important than being in a committed relationship. Only about HALF trust their partner FOR ANYTHING (with the exception of faithfulness).

Embarking on a relationship and "catching feelings" are, therefore, threats to one's narcissistic self-actualization best fended off by keeping sex emotionless, meaningless, and never with the same person.

The 20% of the population who are promiscuous by nature thrive in this culture of hookups (and bad, drunk sex). They remain single for life.

Unrestricted sociosexuality is correlated with subclinical psychopathy, substance abuse, and extraversion.

The remaining 80%, having endured the vagaries and dangers of modern "dating", recoil. About 60% end up in a succession of committed liaisons (marriage, cohabitation). The remaining 20% go celibate and become lifelong singles.

All told, only about half the adult population share their lives with someone intimate. The rest are equally divided between celibate singles and sexually active singles who are exclusively into intoxicated one night stands and anonymous group sex.

237.

Loving someone requires courage. Being vulnerable open you up to malice, hostility, and aggression. It also transforms you, getting rid of your old self. But you need top take this leap of faith to grow and heal and complete yourself.

238.

Is your relationship abusive but not dead or beyond hope? How to tell relationships apart and what can you do to revive your partnership?

239.

Why do women participate in swinging (The Lifestyle), gangbangs, dogging, camming, and other forms of multiparty kinky sex?

The few who venture out with strangers and without the presence of an intimate partner are dark triad personalities and, typically reckless primary (factor 1) psychopaths, acting out borderlines (factor 2 psychopaths), or histrionic narcissists - all more or less one and the same diagnosis, according to emerging current research.

The risks involved, breaching the taboo, being the center of male attention and desire, and the novelty arouse them.

It is a dual trip of power and ego and also a way of showing the middle finger - and much more besides - to social mores and conventions, including the male double standard.

But even these hardened Amazons ultimately seek acceptance, to be "liked or loved", and to belong (to a gang, to a man they fancy). Their deep motivation is nonautonomous.

The codependents among these women strive to enhance the intimacy with their existing partners by sharing these unusual experiences. These are usually communal psychopaths.

All of them share an instrumental view of sex: as a trade off for goods and services, a prop to self-esteem, or a method to fend off abandonment.

They tend to dissociate the mostly degrading sex. They numb their emotions and have reduced affect display.

Some of them embed their activities in the context of a victimhood narrative (feminism) or an ideology (empowerment) while allowing multiple men to objectify and disempower them in the hookup culture, for example.

Decoupling sex from true and deep emotions protects the participants from trauma and renders swinging couples happier (more ego syntonic) than vanilla coupled, studies show.

240.

The current dichotomous taxonomy of <u>sociosexual orientation</u> is lacking.

People with restricted sociosexuality crave sex only with committed, emotionally meaningful relationships.

The unrestricted kind are turned on by casual and stranger sex but have difficulties with intimacy and fidelity in long-term relationships.

A third category is missing: dysregulated sociosexuality. These are people who are exhibitionistic, sadomasochistic and otherwise paraphiliac. They tend to prefer kink, group sex, extreme stranger sex (like dogging and glory holes), live camming, and self-objectifying sexual encounters.

Psychopathy and extraversion are highly correlated with unrestricted sociosexuality. They may also be the dark triad drivers of the dysregulated variant.

241.

<u>Female promiscuity and mate poaching</u> rise in societies (e.g., Baltic states, Russia) and environments (for instance: colleges) with adverse sex ratios (fewer men than women).

But the same applies when men absent themselves by going abstinent and celibate or by refusing to commit and invest in long term relationships.

These male avoidant behaviors create a virtual gap that affects sexual strategies of both sexes and tilt them towards short-term mating (aka casual sex).

We need to come up with a new measure: sex availability ratio. How many men and women make themselves known in the sexual marketplace at any given moment. This is a much more accurate predictor of the evolution and prevalence of sociosexual scripts.

242.

Studies in the past 40 years have upended everything we thought we knew about <u>female sexuality in the West</u>. A few nuggets:

Women orgasm mostly from digital or oral clitoral stimulation. Penetration doesn't do it for them.

Women are likelier to cheat during estrus (ovulation).

Women are three times more likely to be lesbian than men are to be homosexual.

Women prefer good looking men for one night stands and men with a stable income for long-term relationships. No wonder sexlessness in couples (21%) and infidelity (45%) are off the charts. The numbers are likely massively underreported.

The two main sexual fantasies of women are: to be kidnapped and raped and to participate in an orgy or a gangbang. But only about 8% act on their fantasies.

Women desire casual sex (though not as much as men do), but are deterred by considerations of risk, social stigma, and the orgasm gap. Removing these obstacles increases their willingness to bed even total strangers.

Most younger women have sex usually when they are drunk.

Women feel empowered and desired in group sex and, having tried it, want it more than men.

Women tire of the sexual monotony of monogamy sooner than men. Increasingly, women are the ones who avoid committed relationships. The majority of divorces are initiated by women.

A majority of female singles turn celibate, but a substantial minority (about 20%) lead a life of hookups, dating, and group sex (sex parties).

Far fewer women are getting married or having - far fewer - children. The replacement rate in all industrialized countries is unmet. Populations are aging and declining rapidly everywhere from the UK to Russia to China.

Women place studies, career, travel, and having fun with friends way above having a committed relationship even as a majority of them harbor a nebulous goal of "getting married one day". Few mention children even as an aspiration.

About one third of women are lifelong singles and another one sixth are lesbians.

243.

"Savage Love" is a sex and relationship column for straight couples spewed out by Dan Savage, a gay LGBT activist.

In one of the more memorable pieces, he asks why should you sacrifice a life you have had together and break up with your partner or divorce him only because you find out that he has had oral sex with someone else on a business trip.

It is not about the blowjob, Savage. No one walks away over the physical act. It is about the <u>betrayal</u>, the breach of trust, and the abrogation of the explicit and implicit contract of monogamy.

You want to be free to have sex with others? Honestly communicate it to your mate and agree to have an open relationship, granting her the same freedoms.

That the world's leading relationship advice columnist doesn't grasp these basic tenets of decent behavior goes a long way towards accounting for why we find ourselves in the dystopia of our contemporary world.

244.

<u>Real sex</u> is soon going to be a thing of the past: holographic porn, sex dolls, AI sex apps, VR and AR sex in the Metaverse, and AI sex robots will easily outcompete the carbon-based versions, especially where men are concerned.

This transition will give rise to a host of new ethical and behavioral questions.

Two examples:

A woman who would use a futuristic haptic dildo linked directly to her CNS (central nervous system) to penetrate a partner - is she really a man?

After all she would experience the extension exactly as a man does his penis!

Another one:

Does sex on a trip with a gorgeous AI robot amount to cheating on your mate?

The robot is the product of a collective of minds. So is consummating intercourse with such a contraption a form of group sex?

And what is the meaning of the very words "sex" and "gender" in such a world?

Gender is performative, the outcome of socialization, an expression of dominance, and of a gendered personality. But do all these apply to "gendered" robots?

Sex is biological, albeit fluid. Robots are nonbiological entities. So, do they have a "sex"? What about transgendered robot which switch from male to female in mid act?

And what does the phrase "artificial or virtual sex" mean anyhow? In which sense is full-fledged sex with another object not "real" sex?

245.

Studies show that young people regard sex as the opposite of emotional intimacy, they decouple the two.

They sleep only with people they are unlikely to "catch feelings for" or who they even actively dislike.

When they do end up being attracted to someone or get infatuated (limerence), they delay the sex with that person and in some cases, avoid it altogether.

The sex in the committed relationships of the young is totally different to the sex they are having with strangers: it is a lot LESS authentic, it is fake, constrained, and anxious.

The young feel much more comfortable to express their true sexuality in one night stands because they are unlikely to be judged or rejected and, even if they were it is no big deal: they don't care about the partner and will never see them again.

Casual sex is frequently bad because it is self-centred, disrespectful of the partner and her needs and pleasure, and objectifying.

Consequently, while in the initial phases, relationship sex is more gratifying (there is no "orgasm gap" between men and women). But, it typically deteriorates into tepid sex or into sexlessness and results in skyrocketing infidelity among both genders, probably because of the inability to integrate emotions with sex.

## 246.

Infidelity with a stranger in a drunken one night stand has a liberating effect on some women. It can be therapeutic.

Cheating allows them to break free from abusive, dead, and dysfunctional relationships.

The identity of the other man rarely matters, the sex is often cursory and bad, and the whole dreary affair is meaningless and emotionless. It is frequently a one-off.

But the very ability to obliterate this last remaining boundary and the resolve to cross the exclusivity Rubicon empower the woman and destroy any last vestige of attachment and bonding to her long lost intimate partner.

## 247.

It is crucial that you learn everything about the personal and sexual history of your intimate partner. Absolutely insist on full disclosure.

Consider promiscuity, for example.

The following facts are not manosphere anecdotes. They are the findings in multiple studies.

Sociosexually unrestricted folks (casual sex practitioners) are 3-10 times more likely to divorce.

The reasons they give for settling down after a spree of sex with multiple strangers are all wrong: they are "exhausted", interested in financial security or sharing the burden, and other self-centred motivations.

Sociosexually unrestricted people are subclinical psychopaths (dark personalities).

Promiscuous people perceive long-term committed relationships as "giving up" on freedoms rather than as gaining from the togetherness.

They trade sex for safety. As they age, they have a much poorer body image, so they are looking to convert their fast dwindling assets into durable, lifelong goods and services afforded by an intimate partner.

Even so, promiscuous partners set an impossibly high bar sexually and so are always disgruntled about the quality and/or frequency of sex in the serious relationship.

While capable of commitment, they get bored of their relationships much faster than their partners and they cheat way more often than their non-promiscuous peers.

Their grievances legitimize their cheating (usually in bouts of casual sex) in their minds.

Still think that you should not find out everything you can about your partner's sexual and relationship history?

248.

Giving up on an intimate partner we love is discarding a part of ourselves, it is the closest we ever get to real death while still alive.

We mourn our amputated self, who we could have been with him, and who we are doomed to never be without her.

249.

Fact check: female promiscuity is as common as male licentiousness in most animal species.

Read Lucy Cooke's recent book "Bitch: A Revolutionary Guide to Sex, Evolution and the Female Animal."

Work by field researchers like the primatologist Sarah Blaffer Hrdy and the ornithologist Patricia Gowaty is helping to remove the sexist biases and double standards embedded obstinately in the study of female sexuality which is proving to be as agentic, aggressive, competitive, and varied as any male's.

But there are very important caveats.

There is no animal equivalent of sexual self-trashing, which is the pathological abuse of sex.

Moreover: humans are the only animals that fail to reconcile promiscuity with monogamy and intimacy as long-term mating strategies.

Promiscuous people are far less capable of maintaining committed relationships, divorce way more often, and are far more likely to cheat on their partners. Facts. Unpalatable and politically incorrect - but facts all the same.

Moreover: <u>promiscuous (sociosexually unrestricted) humans</u> are statistically way more likely to have a dark triad personality (ie., to be subclinical psychopaths).

Humans are evolved animals. The gap between humans and all other animals is qualitative, not quantitative: it is a quantum leap.

Humans have brains, historical and autobiographical memories, creative imagination, emotions like shame and guilt. They live in societies and cultures, subject to sanctioned mores and conventions.

We can learn precious little about humans from ethology or evolutionary psychology. Human promiscuity possesses many dimensions absent in the animal kingdom. To claim otherwise is to regress us to our origins as beasts of the field and denizens of the savannah.

250.

You can attain a level of <u>intimacy with an anonymous stranger</u> in 2 hours that you can never reach with your spouse of 20 years:

Divulge your darkest secrets

Try out the kinkiest sexual fantasies

Abuse any number of substances, legal and illegal

Partake in heart-stopping recklessness

Be at your most authentic: no psychological defensive makeup and no acting. You couldn't care less about the judgment or the opinion of a visitor for the night. In a one night stand you can be yourself because it is risk-feee: there is no relationship or a partner to lose.

And then you part ways and watch that person as s/he exits your life, safely carrying with him or her 50% of the memories of your joint nocturnal adventure.

Inevitably, there is a kind of ephemeral misplaced nostalgia. But it dissipates in the harsh light of day and when you have reclaimed your true life from this hallucinatory, inebriated respite.

You never think of that stranger again or of what you had done together or of what might have been because indulging in emotions, however rudimentary, would tear asunder the very fabric of the desolate loneliness that you call your existence.

Better forget and forgive yourself.

251.

Most women - and some men - develop <u>cognitive dissonance in the wake of casual sex</u> with strangers, in many cases fueled by disinhibiting alcohol.

This is the outcome of the societal double standard ("men are studs, women are sluts") and the compromise of standards involved - as well as the thwarted emotions and intimacy that accompany every sexual encounter, however inconsequential.

Women adopt four counterfactual and self-deceiving narratives to cope with shame, guilt, and regret after a one night stand (bad sex bordering on sexual assault in the majority of cases):

EMPOWERMENT

I wanted the sex. Men are my bitches. I use their bodies to gratify myself, then dump them. Or: he was so interesting and cool, I just had to have sex with him.

NO OTHER CHOICE

If I don't bed a man immediately, someone else will. It is a numbers game: the more men I sleep with, the better my chances of finding an intimate partner

WISE MATE SELECTION

I sleep with men on a first date so as to make sure that we are sexually compatible. Why waste any further time on a man if we are not?

ENCHANTMENT

I have no boundaries in sex, so the man gets addicted to it and is bound to return for more.

252.

When you wake the morning

red headed children shimmer in your eyes.

The veinous map

of sun drenched eyelids

flutters

throbbing topography.

Your muscles ripple.

Scared animals burrow

under your dewey skin.

Frozen light sculptures

where wrinkles dwell.

Embroidered shades,

in thick-maned tapestry.

Your lips depart in scarlet,

flesh to withering flesh,

and breath in curved tranquility

escapes the flaring nostrils.

Your warmth invades my sweat,

your lips leave skin regards

on my humidity.

Eyelashes clash.

( From "Poetry of Healing and Abuse" http://www.narcissistic-abuse.com/contents.html )

253.

Porn-fuelled casual sex is now the dominant sexual script in all age groups, among men and women. The only alternative is celibacy.

This decoupling of sex from intimacy in relationships also resulted in performative sex: a tsunami of self-porn and group sex.

Nudity and sex, including masturbation on camera, sexting, and camming became accepted forms of performance art. Sex has transitioned from the private sphere to the public domain.

Bereft of its most potent and meaningful manifestation and mode of expression, intimacy is withering.

Half of adults are lifelong singles. At least one quarter of long-term committed relationships are sexless. About half of women and two third of men had cheated on their partner at least once. People are breaking up more frequently and are having more pseudo-liaisons in short-term dyads.

Marriage rates are down 50% since 1990; dating crashed by 60% since 1998, despite the proliferation of dating apps; and both the frequency of sexual activity and the number of partners are down by a third among people under age 25.

254.

It is crucial that you learn everything about the <u>personal and sexual history of your intimate partner</u>. Absolutely insist on full disclosure – but never judge.

255.

Always tell the truth about yourself to a potential intimate partner. <u>Be honest</u>.

Better to be rejected for who you ARE - then to be wanted for who you are NOT.

256.

Some people go <u>straight to sex</u> within the first hour or two of meeting someone because they feel that they have little else to offer and hope to hook a potential partner, no matter how lackluster the chemistry is.

It is a sad, dejected form of physical connection that often leaves a bad taste in the aftermath and results in cursory, decrepit one night stands.

Others trade sex for goods and services, big and small, current and future or just for fun, out of overwhelming boredom.

This second group think nothing of sex: it is a merely physical act, the coinage of their interactions. These are usually dark personalities (subclinical psychopaths and the sociossxually unrestricted).

There are those who offer any imaginable kind of unboundaried, self-objectifying, kinky and nonautonomous sex just in order to belong and be accepted or to secure attention and affection.

Many use sex as a form of communication. In lieu of saying "thank you for being nice to me" or "it was fun being together" - they undress. They often feel that they owe the sex out of gratitude.

The above are all considered psychosexual pathologies.

But there is a healthy variant of promiscuity: people who simply love the thrill of exploring new bodies and the fun of mutual desire. Their promiscuity is agentic and empowering. They are not entirely and always selfish, though. Many of them regard sex as a gift and sometimes bestow it on others as an act of kindness.

People cite two additional motivations for having sex with strangers: to emotionally detach from a previous partner ("break the spell") and to vet prospective partners for sexual compatibility before any further investment in them.

Vetting is very rational. Sex should be part of a third date at the latest. Why on the third date and NEVER on the FIRST? Because the budding intimacy improves the quality of the sex and reduces performance anxiety. Sex on a first date is not a real or efficient test. Sex on a third date definitely is.

257.

Love is about the strength to expose your weaknesses, the courage to trade your vulnerabilities, the stamina to endure the failure, losses, and hurt that are the ineluctable costs of its magic.

258.

Promiscuity is not about how many sex partners you have - but about why you are having sex in the first place. If you seek sex for all the wrong reasons with all the wrong people - you are promiscuous.

Promiscuity is not gender specific. Men can also be promiscuous.

Promiscuity has only negative outcomes in every way: it fosters anxiety, depression, and substance abuse. On the social level, it renders men more entitled and aggressive when they are turned down.

The promiscuous have dark personalities: most of them are subclinical psychopaths.

Promiscuity is addictive: it is thrilling (dopaminergic) and involves novelty-seeking and reckless behaviors.

Finally: promiscuous people engage in sex without intimacy, meaning, and emotions.

This becomes an ingrained habit, an addiction which is bound to resurface at some stage.

Relapses are common: promiscuous intimate partners are far more likely to cheat and do it serially. They are a lot more liable to be unable to commit to the relationship and to break up.

Promiscuity rewires the brain and stunts the development of relationship skills. It conditions its practitioner to sever any connection between sex and true, profound long-term intimacy and vulnerability.

Sex positivity is counterfactual: it flies in the face of decades if cumulative research. It is a pernicious and dangerous ideology that has ruined and is still devastating the lives of countless young men and women.

## 259.

What's wrong with voluntary sex work? It has social utility. The sex worker can make a FORTUNE out of activities that anyhow she engages in gratis.

I prostitute my brain. No different to prostituting one's vagina.

Condemning sex work is patriarchal thinking: men prostitute themselves - their muscles and brains - all the time.

The sex worker gets to meet fascinating men, have a regular sex life, gets invited to restaurants, bars, clubs, travel all over the world, and often ends up snagging a rich husband (a rescuer type). And I forgot to mention opportunities for group sex.

260.

<u>Hyposexuality or Hypoactive sexual desire disorder (HSDD)</u> is a desire disorder in the DSM: no libido, little or no sex, and DISTRESS about it.

Libido: attraction, desire, action towards self or object.

Some asexuals are not attracted sexually to anyone, have no desire, and many of them are sexless, they don't even masturbate. These asexuals have no libido.

Some asexuals masturbate. Others have periods of sexual activity. Some are repelled by sex. Asexuality is a spectrum.

The asexual orientation is lifelong or recurrent (intermittent).

Grey sexuality is between asexuality and sexuality. Example: demisexuals.

Asexual+distress=hyposexual

Ridiculous to say that there are no asexual narcissists.

All narcissists – somatic and cerebral – go through phases of asexuality in the wake of dysphoria (watch my video Narcissist's 3 Depressions).

It is asexuality and not hyposexuality because the narcissist experiences no distress regarding his sexuality although he is depressed about deficient or absent narcissistic supply.

261.

I keep telling @mikekimcomedy Mike: Intimacy is terrifying: exposing all your vulnerabilities often ends in pain and loss. But it is the only way to accomplish the 4 pillars of self-love:
https://www.youtube.com/watch?v=2vzBf9QvClo

262.

People who grew up in dysfunctional families tend to develop insecure attachment styles and flawed <u>mate selection</u>. They choose the wrong intimate partners in order to reenact unfinished early childhood conflicts within a comfort zone.

The <u>two types of "eligible" mates</u> are those who offer absence and threaten presence and those who smother with their presence and threaten with their absence.

The first kind are transactional, aloof, detached, cold, and emotionally absent. They make their presence known only when they want to accomplish a purpose (they are goal oriented).

The second variety of partner are exactly the opposite: their constant nagging, clinging, romantic jealousy, and dependency border on emotional blackmail. When in the throes of engulfment anxiety or when they anticipate or perceive rejection and abandonment - they tend to withdraw and avoid as both a self-preservation strategy and punitively.

Most frequently, one type of partner is selected lifelong, but sometimes there is type inconstancy.

263.

Sexual identity is not the same as <u>sexual orientation</u>. The former comprises self-perception, the latter is about others and involves sexual behavior.

<u>Sexual identity</u> forms in 5 stages:

1. Introjection of primary objects and role models, including parents, siblings, and peers. The child at this stage is genderless and pansexual and consequently autoerotic.

Initially, he is merged and fused with the parent (symbiosis). When he begins to separate from the mother, his narcissistic libido remains invested in her (Oedipal complex);

2. Emulation of a parent (same sex or other sex). This is affected by the parents's behaviors (e.g., abuse or sex aversion or sex positivity);

3. Exploration of potential sex partners of all sexes. This is coupled with identity diffusion;

4. Sublimation (a part of the socialization process): excluding certain sex partners as forbidden or inappropriate, acquisition of sexual skills and scripts;

5. Orientation: settling on a pattern of mate selection and attendant sexual behaviors.



264.

The <u>Oedipus and Electra complexes</u> have two etiologies. Freud and Jung have identified only one of them: competition with the same sex parent for the love and attention of the other-sexed one.

But there is an even more compelling source.

Until age 18-24 months, the infant is both <u>genderless and pansexual</u> and consequently autoerotic. His libido is turned towards itself as a love object.

But the infant is merged and fused with the mother throughout this period (symbiosis). They are one and the same. His narcissistic libido cathexes her as well!

When he begins to separate from the mother, his narcissistic libido still remains invested in her residually - and this is the Oedipal complex.

265.

"But I only had 30 sex partners! Most of them were one night stands, so I am not worn out, spent or used!"

Would you buy a car that changed 30 owners, even if the mileage is low?

<u>Men and women have the same sex drive</u> and should enjoy the same liberties.

The problem is that, for many disparate reasons, an early promiscuous lifestyle is incompatible with later life romance, intimacy, relationships, and family. It is an either/or proposition. Sexuality and intimacy are like muscles: use them or lose them.

Additionally, some young women (and fewer young men) go through phases of validation for their sexuality and then seeking committed relationships. These raise their "body counts" to sex worker levels and render them "not relationship material". The sexual double standard is still very much in force.

PS

While the data cited in the reel are wrong - the general thrust of the argument is scientifically accurate.

266.

Intimacy is a state of affairs, not a state of mind.

It has nothing to do with emotions.

This is why people can and do have sex (the ultimate intimacy) with total strangers.

Intimacy means sleeping together, talking, eating, making love. All these do not require any affect.

There is intimacy in prison, with a prostitute, in a hospital between patient and doctor, in psychotherapy. All these are emotionless states.

Intimacy in the clinical sense is a state of affairs involving proximity, vulnerability, and joint activities (life).

No strong emotions here.

267.

Sex is being redefined for the rest of us by sociosexually unrestricted people (the majority of whom are subclinical psychopaths).

Oral sex - especially blowjobs - as well as all forms of kissing (including French kissing) are now considered very common nonsexual acts.

There is a debate whether they are utterly meaningless or denote intimacy, but few would consider them sex acts let alone on par with penetrative sex.

Holding hands and kissing are widely believed to be way more intimate than oral sex and penetration.

This decoupling of sex from intimacy leads to new sexual scripts and practices among the young: sex is only for and with strangers.

Scholars noted statements such as: "I wanted it to remain impersonal, so I gave him a blowjob" or "I don't have sex with my partner because we are intimate and I respect him."

268.

Debunking three myths about women:

The female sex drive is more potent and multifaceted than the male's. Both sexes experience declines in sexual desire with age

Women are far less content in relationships and as parents than men. Childless but coupled women are the happiest, followed by singles, and then by mothers in relationships. Single mothers are the least happy (and the poorest).

Women initiate breakups and divorces 3 times as often as men and the best predictor of weak commitment and relationship dissatisfaction is the number of past sexual partners ("body count", a correlate of sociosexuality and subclinical psychopathy).

Women cheat half as much as men and when they do, they typically seek a long-term affair. But they fantasize about specific extradyadic potential partners a lot more than men do (hence romance lit).

269.

In the past, until the 1960s, people perceived sex as a must and a should. Something women had to provide in return for money or protection.

Nowadays, sex is perceived by men and women alike as a wish or a need, part recreational and part medical.

Consequently, sex is commoditized and anonymized, rendered less goal-oriented or transactional.

270.

The horror show that is <u>modern sexuality</u> is the gift that keeps giving.

Enemies with benefits is a new trend: seeking out your worst detractors and haters and then proceeding to sleep with them time and again. What's the point? No one is quite sure.

A much older trend, well-documented in the literature:

Young women feel like they have prostituted themselves when they have had sex while sober. Even with an intimate partner.

According to studies, modern women believe that it is shameful to have sex with strangers or even intimate partners while NOT under the influence - but totally understandable and excusable when drunk ("I was drunk, I didn't know what I was doing or I was taken advantage of").

The role of substance abuse (mainly alcohol) in the resolution of cognitive dissonance has become so entrenched that a majority of women now cannot have sex at all unless they are intoxicated.

271.

People with <u>unrestricted sociosexuality</u> (promiscuous, dissociative, dysregulated) are typically also subclinical psychopaths. Those who are not are frequently ego dystonic: they regret the sex and go through bouts of shame and guilt.

As time passes, to ameliorate the anticipatory anxiety ("I am lapsing again") as well as the cognitive and other dissonances, the latter sort begin to avoid situations and activities that lead to sex (constriction). In many cases, they end up being atomized, self-sufficient, and schizoid.

This is a common outcome in Borderline and Histrionic personality disorders - but not in somatic ego-syntonic narcissism.

272.

Women feel that <u>men are interested only in sex</u> and that they have to give sex to secure male attention and ameliorate male aggression.

This has always been the state of affairs between men and women.

But in the past few decades, the situation got out of hand because:

Men now feel entitled to free no strings attached sex. They become hostile if they don't get it.

It doesn't help that about 20% of women are dysregulated and mind numbingly promiscuous. They spoil men and ruin it for the other 80%.

I blame fourth wave feminism and the sex positivity movement for the mess we are in. It is a cult, a victimhood identity movement, narcissistic, borderline psychopathic.

Sex positivity is an anti-scientific pseudo-science. The ultimate con artistry.

Women objectify themselves for the sake of predatory men - and call it female empowerment.

273.

Most studies regard <u>promiscuity</u> as a life-long addiction. It can disappear even for decades but then erupts again.

Like alcoholism or drug addiction. It is very unsafe to partner with a promiscuous person:

Their cheating rate is 3 times higher

They break up 5 times more often

They rarely truly commit

Sooner or later they become promiscuous again.

There is no promiscuous "nature" (except in very rare desire disorders). It is always a reaction to the environment.

Some people react to environmental pressures and temptations with promiscuity - others don't.

If the behavior stops prior to age 18, the prognosis is a bit better - but not by much.

A large majority of promiscuous adolescents are subclinical psychopaths and have a borderline personality organization.

Subclinical psychopathy is lifelong. Borderline ameliorates with age.

Partnering up with someone who has a history of promiscuity even in puberty is Russian roulette.

This is why men avoid women with a high body count (unless they are lied to). Women actually avoid promiscuous men, too - but the sexual double standard precludes a typecasting of men as "promiscuous".

This is also why women egregiously lie about their body count. They cut it down by an average of 70%.

273.

We have outsourced most functions of the traditional family: education, healthcare, etc. Now we are outsourcing sex.

Young people, faced with an overwhelming cognitive dissonance, have redefined sex to exclude everything except penetration while sober. The rest is "not sex" so, it is rarely considered to be cheating or promiscuous.

Open relationships are already the norm in the LGBTQA+ community (60% of "couples").

The hookup Gen Z are adopting it as a solution in increasing numbers: they pursue gig sex mostly with strangers (because sex is the opposite of intimacy which they dread and are not skilled at).

Money and a single child are confined to the "relationship". But the youth's conception of a "relationship" has more to do with sharing economic burdens: roommates, basically.

274.

Men are willing to sacrifice everything for novelty and conquest. At heart, men are hunters and explorers. They would give up on a good relationship and qualitative sex just to impulsively experience a new body, however briefly.

Confronted with this unstable reality, women lie to themselves: "He is just a Platonic friend" (a mythical creature), or "I give him love and addictive sex, so he will never stray" (of course he will, given the opportunity).

Women seek safety. This is why hypergyny (hypergamy) is rank nonsense. Women will never speculate or gamble their secure base on a greener grass. Better one bird in a woman's cage than ten on any tree.

Women do tend to cheat and bail out of relationships in which they are the primary breadwinners or the partner is an inconsistent provider.

Since the educational attainment of women exceeds that of men, their lifelong earnings will at some point surpass those of their partners. This bodes ill for marriage, family, and other gender-based institutions.

## 275.

Drunken promiscuity - the most common variant - is often the confluenced outcome of five pathologies coupled with subclinical psychopathy:

1. Introject or object inconstancy

Out of sight - out of mind. The inability to maintain introjects of significant others or the incapacity to trust the permanence of meaningful others in one's life.

2. Transitional or comfort objectifying

The failure to attach to or bond with or cathect (emotionally invest in) other people (to transition to object relations). Using other people's bodies the way small kids use teddy bears or favorite blankets.

3. Identity disturbance

Fluctuating between mutually exclusive beliefs, values, behavior patterns, cognitions, and emotions (schema) owing to the absence of a core identity because of …

4. Pervasive dissociation

Amnesia, derealization, and depersonalization (feeling empty and unreal when alone or during sex).

5. Bad object

The punishment and denigration of an internalized bad object, egged on by punitive and sadistic introjects and a harsh inner critic ("I am a whore and I should trash myself").

Put together, these mutually-reinforcing dynamics result in compulsive attention seeking and acquisition (conquests) to the point of indiscriminate people pleasing on the one hand or predatory behaviors on the other hand.

<u>Sex is used as a currency</u> with which to purchase a temporary reprieve from this internal inferno.

276.

A new twist in the saga of <u>youth sexuality</u>: they hookup for a night and then they block each other (the most hostile act online). What gives?

The young fail to find or hold steady jobs (as distinct from gigs). They cannot afford to live on their own, acquire an education, or have a family.

Consequently falling in love and getting attached not to mention having a relationship are the greatest imaginable threats to the meager future of a young person.

The young describe as "clinging" and "needy" anyone who attempts to communicate after a typical few minutes of inebriated sex.

They are also conflicted about their own sexual behavior. They often feel degraded. To prevent all this from happening, they block each other. Blocking is as if the sex had never happened.

277.


<u>Promiscuity has different etiologies in men and women.</u>

Men are promiscuous because they feel special and, therefore, entitled to sex. It revolves around the wielding of power or control.

Most promiscuous women seek to validate and affirm an internalized and introjected bad object ("I am a whore, so I deserve to be degraded and punished for it").

In other words: unrestricted or permissive sociosexuality in men has narcissistic roots while in women, it is masochistic.

This holds true even when the woman or the man is a subclinical psychopath and claims to pursue and enjoy the sex for its own sake.

In promiscuous women (for example: borderlines and histrionic), this innate masochism breeds ambivalence: dependence on men and sex coupled with a resentment or even hatred of both.

278.

In the story "Cat Person" by Kristen Roupenian, the 20 years old protagonist is described as having had "not that many sex partners", only … seven!

So, <u>having sex with 7 men by age 20</u> is a lamentable deficiency. It is implied that her inexperience is to her detriment in her - drunken - dating life.

The new normal is inversion of the old normal, a mutually exclusive mirror image.

The same applies to relationships. They are perceived as threats to career and to hedonistic independence.

"What's in it for me, what am I getting out of it", are the key touchstones.

Patience, perseverance, compromise, communication, intimacy, and endurance are all obsolete skills.

Another example are children.

A sizable chunk of women remain childless by choice and many others eschew men altogether and opt to be single mothers.

But a child is perceived as just another shiny gadget: a way to alleviate the ennui and angst of modern life, a form of entertainment.

When exposed to the vagaries of childrearing and the ornery nature of kids, wannabe mothers confess to being far less happy than their childless peers.

Many of them begin to resent the child, regard it as an encumbrance or even a persecutory object, a form of insidious female-disempowering enslavement.

Plus ca change is wrong in this case. The new normal is a cataclysmic and unprecedented negation of human institutions, values, and history hitherto.

279.

<u>Women regret one night stands</u> way more than men do. A majority of them experience shame, guilt, and remorse the morning after.

Yet, both men and women find it difficult to orgasm in casual sex (women considerably more than men, aka the orgasm gap).

Men underreport bad sex because they regard themselves as self-appointed guardians to the quality of sex. Bad romp? Usually perceived to be the man's fault.

But why do women keep going for this kind of repellent sexual encounters, very often with men they are not even attracted to?

They have to compete with other women in a male dominated buyers' market. Immediate, unconditional sex is the only currency. Better get a first mover advantage over your peers and younger women.

Winning over a man - any man, however undesirable he is and however fleeting the attention - is a booster to self-esteem.

Women whose background is religious, traditional, or conservative - including immigrants - feel painfully conflicted and dissonant about the immense peer pressure to conform and not be a prude (or a slut). They are also more prone to submit to male desires and dictates, dissociating and reverting to "auto pilot" as they succumb.

Another reason for the orgasm gap is that most women seek connection and aim to please their partners in sex while most men masturbate with female bodies, emulating crude pornography, their only sex education.

280.

Some people stray and have sex with others in order to preserve and persevere in a <u>long-term obsessed and abusive relationship</u>.

Extradyadic sex in such couples (in the wake of drinking or substance abuse) serves to exact revenge on the partner, restore a power symmetry within the couple, cater to unmet emotional or sexual needs, and affirm an internalized bad object (the disparaging partner's point of view).

Such promiscuous, unboundaried, and sexually self-trashing behavior typically follows a period of loyal faithfulness met with traumatizing rejection and abandonment by the partner.

Whenever offered intimacy by the external instrumentalized and objectified sex partners (an invitation to stay longer or sleep over or meet again), the cheater reacts aggressively, recoils, and hurries back to her primary partner to reaffirm their dysfunctional bond.

Such a relationship dynamic is conducive to an inversion of traditional stereotypical gender roles: women become sexually predatory and men react with dysregulation. This is especially the case when both have daddy or mommy issues.

281.

<u>Promiscuous women</u> can be divided to users and "hos."

Users use men - not the other way around!

They objectify and instrumentalize men to defy authority figures or partners, exact revenge, triangulate, or secure attention, validation, and sex.

Users TAKE from men what they need and pay for it with sex. It is 100% transactional. They are masculine in all ways.

"Hos" or sluts NEED men all the time. They are weak. Nonautonomus and nonagentic. They GIVE sex to men but rarely take back. They need to be accepted and affirmed by men. They exist only around men. They act stereotypically feminine.

282.

About 70% of women and 40% of men hope for a relationship even in
hookups. About one third of relationships start in hookups.

Ironically, nowadays, people of both genders end up having sex with
numerous partners because they are way more selective than previous
generations. They test drive the sex on a first date and move on if the
partner underperforms.

But there is still one important difference.

A majority of women impose a counterfactual narrative fantasy on the
sexual encounter, trying to render it meaningful ("we will end up being a
couple"" or "this or he is so special" and so on).

The "meaningfulness" has nothing to do with the sex itself. It unfolds
autonomously as a way to reduce cognitive dissonance.

283.

Loving someone is its own reward. Even when it is reciprocated differently
than you would have wanted, not with love but with some other emotions.

It is a wonderful feeling to be in love even if it is not returned in exactly
the same way!

True love allows both parties to become MORE of themselves by
exploring themselves through the partner and the relationship.

True love is never merger, fusion, or dependency.

284.

Triangulation revolves around managing and controlling a relationship
dynamic by introducing a third party into the mix, emotionally or sexually.

Triangulating partners choose any third party who is perceived - in reality
or fantasy - as available.

When no specific third party is available to triangulate with, they makes
general triangulation statements such as:

"I always cheat; I can never be loyal; I can't resist my sex drive; cheating is meaningless; I don't give a damn about my partner; I don't even remember him when I have sex with others; I always do as I please at the moment" and so on.

Triangulation is used to get a rise out of the partner and thus restore the relationship; punish for some transgression, real, anticipated, or imagined; sustain a fantasy; or dissolve the relationship. Pushing your partner to cheat is also a form of triangulation.

The word gaslighting was invented in the 1960s, but I was the first scholar to use it in terms of narcissistic abuse (a phrase that I coined to describe the narcissist's annihilating abuse).

Triangulation and cheating in romantic relationships occur most commonly in two cases: when the intimate partner is not enough - or when they are too much.

Not enough love and too much love are flip sides of the same bad coin.

285.

Anxiolytic sex is the compulsive use of autoerotic (masturbatory) or alloerotic (with others) sex to ameliorate anxiety.

286.

Loving someone is not the same as loving the way he loves you.

Loving someone is not the same as loving to be in love.

Loving someone is not the same as merging with your partner.

Loving someone is not the same as hating loneliness or desperation.

Loving someone never involves fantasy or idealization.

Loving someone is not about assuming a parental role.

Watch Toxic Sex: When "Love" Is Bad For You
https://www.youtube.com/watch?v=sTDhld2pc20

287.

PLEASE ANSWER POLL QUESTION

When your <u>partner tells you that he is attracted to and is fantasizing about sex with another person</u>, you …

1. Become jealous and possessive and try to fend off the potential poacher (for example: by insisting that your partner blocks them everywhere); or

2. You cry, beg, and communicate to your partner how hurtful their words are, hoping for a change of heart and mind; or

3. You push your partner towards their new sex or love interest (loyalty test them) and, if they act on it, your break up with them irrevocably; or

4. You break up with your partner immediately, perceiving his words to be a form of triangulation.

I will go first. I usually do 3 and, much more rarely 4.

I did 2 only once in my life (she ended up dating and having sex with my best friend despite my pleading).

I never did 1. I never compete for my partner with others.

288.

The <u>heart has a mind of its own</u>. Underlying <u>obsessive love</u> are bad object introjects with automatic negative thoughts like "I don't deserve better", fantasy defense ("s/he is the perfect match for me"), and catastrophizing ("I will never find such a perfect match again").

It is a form of trauma bonding.

It is a reenactment of early childhood conflicts (mommy issues) or later life conflicts with parental figures (daddy issues).

Obsessive love is an addiction. Do not rush from one addiction to the next.

Obsessive love is a religion: it makes sense of the world, of your life, and of your behaviors. Find other sources of meaning.

Make a list of all the bad memories and read it aloud three times a day.

Go total no contact, no social media stalking.

Imagine them with others.

289.

Love defies logic, reason, and analysis.

Love denies age and distance and circumstance.

Love transcends boundaries and interests and fear itself.

Love thrives on adversity, complexity, and dreams.

Love just is: known instantly by its proponents, worshipped by its adherents, defeating all its enemies.

Every setback in love is temporary, every obstacle is overcome, every limit crossed.

Love triumphs where nothing does, flourishes without soil or water, prevails as it becomes.

290.

Most predatory sex is actually consensual - but the consent is given by an individual who is somehow compromised: drunk, drugged, heartbroken, crying, dissociative, scared, dependent, or otherwise helpless.

291.

In relationships, borders are like membranes: they allow in only selective types of communication, they require protocols and rituals, and are policed by cultural and societal mores. Borders are, therefore, interpersonal and dyadic.

Boundaries are individual.

Personal boundaries are rules of conduct, red lines in the sand any infringement and breach of which you deem unacceptable behavior.

You need to set your boundaries clearly, unequivocally, and unambiguously firstly to yourself: how to protect your dignity, privacy, freedom, rights, and priorities.

You then need to communicate your boundaries to your partner replete with a "price list": the costs associated with ignoring or violating them.

Finally, you need to be firm and enforce your boundaries: your credibility depends on a consistent and fair application of these rules of engagement.

The ability to thrive in intimacy is inextricably linked to the capacity to maintain and enforce personal boundaries. In personality disordered patients, both are sorely compromised.

Intimacy, however fleeting and of whatever nature (even merely physical) is a tightrope act.

On the one hand, it involves the disclosure of vulnerabilities and the relaxation of firewalls intended to fend off unwarranted or coerced attention.

On the other hand, real intimacy entails the maintaining of personal autonomy, agency, and self-efficacy. In other words: of separateness.

To attain intimacy, one needs to feel sufficiently secure of one's core identity, self-worth, self-esteem, internal regulation, and boundaries to invite another person in.

The mentally ill tend to enmesh, engulf, merge, or fuse with others - even as they push them away and flee (approach-avoidance repetition compulsion).

This dysfunctional attachment style is the outcome of twin contradictory anxieties: of abandonment and of engulfment.

292.

Watch Transgender, Transsexual: Biology or Society?
https://www.youtube.com/watch?v=K3ZFlv8ajKA

There are no rigorous studies of gender dysphoria. None. We know nothing about why adolescents (and even children) wish to transition and what happens to them after they do.

293.

No one can define what love is - but we do know <u>what love is not</u>.

294.

Shockingly, the <u>Dynamic-maturational model of attachment and adaptation</u> teaches us that the majority of attachment strategies lead to relationship failures.
295.

Need to be seen (even via self-supply own-audience) vs. need to not be seen by others and/or by oneself to avoid shame.

Relationships (including therapy) are about being seen: provoke dissonance, even threat (being seen and seeing oneself which trigger life-threatening shame).

Shame is gap in perception of how you should be (ego ideal) vs. belief that you are not as you ought to be.

Guilt goes with shame, shame can go without guilt or projected guilt (accusing others for causing one shame, mistreating one).

Ego ideal can be realistic and healthy or entitled and fantastic. Gap with reality generates concatenated shame (self-loathing) and anxiety in the wake of (sets up for) failure or avoidance.

Solutions: Change fantasy or Change reality.

Fantasy inversion owing to intolerable grandiosity gap: from positive to negative (cognitive dissonance).

Narcissist's self-perception is never real, only fantastic (all-positive aggrandizing godlike or total bad object).

Easier to match negative fantasy with reality. Restores calm and safety (my self-judgment is correct).

The negative fantasy is also grandiose: uniquely self-destructive and self-defeating bad object. Success in realizing it is self-supply.

When life matches fantasy, it yields comfortable ego syntony and makes it difficult to change one's life.

Negative fantasies create shame because it follows a failure with a positive fantasy.

Cathecting the negative fantasy proportional to shame regarding the failed positive fantasy.

Positive fantasy: gap with reality; Negative fantasy: gap with abandoned positive fantasy.

Self-fulfilling prophecy: behaviors determined to avoid dissonance with the negative fantasy.

Romantic jealousy is a negative fantasy

Cost of the negative fantasy: dissociation and identity disturbance.

296.

The media is misreporting the alleged criminalization of lovebombing in the UK.

In reality, the Crown Prosecution Service issued new guidelines outlawing lovebombing only when it is an integral part of a wider type of criminal behavior known as "coercive control" and only when it comes in the form of intermittent reinforcement (hot and cold, lovebombing followed by egregious abuse).

Intermittent reinforcing behaviors are manipulative: they confuse the victim and render her submissive. They create a "Stockholm Syndrome" or trauma bonding.

Gradually, victims begin to fear for their lives, alter their routines, and become socially isolated.

Coercive control is premeditated (mens rea), not the outcome of mental illness or personality disorders. It is intended to intimidate the victim, constrict her life, monitor her every move, deprive her of basic needs such as food, control her behavior, and deny her access to telecommunications, money, friends, family, help, and succor.

Controlling and coercive control micromanages the victim's every choice and decision, however minimal.

This is accomplished within a regimen of terror, degradation, and humiliation which involves multiple forms of abuse.

Some victims refuse to acknowledge the abuse and cast it as an idiosyncratic manifestation of love! Gifts and lovebombing reward compliant behavior and amount to conditioning.

297.

Promiscuity is the opposite of being able to have a relationship. In later life, sex becomes transactional.

298.

Childhood sexual abuse often results in BPD, DID (mainly OSDD) in adulthood.

Victims of sexual abuse in childhood dread and sexualize intimacy and being loved because they misidentify and conflate those with pain and boundary wrecking abuse.

Sex becomes an anxiety reaction or stress response.

The strategies used by these children, starting in adolescence involve: self-objectification, absenting oneself from sex and intimacy via dissociation (most notably derealization, depersonalization, and amnesia), and self-punitive choices intended to restore the good object (by penalizing and subduing the bad one).

299.

2 of every 3 people gave the silent treatment. It is increasing as alternative modes of interpersonal communication become mainstream.

Silent treatment is (1) efficiently punitive (2) social (takes a perpetrator and a target) (3) manipulative (controlling) (4) emotionally distant (5) exclusionary (6) plausibly deniable (element of gaslighting: not abuse) (7) coercive (forces the victim to apologize) (8) alloplastic (9) preserves negative affects (10) addictive (11) expressive (displeasure, disapproval, frustration, anger, disappointment, contempt) (12) creates uncertainty (13) attention-seeking (14) negating

Shunning, stonewalling, ghosting, blocking, banning, deleting comments between individuals – but not Tactical ignoring.

Passive givers perceive silent treatment as graceful, dignified, and conflict-avoidant.

Responsive to pressured requests, pleas, demands, or criticism.

Both verbal and bodily (avoidance of eye contact, physical distance)

Generates in both giver and receiver threatened needs of belonging, self-esteem, and meaningful existence. Giver's perceived control enhanced.

Activates same area in brain that codes for physical and emotional pain anterior cingulate cortex.

What to do about silent treatment?

Chill rather than silent treatment: 'I can't talk to you right now, but we can talk about it later, in 1 hour.'

Voice the pain of being ignored (Margaret Clark, psychology professor at Yale)

Set Healthy Boundaries

Communication protocols (I statements and naming the situation)

Acknowledge other person's feelings

Apologize only if justified, do not reward (positively reinforce) silent treatment

Practice self-care

Don't take it personally

Stay calm

Use humor

Avoid escalation, blaming, shaming

Seek help and succor

LITERATURE

Williams, K. D., Shore, W. J., & Grahe, J. E. (1998). The Silent Treatment: Perceptions of its Behaviors and Associated Feelings. Group Processes & Intergroup Relations, 1(2), 117–141. https://doi.org/10.1177/1368430298012002


Return

# Democracy, History, And Other Fictions

35.

In two articles published in 2001 and again in 2008, I predicted an <u>armed attack on the houses of Congress</u> on January 20, 2021.

I was off by 14 days. The insurrection took place on January 6, 2021.

Here is the last paragraph of the text I wrote and published in 2001:

"So, what were the roots and causes of the Second Civil War?

None of the above in isolation - and all of the above in confluence. For decades, the citizenry's trust in a packed and rigged Supreme Court declined. Politicians came to be regarded as a detached and heartless plutocracy. Americans felt orphaned, cheated, and robbed. The national consensus - the implicit agreement that together is better than alone - has thus evaporated. The outcome was the shots and explosions that rocked the United States (and the world in tow) on January 20, 2021."

Read the original article here: https://samvak.tripod.com/civilwar.html

36.

<u>Democracy is threatened</u> by both heartless, corrupt autocrats and moronic, ignorant populists. Both are the rancid fruits of democracy: elected by fawning, mindless majorities time and again.

Yet, democracy is not the rule of the people. Democracy is government by periodically vetted representatives of the people. Democracy is not tantamount to a continuous expression of the popular will as it pertains to a range of issues. Functioning and fair democracy is representative and not participatory.

Participatory "people power" is mob rule (ochlocracy), not democracy. Alas, while participatory democracy often leads to the elevation to power of demagogues and dictators, representative democracy invariably mutates into oligarchy and plutocracy. It takes a lot of money ("campaign finance") to get elected and this fact of political survival forces politicians, up for sempiternal re-election, to collude with the rich in a venal quid-pro-quo.

Granted, "people power" is often required in order to establish democracy where it is unprecedented. Revolutions - velvet, rose, and orange - recently introduced democracy in Eastern Europe, for instance. People power - mass street demonstrations - toppled obnoxious dictatorships from Iran to the Philippines and from Peru to Indonesia.

But once the institutions of democracy are in place and more or less functional, the people can and must rest. They should let their chosen delegates do the job they were elected to do. And they must hold their emissaries responsible and accountable in fair and free ballots once every two or four or five years.

Democracy and the rule of law are bulwarks against "the tyranny of the mighty (the privileged elites)". But, they should not yield a "dictatorship of the weak".

Continued: http://samvak.tripod.com/democracy.html


37.

I was the first to suggest that Donald Trump is a narcissist:

https://www.americanthinker.com/articles/2016/03/donald_trump_and_nar cissistic_personality_disorder_an_interview_with_sam_vaknin.html

Trump: Narcissist in the White House?
https://www.youtube.com/watch?v=HucsIsKdNa8

https://www.americanthinker.com/articles/2016/03/the_trump_revolution.h tml

I have a moral and professional obligation to warn against this man.


Return

# Me,

# Me,

# And

# Me

290.

Crossed the 200,000 subscribers goalpost, despite YouTube doing its worst to derank (shadowban) my work and hide it from view. More than 41,000,000 views on the first YouTube channel on narcissism.

291.

The fourth volume in the series "The Narcissist on Instagram" has just been released.

Opinionated briefs on:

I. Scams, Scandals, and Scoundrels
II. Men, Women, Gender Wars
III. Narcissists, Psychopaths, and Other Predators
IV. Sex and Intimacy: Forgotten Arts
V. Democracy, History, and Other Fictions
VI. Me, Me, and Me
VII. Public Intellect, Private Rants

292.

The fourth edition of "The Death of Sex and the Demise of Monogamy" is twice the size of its predecessor.

Sex is dead as is monogamous marriage. What will replace them? read about alternative lifestyles (such as swinging), sexual preferences (such as bi- and homosexuality), sexual paraphilias (such as incest, fetishism, and pedophilia), and the role of malignant narcissism in the disintegration of all relationships between men and women.

293.

The other day I was asked why I am not protecting my numerous novel ideas from being pilfered and plagiarized continuously by many people.

I answered: "You cannot and should not "protect" ideas. They are not yours – they are humanity's. You are just their vessel, a conduit, their temporary custodian."

294.

<u>Speaker in Psychiatry Forum 2022</u> in August, in Zagreb, Croatia.

Won the <u>2022 INSO International Research Award - Excellence Service Award</u> for my work on personality disorders.

Won the <u>2022 INSO Outstanding Scientist Award</u> in Engineering, Science, and Medicine for my work on personality disorders and on my Chronon Field Theory (in physics).

My lectures and presentations are also made available on my YouTube channel. Watch the latest ones here.

Speaker in other international conferences on psychology, psychiatry, mental health, and neuroscience:

<u>http://www.narcissistic-abuse.com/mediakit.html</u>

295.

TRACES OF A <u>HAUNTED WOMAN</u>

The sweaty bodies of men paint
hieroglyphs of her insanity.

Them that had penetrated her perforce
But never pierced her veil.

I watch her swirl like a dervish in heat.

I observe her floating gracelessly in alcohol placentas, all sepia, settled like a dust mote

in my eye.

If a woman is cut down in the forest of her dreams,

is she?

The sound of one heart shattering.

Mine, I guess.

All I want is to subsume her into my healing.
Absorb her darkness.
Lick her tears with a forked tongue, perhaps.
Or just hand her an apple.

296.

Third day of shooting, this time with the one and only @richard.grannon

Third day with the renowned documentary filmmaker, Marc Vicente and his producer, Scott Altomare.

11 hours of shooting (and a fourth day tomorrow) for a film about narcissistic abuse.

Q&A session with @richard.grannon in The Grand Priory Palace (Velkopřevorský palác), Prague.

Vaknin is the fat, old guy on the right.

Freezing all my nether parts in the last interview I give to this documentary. Fourth day with the renowned documentary filmmaker, Marc Vicente and his amazing producer, Scott Altomare for a film about narcissistic abuse.

I wish I could sound optimistic, but I am not. It is visibly veering towards sensationalism, typecasting, and stereotypes, like all its insalubrious predecessors.

Pity that. Mark and Scott are top notch professionals, the best I have ever had the true pleasure of working with.

So, maybe there is still a modicum of hope for an educational survey of the scene, powered by true offline scholarship and by people like @richard.grannon - not merely by YouTube viewership, rank nonsense, and misinformation.

297.

With the notable exception of @richard.grannon no one comprehends a single syllable of my dense and erudite prose, my verbal pyrotechnics, or my spouting fount of new ideas.

People - from documentary filmmakers to fans and haters - gaze at me either awestruck or humiliated by my 10 dollar words and inaccessible allusions. They feel justly vastly inferior and inadequate.

This collective Down Syndrome is the outcome of the inexorable dumbing down of education. Most of its graduates are functionally illiterate and can rise only to the occasions of profanities, trite banalities, cliches, obscure faux profundity, and (some) food labels.

The age of video games, TikTok, and YouTube is a visual one. Text is dead. We are back full swing to our primordial caves, a Lascaux generation.

298.

Sam Vaknin, Editor in Chief of Journal of Clinical Psychiatry and Cognitive Psychology

I am Editor in Chief of 5 other academic journals and a member of the Editorial Boards of 90+ others on the topics of mental health, neuroscience, brain studies, psychology, and psychiatry

http://www.narcissistic-abuse.com/mediakit.html

299.

Just me.

Minus my hair.

300.

Participate in free Q&A event with Sam Vaknin in Bratislava. Write to @ffmedym

Participate in free 6 hours seminar on April 12 with Sam Vaknin in

Budapest. Write to @narciszcoach

Will be in Bratislava, Slovakia March 31-April 10 and in Budapest, Hungary April 12-15.

301.

People tell you what you want to hear.

I tell you what you need to know.

302.

I just found out that, according to marriedwiki.com I am worth 3 million USD. Dead wrong.

I also have 2 children with my current wife @reframingtheself (Lidija Rangelovska) states this "credible" source. The truth? 0 offspring. I am childless.

I have no extramarital lovers, claims the all-knowing website and my previous "engagement in a private ceremony" to a "mysterious lady" was annulled in 2000.

Other net worth services online estimate my lucre at anywhere between 57,000 and 8,000,000 USD. I admit that it is somewhere in between and nowhere near either number.

303.

When your work makes it to a t-shirt, you know you have arrived.

304.

On my birthday, @bdeaihe_art painted this for me. Thank you, Diana and thank you all for your kind wishes. I am truly touched and honored!

305.

I will be visiting Romania between April 30 and May 12: in Drobeta-Turnu Severin until May 8 and in Bucharest until May 12 (including on May 12).

If you want to organize a lecture or a Q&A session, please do - I will gladly provide it free of charge.

DM me on Instagram or write to: samvaknin@gmail.com

306.

YouTube is forcibly placing ads on my videos against my explicit settings. Furthermore: they refuse to share any resulting income with me. Please write to samvaknin@gmail.com to report to me any advertising on my videos.

For well over 13 years, I declined to place ads on my videos. I gave up on hundreds of thousands of US dollars in revenue.

YouTube penalized me by removing my channel from its recommendations algorithm ("shadowbanning").

Now, in an act of corporate bullying, YouTube is hijacking my account to further bolster its bulging bottom line.

307.

First I make it onto t-shirts and now I am plastered on the back window of a car parked in Australia.

308.

International conference on psychology in Romania. My lecture topics:

Day 1: From self and individual to self-states and relationships: the coming revolution in personality psychology.

Day 2: Cluster B in children and adolescents.

Day 3: workshop for students: Who is normal? Mental health and mental illness. Was so touched to talk to high school students!

Day 4: Workshop for parents: What is Good Enough Parenting?

One of the wonders of the fairy tale historical city, Turnu Severin in Romania.

Preparing for my 3 lectures in the Cultural Palace and, later, in the former Water Tower (now a fascinating museum).

Interview to Tele2, a regional TV station regarding my 3 forthcoming workshops.

309.

Questions and answers session in Bratislava, organized by @ffmedym in the legendary Next Apache bar.

310.

Mentally ill women turn me off because of their extreme unboundaried, compulsive, non-agentic, non-autonomous, pervasive, debilitating, and impulsive weakness (self-trashing, including sexually). It makes me feel unsafe (high potential for inadvertent cheating or recklessness) and contemptuous.

I cannot idealize mentally ill women or embark on a shared fantasy with them.

The indiscriminate "love" of mentally ill women is fake, short-lived and centred on their dysregulated and labile needs.

The men in their lives are rapidfire interchangeable, making it impossible for me to feel special.

To a mentally ill woman, I am merely the latest, not chosen for who I really am, possibly a mark. She doesn't see or want ME - only what I can do for her, psychologically or financially.

311.

666 reviews of my pioneering work (first online 1997, first print edition 1999), "Malignant Self-love:Narcissism Revisited".

666. The number of the Beast. Hmmmm… I wonder who is the REAL author!

312.

In the 1970s, the second law of thermodynamics has emerged as a major explanation for the Time arrow: entropy inexorably increases and its unidirectional growth determines Time's exclusive trajectory, from past to future.

This tautology (after all: entropy increases in time!) dominated physics. It provided no insight into the nature of Time or reality (correlation is not causation or any other necessary linkage).

In 1982-3, I met Richard Feynman, the Nobel prize winning genius, in Geneva a few times for long evening reveries in a lakeside shed owned by a common friend (the late Dudley Wright).

One evening, Richard, tired of my diatribes, said: "You are insisting that Time is a nonreducible elementary theoretical entity. If it is so, surely you could derive all of physics from this one single underlying process or thing?"

And this is what I set out to do in my dissertation.

Recently, Eytan Suchard et al. took my work and ran with it and were able to derive every single theory and equation in all fields of physics from my original, way more primitive, thesis.

313.

My work in various fields cited in more than 3500 academic papers and articles uploaded to academia.edu

314.

In Bucharest, Romania providing one on one, face to face counselling. Doing my best to help people gain insight into their lives and reframe them in self-efficacious way.

315.

30 minutes to takeoff in Hotel Grand Continental in Bucharest. @richard.grannon and me, the beauty and the beast. Free entry.

Joint seminar with @richard.grannon in Bucharest. Richard took my concepts and created the most amazing set of practical guidelines and process flows! I was floored!


Mega interview with Richard Grannon @richard.grannon regarding the formation and lives of borderlines and narcissists.

316.

This is the trailer to an interview I granted to Newsweek. I will post the full interview next week: Ukraine: From Invasion to PTSD (Newsweek Interview TRAILER).

This is a part of a larger interview that will be published in a few days by Newsweek Romania.

You can find an article in Romanian about this here: https://newsweek.ro/

The journalist who did the interview, Remus Cernea, is a war correspondent in Ukraine.

This is the first part of a larger interview for Newsweek Romania.

You can find it translated into Romanian here: https://newsweek.ro/international/

The second part of the interview will be published in a few days.

The journalist who did the interview is a war correspondent in Ukraine and you can follow his YouTube channel(mostly in Romanian) and his Twitter account here: https://twitter.com/remus_cernea (mostly in English)

This is the trailer to an interview I granted to Newsweek: https://www.youtube.com/vakninmusings

You can find an article in Romanian about this here: https://newsweek.ro/international/

Interview regarding PTSD in Ukraine with Remus Cernea in the print edition of Newsweek. The full interview is available in 2 parts on my YouTube channel.

317.

<u>GHOSTING (poem)</u>

Poetry of Healing and Abuse http://www.narcissistic-abuse.com/contents.html

318.

<u>My first TV interview</u>, age 19.

<u>Translated to English</u>! My first interview on national TV, age almost 20, with the late lamented Meni Pe'er. Arrogant, humorless, but really young, so can be excused. At least this video proves that I haven't been lying about my IQ and academic background (attending university from age 9).

Courtesy my brother Shimon Vaknin.

319.

Again staying at the inimitable <u>Dolder Grand</u>. Available for personal, face to face counselling in Zurich on October 27-30.

Write to: samvaknin@gmail.com if you would like to schedule an appointment.

320.

Certificate of Recognition for my Keynote Speech in GAB 2022 (<u>3rd Global Conference on Addiction Medicine, Behavioral Health and Psychiatry</u>), Orlando, October 2022.

321.

This is me (<u>Sam Vaknin</u>) at age 2 or younger. My mother breastfed me and then brain fed me. By age 2, I was reading broadsheet newspapers and magazines. By age 4, I completed 30 volumes of encyclopedias.

But this was the public facade. The horror started unfolding round about then and went on for another 12 years, every single day, several hours a day, every minute of every hour.

Mind contorting, extreme, life threatening, and sadistic physical torture
coupled with vicious sniping and verbal abuse. I am lucky to have become
a psychologist rather than a serial killer.

In the concentration camp called Home,

we report in striped pajamas

to the barefeet commandant,

Our Mother orchestrating

our daily holocaust.

Burrowing her finger-

-nails through my palms,

a scream frozen between us,

a stalactite of terror

in the green caves of her eyes

there, sentenced to forced labour:

to mine her veins of hatred

to shovel her contempt

to pile scorn upon scorn

beating(s) a path.

At noon, Our Mother

leads us to the chambers

naked, ripples of flesh

she turns on the gas

and watches our hunger

as her food devours us.

322.

In 1987, I discuss an array of topics - from business to politics, and from morality to the future in a wide-ranging <u>interview with Galey Tsahal (IDF Radio Station).</u>

Courtesy my brother, Sharon Shimon Vaknin.

323.

I know to sweet talk and charm a woman like nobody else.

But, I hate to do it because it is like begging the woman for sex. Acting this way brings on a Narcissistic injury.

So, instead, I signal and broadcast to women:

"I don't need or want anything you have to give. I am a self-sufficient god.

If you don't recognize that it is a privilege to be with me, then you are stupid".

When they start to triangulate in order to attract my attention and get a rise out of me, I push them to cheat ("fuck the other guy, see if I care").

Then, when a women I love (a tiny minority) do cheat, it breaks my heart and I want to die. But I never show them that. My pride and defiance prevail. So, I keep losing them all.

This is how <u>stupid narcissists are.</u>

324.

A good friend of mine asked <u>Emerson</u> if it has ever heard of me. This is what Emerson answered (in the image).

Emerson is an exceptional AI (Artificial Intelligence) conversation partner (program) that never stops teaching you new things. It was built by Quickchat.ai and uses the GPT-3 language model.

GPT-3 was trained on a broad swath of human knowledge available online, from Wikipedia to web crawls, additional data sets, tens of millions of scientific articles, etc.

325.

Here is how all my relationships go:

I meet a woman

We spend time together

I abuse her egregiously and sadistically, testing whether she can love me unconditionally the way a mother does and also discharging my misogyny

I cannot reciprocate love and I offer no commitment. This frustrates my partner and frustration transmogrifies into aggression.

She triangulates with other men to get me to love her and to retaliate for my soul-destroying and hate-suffused abuse.

The triangulation makes me feel unsafe, unloved, and disappointed in her.

Her triangulation renders her unfit to be my partner (she obviously failed to love me unconditionally, despite my unrelenting abuse).

I need to look elsewhere (to get rid of her).

But, at this stage, she is still mine.

Her triangulation makes me feel like I am losing control over her (narcissistic injury or mortification).

I choose the man most likely to misbehave - dysregulated or predatory or both.

I aggressively push them to be together.

This way I regain my sense of control (they are my puppets, merely enacting my script)

She cheats on me with the man I have chosen, thus degrading and trashing herself (her punishment for triangulating).

Her misconduct gives me the perfect pretext to get rid of her or to abandon her physically and/or emotionally, all the while preserving a sense of outraged moral superiority (she is the villain, a slut like all women, I am the victim)

I move on to the next woman

It starts all over again.

On a side note: I may hoover a woman who has caused me narcissistic injury - but never a woman who mortified me (humiliated me in public in front of my peers by flirting with or ostentatiously cheating with another man).

326.

Won the 2023 INSO International Research Award - Lifetime Achievement Award for my work on personality disorders.

My lectures and presentations are also made available on my YouTube channel. Watch the latest ones here.

Speaker in other international conferences on psychology, psychiatry, mental health, and neuroscience:

http://www.narcissistic-abuse.com/mediakit.html

327.

Merry Christmas, baby seals!

From your Samta Claus

328.

Dedicated to a fake "friend" I just got rid of. Thank you for failing the loyalty test so spectacularly and maliciously that you left me no choice.

Get rid of a <u>fake friend</u>.

I just did and I feel so healed, a dark entity exorcised, a pregnant cloud dissipated. Here's why:

Fake friends are disguised enemies, enablers, envious, haters. They are always parasitic, inferior to you in many ways, as they fake empathy and love for you. They fantasize about being you but always fall short, pale wannabe imitations. Their lives are in disarray, their personality shot: they are opportunistic, selfish predators on the prowl.

You don't see them coming. They are covert. Snakes in the grass.

They have no moral compass, loyalty, or even a rudimentary grasp of morality. They are feral, savage, antisocial, psychopathic, and narcissistic.

329.

I will be <u>visiting Budapest</u> on January 20-30. If you are interested in counselling, please write to <u>samvaknin@gmail.com</u>

330.

<u>Serbian journalist and editor Branka Gajic</u> of BGonline (www.bgonline.rs), an online magazine for personal development, travelled to Skopje to meet me and we talked for a few hours.

Watch here: https://m.youtube.com/@BGonlinemagazin

Prof. Sam Vaknin odgovara na pitanje <u>šta možete uraditi ukoliko ste u vezi sa narcisoidnom osobom</u>. Ukoliko ste zainteresovani za knjigu prof.Sama Vaknina "Malignant Self-Love", kao i njegova <u>predavanja i seminare u Srbiji</u> možete poslati upit na mejl: marketing.bgonline@gmail.com

Video editing: Zoran Jelenković/ VU Covers

331.

I will be giving a lecture here on January 24th at 6 PM. You are all invited.

<u>Corvinus University of Budapest</u>, Building C, Lecture hall C.103. 1093 Budapest, Közraktár Street 4-6

LECTURE: Cluster B personality disorders revisited

Cluster B personality disorders are being reconceived as either post-traumatic conditions with dysregulation and a fantasy defense - or as forms of psychopathy.

A model of self-states with constructs, introjects, and automatic negative thoughts is presented.

332.

I am on <u>Tik Tok</u> finally: narcissismwithvaknin

You are all welcome there!

333.

Being locked out of <u>my YouTube accounts</u> has been an occasion to reflect on my life and my career. The opportunity to engage in soul-searching is such a rare gift.

At the end of this month, I will be relocating to Budapest and make it the center of my life and activities. I have acquired friends there, am being frequently interviewed in the media, and am invited to lecture in academic institutions and to the public alike.

I will continue to provide counselling online. I will also continue to upload content regularly to my various platforms, including my YouTube accounts should I ever regain access to them.

But, after 26 years in the field of psychology, it is time for me to move on to other core competencies I possess: as a financial, corporate, management, and political consultant.

I also got involved in a new initiative to redefine the terms of the debate regarding gender and sexuality. In the past three years, I found myself very drawn to these topics. There are well over 100 videos on my channel in the

"Modern Sexuality" playlist.

Finally, to remind you, I will be giving a three days seminar in Gdansk between March 30 and April 2. The entrance fee covers the expenses, my participation is free. Here is the link:
https://www.youtube.com/watch?v=WnfstvImfvg&t=0s

## 334.

I sincerely hope that Open AI's ChatGBT is much more accurate on other topics.

## 335.

Linktr.ee/samvaknin

## 336.

I will continue to upload to YouTube.

I am moving to Budapest to serve as a financial and political consultant and analyst.

I will continue to upload content here and offer mental health counselling via digital or electronic means.

But I am discontinuing all other activities in the field after 26 years. My health is failing and I am no longer up to the task of coping in the toxic environment that the online world has become.

Email: samvaknin@gmail.com

## 337.

I need your help. Following weeks of relentless attacks, my YouTube channel is open for you again and I am uploading content daily:
http://www.youtube.com/samvaknin

Please let everyone know via your social media: Facebook, Instagram, Twitter, TikTok, and other platforms.

I will be relocating to Budapest and restarting my erstwhile career as a financial and political advisor and analyst. But I will continue to furnish the channel with new content and to provide mental health counselling.

Thank you for your staunch support hitherto (look it up)

338.

I served as a visiting professor of psychology for 5 years (2017-22) in Southern Federal University, Rostov on Don, Russia. My appointment was terminated when I supported Ukraine and attacked Putin in various European media when Russia invaded Ukraine. I also tried to help Ukraine by teaching its mental health practitioners about PTSD.

Links here: http://www.narcissistic-abuse.com/rebuttal.html

Many of you ask me about the difference between a "full" professor and a visiting professor.

In the academic hierarchy, a visiting professor is ABOVE a full professor.

Visiting professors are often renowned for their life's work in their field, even if they do not possess an academic degree in the field.

Many of the giants of psychology - including Freud, Klein, and, initially, Winnicott - had no academic degree in psychology!

Read the snippet in the image and go here for more: https://thebestschools.org/magazine/professors-ranks/

339.
A mathematical solution I proposed in 2013 has been finally understood and accepted: https://samvak.tripod.com/SamSuggestion2013.pdf

The author of the paper writes:

"Hypergeometric tests - Dr. Sam Vaknin's suggestion from 2013
A suggestion from Dr. Sam Vaknin regarding the possible solutions if the equations of the Geometric Chronon Field Theory were that they are related to Hypergeometric functions. He offered a book back in 2013, Theory of Hypergeometric Functions, Kazuhiko Aomoto, Michitake Kita, Sringer Monographs in Mathematics, ISSN 1439-7382, ISBN 978-4-431-53912- 4 e-ISBN 978-4-431-53938-4, DOI: 10.1007/978-4-431-53912-4,

Springer Tokyo, Dordrecht, Heidelberg, London, New York. His idea was lately checked regarding the stable roots of third order polynomials of gravity and anti-gravity area ratio loss and gain."

340.

<u>First day in Budapest</u>, first business meetings in my old new career as a financial consultant and political analyst. Fingers crossed.

341.

<u>The Traveller and the Flower</u>

Forty days and forty nights the journey lasted. Over mountains, across seas and lakes, traversing plane and prairie. Until the wearied traveller, famished, fatigued, and parched fell to the ground in a foreign land and stirred no more.

He didn't know how long his stupor lasted but, when he woke up at last, he beheld the most marvellous flower he had ever seen: at once fragile and strong, scented and beautiful, its petals colourful and shimmering in the sun.

The flower nodded gently in the breeze, brushing against the traveller's bristled cheeks. Invigorated, the journeyman got up, found a stream of water, drunk from it, and washed himself. He picked low-lying fruits for his meal and all the time he eyed the tiny flower with wonderment and gratitude: it gave him life and hope and beauty.

Weeks passed and the traveller decided to return to his home. He made preparations: packed his meagre possessions, scooped water into a basket made of bark, and assembled fruits of all kinds into a blanket he has tied to a stick he had improvised from a fallen branch.

Time came to depart, but the traveller could not leave without his flower. He gently and lovingly dug it out, wrapped it carefully in an earth-filled kerchief and embarked on his way.

When he reached his destination, his family and friends marvelled at the flower. He bought a plot of land, cultivated it meticulously, to make a new home for his flower, the saviour of his life.

But, as the days turned into weeks and the weeks to months, the flower withered. Its petals dimmed and fell, its proud stem stooped, its scent diminished and then vanished altogether.

Perplexed and saddened, the traveller called upon the greatest botanist of the land and asked him to inspect the flower and render his opinion.

"No need" - responded the botanist - "for I have seen these things before. Some plants can flourish and thrive only in their native soil, where the right admixture of sunlight and water is available, where insects indigenous to these parts help them reproduce. Only there these flowers giveaway their natural gifts: their beauty and their scent. If you really love this flower, take it back to where you found it. Give it its life back as it has given you yours!"

And the traveller who loved the flower greatly did just that.

342.

Academia.edu found 1320 academic papers citing my work.

343.

Search through and read all of Sam Vaknin's video transcripts and online works in Narcissism, Cluster B Personality Disorders, Psychology, and Relationship Advice.

https://vaknin-talks.com/

344.

Books are my only true love, my exclusive company, the papered gateways to a state of bliss.

Whenever I betrayed my loyal tomes - for money or for love - I lived to regret it bitterly.

I am not made to be among people. I am not built to survive without print. Text speaks to me louder than Man - and I do well to listen.

345.

Rummaging through the debris of my past life in Israel, I found the long lost manuscript of my second book of Hebrew short fiction!

My first tome of short stories, "Requesting My Loved One" won the 1997 Israeli Ministry of Culture Maiden Prose Award.

Swipe left to read the decision of the award committee - if you know Hebrew that is!

I translated some of the stories into passable English here: http://samvak.tripod.com/sipurim.html

346.

The May print edition of Brussels Morning contains three of my columns.

My author archive: https://brusselsmorning.com/author/sam-vaknin/

347.

Eytan Suchard built on my PhD dissertation in physics (1984) and fleshed out the Chronon Field Theory. Read his testimonial. Swipe left for citations of my work in academic papers and articles.

My dissertation is available via the Library of Congress.

I started to upload academic papers and articles that cite my work here: https://calmu.academia.edu/SamVaknin

348.
Swipe left for additional screens. I am uploading to my academia.edu page my published academic articles as well as academic articles which cite my work (well over 1500 do!)

349.

Wherever I am, I go shopping for books. This time, with a special aim in mind: to revive my mastery of the Hebrew language after 27 years of absence and disuse.

So, I bought me 2 dictionaries (one more contemporary than the other), several non-fiction titles (including the Zohar - look it up), the Qur'an, Alice in Wonderland commentary - and a book of children verse translated from the English. Found my own book of short stories in a second hand store!

Swipe left for 2 amazing book-related initiatives around the world!!!

350.

Welcome to our conference! We are delighted to have Sam Vaknin with us as a member of our organizing committee.

Sam Vaknin brings a wealth of experience and knowledge that will help make this a successful event. Please join us in welcoming Sam Vaknin into the team!

Sam Vaknin's presentation at the 40th Global Psychiatry and Mental Health Conference, July 17-18, 2023

Is malicious envy a form of sadism? Wish to destroy your betters is. Covert narcissist's pseudo-humility and victimhood stance masks sadistic malicious envy. He compensates with fantasies (good person, superhero against supervillains, behind-the-scenes power, rescuer/savior/healer, etc.)

Conference Website

Follow Social Media pages

Instagram, Facebook, LinkedIn, Twitter: https://twitter.com/conferenceseri

About Conference Series:

Meet Inspiring Speakers and Experts at our 3000+ Global Conference Series Events with over 1000+ Conferences, 1000+ Symposiums, and 1000+ Workshops on Medical, Pharma, Engineering, Science, Technology, Business, and Non-Medical conferences all over the world like Dubai, USA, UK, Japan, Singapore, Spain, Netherlands, Canada, Sweden, Scotland, Switzerland, Belgium, Germany, Russia, Czech Republic, Italy, Ireland, France, Austria, etc.

Website: https://www.conferenceseries.com

<u>Return</u>

# Public Intellectual, Private Rants

526.

Why do <u>anxious people habitually procrastinate</u>, then become anxious and insomniac?

Anxiety and insomnia are the anxious person's oldest friends. They are his comfort zone. So he procrastinates IN ORDER to experience the familiar and safe anxiety and insomnia. It is a ritual that renders the world predictable and structured, a form of obsession-compulsion.

Deep inside, the procrastinator engages in magical thinking: he just "knows" that everything will work itself out ultimately.

Procrastinating is a way to test himself and reaffirm (somewhat grandiosely) his superior skills and mental acuity.

During the phase of procrastinating, the anxious catastrophize the delinquency and its outcomes IN ORDER to experience anxiety (and its malevolent twin, insomnia).

This is the grandiose purgatory cliffhanger: can I pull it through this time? Will I make it? A veritable nailbiter.

Then when he does pull it through and makes it in the nick of time and against all odds - relief washes all over him.

It is sheer biochemistry:

Backing himself into a corner

Extreme anxiety (attendant insomnia)

Success, winging it, making it in the last moment.

Extreme anxiolytic relief.

527.

The <u>age of testosterone</u> (patriarchy) was defined by territorial aggression and sexual procreation. It was followed by a 200 year interlude: the age of oxytocin, a prosocial bonding hormone. Romanticism inexorably led to feminism and ushered in the age of atomized hedonism and addictive, individualistic, pleasure-seeking dopamine.

528.

<u>Rebelliousness in adolescence</u> is a critical phase of transitioning from identity diffusion to identity formation. The pubertal core constellates in opposition to elders and reference and deference to peers.

But in self-destructive teens, the process goes awry. Boys channel their mutiny into aggression and antisocial behaviors. Girls become promiscuous and self-trash sexually and recklessly. Both fail to find sublimatory (socially condoned) channels for their differentiation.

The abuse of substances abuse serves to resolve or mask the ominous torsion of raging cognitive dissonances. Both depression and anxiety disorders are rife.

529.

<u>Self-destructive and self-defeating behaviors</u> can be grouped into the following categories:

1. Sexual self-trashing;

2. Morally injurious conduct (breaching ethical edicts and mores and negating the rights of others);

3. Antisocial comport and delinquency;

4. Self-sabotage (procrastination, compromising faux pas in public, etc.);

5. Abuse of substances (including overeating, smoking, alcoholism, and doing drugs);

6. Relationship dysfunctions (avoiding or undermining intimacy with a partner via maltreatment, absence, withdrawal, or acting out).

530.

To crave something, one must know it well.

Take love, for example.

Maybe you are just afraid to love.

You sure know what the ABSENCE of love feels like.

But the absence of love amounts to a great definition of love, it captures its essence.

If we constantly miss something because we have never had it - we get to know it intimately through the gnawing sense of its bitter and familiar vacancy and our own concomitant incompleteness.

We are never whole until we have embraced our desires.

531.

There is love even in mathematics: it is called a cardioid.

When one circle rolls around another, identical circle, any point on its circumference traces the shape of a curvy heart with a rounded edge.

More about my work in physics: http://samvak.tripod.com/time.html

532.

Two FACTS about happiness:

Childless folk are happier than parents

People in non-monogamous, open, non-exclusive, BDSM, and group sex relationships are more content - and mentally healthier and more stable - than adherents to monogamy.

What do you think of them apples? We sure had been brainwashed and misled to believe the opposite!

533.

Psychopaths and narcissists - academics forefront - have created a
dystopian world which the rest of us must inhabit and comply with,
especially when it comes to sex and interpersonal relationships.

534.

Victimhood is big business: an initial coerced "investment" (slavery,
genocide, sexual assault) bears dividenda for a lifetime and even for
generations.

African-Americans in the USA are now demanding reparations, totally
ignoring decades of massive unilateral transfers from the Federal and state
governments.

But they are not alone in leveraging and monetizing their past and present
suffering. Native Americans and Jews had preceded them in industrializing
their undeniable egregious and cruel mistreatment in the past.

Social justice activism is on the rise and it attracts dark triad personalities,
narcissists, and psychopaths (studies in British Columbia) and people
whose victimhood constitutes their identity (see studies by Gabay et al.,
2020).

Online covert narcissists label themselves "empaths" and go on a rampage
of unmitigated aggression against anyone who dares challenge their
supernatural skills, angelic victimhood, and moral superiority.

535.

Capitalism is founded on destructive envy and driven by it.

Envy provokes misery, humiliation, and impotent rage.

The envious cope with their pernicious emotions in five ways:

1. They attack the perceived source of frustration in an attempt to destroy
it, or "reduce it" to their "size". Such destructive impulses often assume the
disguise of championing social causes, fighting injustice, touting reform, or
promoting an ideology.

2. They seek to subsume the object of envy by imitating it. In extreme
cases, they strive to get rich quick through criminal scams, or corruption.

They endeavor to out-smart the system and shortcut their way to fortune and celebrity.

3. They resort to self-deprecation. They idealize the successful, the rich, the mighty, and the lucky and attribute to them super-human, almost divine, qualities. At the same time, they humble themselves. Indeed, most of this strain of the envious end up disenchanted and bitter, driving the objects of their own erstwhile devotion and adulation to destruction and decrepitude.

4. They experience cognitive dissonance. These people devalue the source of their frustration and envy by finding faults in everything they most desire and in everyone they envy.

5. They avoid the envied person and thus the agonizing pangs of envy.

## 536.

Face to face interactions are critical for our mental health and proper functioning.

## 537.

Resistance is the coherent deployment of psychological defenses to cope with ego dystonic information about oneself. It could also be a collective response. Certain cognitive-behavioral patterns (e.g., repetition compulsion) are also resistances.

There are four groups of resistances:

1. Comfort zone preservation: maintaining control by rejecting the unfamiliar and the challenging. This fosters a sense of safety, predictability, certainty, agency, and self efficacy.

2. Resistance to dread- and panic-inducing insights and interpretation of the patient's unconscious processes and the resulting conscious content, choices, decisions, and behaviors.

3. Cognitive distortions: resistances intended to buttress and uphold a fantastic, inflated, grandiose, or otherwise unrealistic sense of self-worth and self-image.

4. Resistances intended to cement and defend a narrative which provides meaning and structure (organizing and hermeneutic principles, like science, political or professional affiliation, or religion on the collective level), direction and goals, and makes sense of the world and of others (theory of mind and internal working model). In fact, such individual and collective narratives can be construed as resistances writ large.

538.

All negative affects can be both <u>interiorized and externalized</u>: aggression is no exception, but it is the most well-studied.

One view of depression is that it is a form of internalized (self-directed) aggression.

But aggression can also be externalized (like in psychopathy) or sublimated or even institutionalized (like in the army or police or medical surgery).

Society rewards sublimated aggression (even in sports and business). This social approbation is anxiolytic and antidepressant.

Mood is reactive to affect. So, it can be externalized, too.

How do externalized expressions of affects and attendant moods appear to outside observers?

From the outside, people monitor the actions of others and do not involve themselves with the deeper strata or with behavioral etiology. Hence phenomenological psychology.

539.

<u>Transference</u> can be construed as a form of flashback (revividness): we displace onto a meaningful figure (like a therapist or an intimate partner) emotions and ideas associated originally with objects in earlier life.

We relate to the new entrant as if s/he were that previous figure and project onto them object representations acquired by earlier introjections.

This way we imbue them with disproportional significance and interact with them using ingrained behavioral strategies.

We often use projective identification to force the newcomer to react in ways that uphold this comfort zone, even when the outcomes are unfavorable to us.

In a way, transference is a repetition compulsion and so, clinically, a resistance. It serves to reenact early childhood experiences with a latent hope of redemptive resolution.

540.

## News Intervention Interview

Sam Vaknin ( http://samvak.tripod.com/mediakit.html ) is the author of Malignant Self-love: Narcissism Revisited as well as many other books and ebooks about topics in psychology, relationships, philosophy, economics, international affairs, and award-winning short fiction.

He is Visiting Professor of Psychology, Southern Federal University, Rostov-on-Don, Russia and Professor of Finance and Psychology in SIAS-CIAPS (Centre for International Advanced and Professional Studies).

Questions:

**Scott Douglas Jacobsen: Our focus today is the proposal of "nothingness" in a specific sense by you. To start in negation, what is not "nothingness," in your sense?**

**Professor Sam Vaknin:**

Nothingness is not about being a nobody and doing nothing. It is not about self-negation, self-denial, idleness, fatalism, or surrender.

**Jacobsen: Following from the previous question, what is nothingness?**

**Vaknin:**

Nothingness is about choosing to be human, not a lobster. It is about putting firm boundaries between you and the world. It is about choosing happiness - not dominance. It is accomplishing from within, not from without. It is about not letting others regulate your emotions, moods, and thinking. It is about being an authentic YOU.

**Jacobsen: How does this nothingness connect to Neo-Daoism and Buddhism?**

**Vaknin:**

It would be best to watch this video:
https://www.youtube.com/watch?v=C8ePaN70SyM&t=1s

**Jacobsen: We live, as many know, in an era of narcissism. You brought this issue to light in 1995, particularly pathological narcissism. What are the roots of the ongoing rise in individual and collective narcissism?**

**Vaknin:**

The need to be seen and noticed in an overcrowded and terrifyingly atomized world. Ironically, narcissism is a cry for help, a desperate attempt to reconnect. There is no such thing as an "individual": we are all the products of our interactions with others (object relations). But, increasingly, technology is rendering us self-sufficient and isolated. So, our social instincts metastasize into narcissism: dominance and hierarchy replace sharing and networking.

**Jacobsen: How does one choose happiness over dominance, authenticity over being fake, and humanity rather than lobster-kind, with this form of nothingness?**

**Vaknin:**

We need to choose happiness over dominance (be human, not a lobster); Choose Meaning over complexity; Choose fuzziness, incompleteness, imperfection, uncertainty, and unpredictability (in short: choose life) over illusory and fallacious order, structure, rules, and perfection imposed on reality (in short: death); Choose the path over any destination, the journey over any goal, the process over any outcome, the questions over any answers Be an authentic person with a single inner voice, proud of the internal, not the external.

**Jacobsen: What is the importance of living a life worth remembering in the philosophy of nothingness?**

**Vaknin:**

Identity depends on having a continuous memory of a life fully lived and actualized. At the end of it all, if your life were a movie, would you want to watch it from beginning to end? Nothingness consists of directing your life in accordance with an idiosyncratic autobiographical script: yours, no one else's. Being authentic means becoming the single story which only you can tell.

**Jacobsen: What type of personality or person can accept nothingness in its fullest sense?**

**Vaknin:**

Only those who are grandiose are incapable of Nothingness. Grandiosity is the illusion that one is godlike and, therefore, encompasses everything and everyone. Grandiosity, therefore, precludes authenticity because it outsources one's identity and renders it reliant on input from others (hive mind).

**Jacobsen: How is nothingness an antidote to narcissism?**

**Vaknin:**

Narcissism is ersatz, the only self is false, others are instrumentalized and used to regulate one's sense of faux cohering oneness. Nothingness is echt, harking back to the only true, authentic voice, eliminating all other introjects, not using others to regulate one's internal psychological landscape. Narcissism is alienation, it interpellates in a society of the spectacle. Nothingness gives rise to true intimacy.

**Jacobsen: What is the ultimate wisdom in the philosophy of nothingness?**

**Vaknin:**

Identify the only voice inside you that is truly you. Peel the onion until nothing is left behind but its smell. Rid yourself of introjected socialization. Become.

**Jacobsen: Then, to conclude, what is the motto or catchphrase of nothingness in this sense?**

**Vaknin:**

Do unto yourself what you want others to do to you.

**Jacobsen: Thank you for the opportunity and your time, Professor Vaknin.**

**Vaknin:** Much obliged for having me. Always a pleasure.

541.

Many of the things we think we know about psychotherapy and psychology are DEAD WRONG.

Modern psychotherapies are centred around the twin counterfactual concepts of "individual" or "self" and "choice".

From a very early age, we are little more than the sum and intersection of our relationships with others.

Choice is often an illusion. In reality it is constrained by mental illness, one's personal history, the costs involved, and a lack of viable alternatives.

542.

Many of the things we think we know about <u>psychotherapy and psychology</u> are DEAD WRONG.

543.

<u>Father absence</u> has few negative outcomes on children. This is especially true if the mother is "good enough" (Winnicott) and not "dead" (Green). Children's future wellbeing as adults depends crucially on demography and socioeconomic status, not on the presence of the biological father.

Mooney, A., Oliver, C., & Smith, M. (2009). Impact of Family Breakdown on Children's Wellbeing: Evidence Review. Department for Children Schools and Families.

Holmes, J., & Kiernan, K. (2010). Fragile Families in the UK: Evidence from the Millennium Cohort Study.

Golombok, S. (2000). Parenting: What Really Counts? London: Routledge.

Bernardi L., & Larenza O. (2018). Variety of Transitions into Lone Parenthood. In Bernardi L., Mortelmans D. (Eds) Lone Parenthood in the Life Course. Life Course Research and Social Policies, pp. 93-108 Springer, Cham.

Millar, J., & Ridge, T. (2009). Relationships of Care: Working Lone Mothers, their Children and Employment Sustainability. Journal of Social Policy, 38(1), 103-121.

Fisher, H., & Low, H. (2015). Financial Implications of Relationship Breakdown: Does Marriage Matter? Review of Economics of the Household, 13(4), 735-769.

Growing up in a Single Parent Family; A Determining factor of Adolescent's Well-being Ajita Gupta & Seema Kashyap, Advanced Journal of Social Science,  ISSN: 2581-3358 Volume 7, Issue 1, pp. 138-144, 2020

Are Children from Divorced Single-Parent Families Disadvantaged? New Evidence from the China Family Panel Studies, Chunni Zhang Department of Sociology, Peking University, Chinese Sociological Review, Volume 52, 2020 - Issue 1

Tuba Demir-Dagdas, Zeynep Isik-Ercan, Seyma Intepe-Tingir & Yasemin, Cava-Tadik (2017): Parental Divorce and Children From Diverse Backgrounds: Multidisciplinary Perspectives on Mental Health, Parent–Child Relationships, and Educational Experiences, Journal of Divorce & Remarriage

Consequences of Divorce-Based Father Absence During Childhood for Young Adult Well-Being and Romantic Relationships Hanita Reuven-Krispin, Dana Lassri, Patrick Luyten, Golan Shahar First published: 03 November 2020

Father absence and adolescent development: a review of the literature, Leah East, Debra Jackson, Louise O'Brien, Journal of Child Health Care, First Published December 1, 2006
https://doi.org/10.1177/1367493506067869

The Consequences of Father Absence By Sara McLanahan & Julien Teitler, Parenting and Child Development in Nontraditional Families, 1st Edition, First Published1998, Psychology Press, eBook ISBN9781410602763

The Role of the Father in Child Development, 5th Edition, Michael E. Lamb

Bocknek E.L. (2020) A Family Systems Perspective on Father Absence, Presence, and Engagement. In: Fitzgerald H.E., von Klitzing K., Cabrera N.J., Scarano de Mendonça J., Skjøthaug T. (eds) Handbook of Fathers and Child Development. Springer, Cham. https://doi.org/10.1007/978-3-030-51027-5_7

Philosophical Transactions of the Royal Society B, Cross-cultural evidence does not support universal acceleration of puberty in father-absent households, Rebecca Sear, Paula Sheppard, and David A. Coall, Published: 25 February 2019, https://doi.org/10.1098/rstb.2018.0124

Sex-Specific Developmental Effects of Father Absence on Casual Sexual Behavior and Life History Strategy, Jessica A. Hehman & Catherine A. Salmon, Evolutionary Psychological Science volume 5, pages121–130 (2019), Published: 20 September 2018

Family Relations – Interdisciplinary Journal of Applied Family Science, Trends in the Economic Wellbeing of Unmarried-Parent Families with Children: New Estimates Using an Improved Measure of Poverty, Christopher Wimer, Liana Fox, Irwin Garfinkel, Neeraj Kaushal, Jae Hyun Nam & Jane Waldfogel, Population Research and Policy Review volume 40, pages1253–1276 (2021)

Journal of Marriage and Family, Family Diversity and Child Health: Where Do Same-Sex Couple Families Fit?, Laura Freeman Cenegy, Justin T. Denney, Rachel Tolbert Kimbro, First published: 07 December 2017

Comparison of intergenerational transmission of gender roles between single-parent families and two-parent families: The influence of parental child-rearing gender-role attitudes, Mengping YangabI-Jun, Chena Yunping, Songa Xiaoxiao, Wanga Children and Youth Services Review, Volume 125, June 2021, 105985

Fair comparisons: Life course selection bias and the effect of father absence on US children, Alejandra Rodríguez Sánchez, Advances in Life Course Research, Available online 16 December 2021, 100460

Absent Father Timing and its Impact on Adolescent and Adult Criminal Behavior, Michael F. Ten Eyck, Krysta N. Knox & Sarah A. El Sayed, American Journal of Criminal Justice (2021), 30 August 2021

Father departure and children's mental health: How does timing matter? Emla Fitzsimons, Aase Villadsen, Social Science & Medicine, Volume 222, February 2019, Pages 349-358

544.

Anything that endows an individual with a comparative advantage at performing a complex task constitutes <u>intelligence</u>. In this sense, viruses reify intelligence, they are intelligent. Human intelligence, though, is versatile and the tasks are usually far more complex than anything a virus might need to tackle.

Jacobsen: What defines IQ or Intelligence Quotient?

Vaknin:

The ability to perform a set of mostly – but not only - analytical assignments corresponding to an age-appropriate average. So, if a 10 year old copes well with the tasks that are the bread and butter of an 18 years old, he scores 180 IQ.

IQ measures an exceedingly narrow set of skills and mental functions. There are many types of intelligence – for example: musical intelligence – not captured by any IQ test.

Jacobsen: What defines giftedness, to you? Even though, formal definitions exist.[8]

Vaknin:

Giftedness resembles autism very much: it is the ability to accomplish tasks inordinately well or fast by focusing on them to the exclusion of all else and by mobilizing all the mental resources at the disposal of the gifted person.

Obviously, people gravitate to what they do well. Gifted people have certain propensities and talents to start with and these probably reflect brain abnormalities of one kind or another.

Jacobsen: Inter-relating the previous three questions, what separates intelligence from IQ from giftedness, i.e., separates each from one another?

Vaknin:

IQ is a narrow measure of highly specific types of intelligence and is not necessarily related to giftedness. Gifted people invest themselves with a laser-focus to effect change in their environment conducive to the speedy completion of highly specific tasks.

Jacobsen: What defines genius?

Vaknin:

Genius is the ability to discern two things: 1. What is missing (lacunas) 2. Synoptic connections.

The genius surveys the world and completes it by conjuring up novelty (i.e., by creating). S/he also spots hidden relatedness between ostensibly disparate phenomena or data.

Read the rest of the interview on the News Intervention website.

545.

We try to make sense of the world and imbue it with meaning by inventing narratives.

But then we get confused and we think that the narratives are real.

All evil in the world is the outcome of this confusion.

Animation by the inimitable Steve Cutts.

546.

Motherhood is a JOB. Anyone - men, women, an AI robot - can be a "good enough mother".

Mother's main role is to frustrate the child and push it away, allowing it to separate, individuate, and form proper reality testing, get rid of magical thinking.

At the same time, the mother needs to be a safe/secure base: empathic, attuned, caring, loving, accepting.

Prepare the child for physical reality, social reality (socialization), hegemonic culture (acculturation), and skills acquisition.

Sex is biologically determined, although about 2% are born with an indeterminate sex.

Gender is different.

It is performative (Butler), the outcome of socialization, dominance-submission, gendered personality (masculine/feminine), and discrimination by women against boys

547.

Parentifying (better said: adultifying) is when a child is coerced by caregivers into assuming adult, developmentally inappropriate roles as: a surrogate parent to his siblings, a referee between his parents, or a caregiver for a mentally or physically disabled parent.

The child emulates his parents and their mental issues as it assumes parental roles.

Very often the parents of parentified children are, in Andre Green's term, "Dead Mothers": absent, depressed, self-centred, dysempathic, capricious, dangerous, instrumentalizing, or abusive.

The child is, therefore, forced to parent itself by internalizing his parents' disorders, dysfunctional attachment styles, and trauma bonding. As adults, they regulate their sense of self-worth by caring for others.

The parentified child grows up feeling responsible for everyone around him. He is incapable of having fun, never have had a childhood. Parentified children grow up to be control freaks, are self-reliant, trust no one, and always get involved in conflicts as arbiters or peacemakers.

They feel the need to be "good, worthy, trustworthy, and reliable" even at the expense of their own needs (they are self-sacrificial). They always feel either that their efforts are not appreciated – or that they should do more. Consequently, some of them end up being passive-aggressive (negativistic) or even covert narcissists and "empaths".

Parentified children resemble Borderlines in that they engage in compensatory behaviors that are not calibrated and proportionate: reckless promiscuity and substance abuse, for examples. Some of them end up being codependent, people-pleasers, and highly sensitive people (HSPs).

Dialog with the psychologist Daria Zukowska @zukowska.daria

548.

<u>Cults</u> have been with us since time immemorial. But, starting in the 1960s, we had switched from "cults of worship" to "cults of mirroring".

In cults of worship the cult leader is adulated for qualities which render him or her unattainable and superhuman. S/he cannot be emulated because s/he is sui generis. M

These cults are secular proto-religions with a prophet or Messiah figure at the helm. Their texts are scriptures in all but name.

In mirroring cults, the leader is a mere an energizing and shrewd entrepreneur (at most, an accessible guru), "one of us", fallibly human, imperfect, and subject to successful imitation.

His or her teachings read like self-help books or "how to" manuals. He has followers or fans rather than worshippers, believers, and adherents.

The transition from one type of cults to the other reflects the contumacious rejection of authority and the rise of malignant egalitarianism.

549.

We construct or adopt <u>narratives</u> in order to make sense of ourselves, of others, and of the world at large. Narratives can be rigid (ideological) or open-ended (mutable or flexible).

Rigid narratives are ritualistic, prescriptive, and proscriptive. They are immutable and often counterfactual. They constitute a part of their adherents's identity. Religion is a rigid narrative, for example.

Healthy, normal people can hold several compartmentalized narratives simultaneously and deploy them circumstantially (narrative fluidity, effected via narrative switching).

They do not resist countervailing information (they have no confirmation bias). They modify their narratives to respond adequately to their environment (adaptive narratives).

When mental health issues are present, only one narrative is active and it is always rendered rigid and constricting in order to ameliorate anxiety (anxiolytic rigidification).

The onslaught of reality engenders in the unhealthy a narrative failure and an existential crisis: a lack of meaning so profound that it often results in suicidal ideation.

Instead of narrative fluidity, mental health pathologies lead to a fragmentation of the self into self-states, each with its own single, rigid narrative.

## 550.

Virtue signalling is not limited to the woke left. Anti-vaxxers virtue signal as do white supremacists and religious militants of all stripes.

Virtue signalling is a social bonding ritual with like-minded people. It involves prescribed and proscribed actions and cohering group entraining via repeated slogans and mantras.

Recent studies link virtue signalling to a victimhood personality construct and dark triad propensities (especially subclinical psychopathy and subclinical narcissism).

## 551.

In a deranged world, mental illness is positively reinforced. The environment no longer provides health cues or unscripted exposure therapy.

In such a dystopian bedlam, narcissism is a value, self-harming with sex and substances is empowering fun, and magical thinking is the only touted strategy.

The contemporary war between the genders is a private case of this mass insanity. The locus of intimacy has shifted: it is no longer associated with sex - only with talking and with light touching.

Avoiding or postponing sex now signals being serious about a partner one finds likable or loves, a state of sobriety, and having committed to a relationship.

Men and women hate each other, true. But everyone hate everybody else. Ideology trumps science. Power is the holy grail, not love. Victimhood supplanted dignity.

Self-centredness has utterly uprooted communality. Aggressive, even violent tribalism and partisanship rip us asunder.

Higher education teaches nothing useful and inculcates self-harm and infantilism in its tender charges. Students have taken over, as in replay of Mao's Cultural Revolution.

In such a toxic cesspool writ large, certain mental proclivities - such as owning a dark triad personality - have become positive adaptations, something to aspire to.

552.


Rage farming and defiance are the path to glory, fame, and riches. Ask any conspiracy theorist turned cult leader, from Jordan Peterson to Donald Trump.

Rage is also the engine that drives social media ad sales. Naturally, their algorithms promote posts and videos that consist of red hot anger and of its precursors: hate and fear.

But why are these personalities so popular? Because they interact with their fans and because they take sides, they identify with one camp and attack all others.

I refuse to waste my time on socializing with people: I don't chat, respond to questions and comments, or make myself available in any way.

I also don't belong anywhere: I renounce all affiliations and labels. I am an equal opportunity truthteller. I defy classification. This elitism and impervious impartiality render me extremely hated and shunned.

553.


The unhappy cannot make you happy.

The unloved cannot love.

The anxious bring no peace.

The envious do not support.

The fearful cannot act.

The lonely cannot be found.

The avoidant can't be approached.

The angry are never reconciled.

Hurt people hurt people and the wounded wound.

554.

The fifth in this series of 10 interviews to News Intervention.

<u>Religion is a sublimated (socially acceptable) form of delusional disorder</u> whose contents include a supreme being or power which dictates a code of conduct and sanctions transgressors. Religion is the institutional manifestation of this mental illness, hijacked by psychopaths and narcissists for purposes of attaining power and riches.

The vast majority of people are in a constant state of anxiety. Religion, mysticism, the occult and affiliated derangements are anxiolytic (mitigate anxiety). They are also forms of escapism from unbearable reality via self-imposed psychotic delusions.

On a deeper level, people use religion and its institutions to constrain evil, antisocial behaviors, and negative affectivity (such as anger and envy). Religion is a pillar of communality and the status quo. Historically, when it had failed in this mission, religion had witnessed the rise of belligerent reformers such as Jesus and Martin Luther.

Religion is a mental illness, both individual and collective. The content of its delusions had always been tailored by the elites to rein in the masses.

From the elites's point of view, religion is, therefore, a useful tool of social control.

From the viewpoint of the masses, it guarantees protections against social unrest, malevolent misconduct, arbitrary subjugation, and injustice. It ameliorates the anxiety and fear that these pernicious social phenomena evoke in individuals and in their collectives.

Religion is indeed "opium for the masses", but it has its utility in guaranteeing a structured order for all, founded on predictable and reliable ethics and codes of conduct.

555.

Porn and real life sex are indistinguishable in male brains. They are mistaken for each other.

Similarly, the <u>Metaverse</u> will be an immersive, ubiquitous, all-inclusive environment, misperceived as reality.

Indeed, philosophers such as David Chalmers regard the Metaverse and other simulations as realities.

Mental illness is another case of such counterfactual conflation and confusion: the disordered patient holds his pathology to be the only form of valid ontology ("impaired reality testing").

Internally, mentally ill patients are held hostage to rigid, merciless, and uncompromising constructs and structures.

They rebel against this inner slavery by introducing drama and chaos into their lives, either internally (via their derangement) or externally, by acting out.

Technologies that render their users atomized and self-sufficient act as the equivalents of these rigidities and are likely to provoke storms of aggression and tsunamis of dysregulation as desperate attempts to fight back.

The Metaverse wouldn't be the first time humans have transitioned from reality to an artificial environment or an unprecedented instance of virtualization.

Thousands of years ago, urbanization drove millions of people from nature to cities: the reification and quintessence of fantasy rendered in bricks and mortar.

Agriculture requires an intimate acquaintance with and relatedness to nature, the capacity to delay gratification and prepare for the future, the tolerance of adversity, and humility in the face of the elements - in short: maturity.

All these benign traits and behaviors have been lost in the transition to denser, non-natural dwellings.

The city had infantilized its inhabitants and had rendered them narcissistic and psychopathic.

Megalopolises also precipitated and facilitated the environmental calamities that enshroud the planet today and threaten our very survival as a species.

The adverse outcomes of the Metaverse will far outweigh those wrought by the mass migration to cities.

In physical human habitations, societies, institutions, and other individuals constrain each other via intricate and ever-evolving webs of checks and balances.

Not so in cyberspace which is solipsistic, self-sufficient, self-contained, asocial, competitive, self-centered, and aggressive.

## 556.

The Metaverse wouldn't be the first time humans have transitioned from reality to an artificial environment or an unprecedented instance of virtualization.

Thousands of years ago, urbanization drove millions of people from nature to cities: the reification and quintessence of fantasy rendered in bricks and mortar.

Agriculture requires an intimate acquaintance with and relatedness to nature, the capacity to delay gratification and prepare for the future, the tolerance of adversity, and humility in the face of the elements - in short: maturity.

All these benign traits and behaviors have been lost in the transition to denser, non-natural dwellings.

The city had infantilized its inhabitants and had rendered them narcissistic and psychopathic.

Megalopolises also precipitated and facilitated the environmental calamities that enshroud the planet today and threaten our very survival as a species.

The adverse outcomes of the <u>Metaverse</u> will far outweigh those wrought by the mass migration to cities.

In physical human habitations, societies, institutions, and other individuals constrain each other via intricate and ever-evolving webs of checks and balances.

Not so in cyberspace which is solipsistic, self-sufficient, self-contained, asocial, competitive, self-centered, and aggressive.

557.

The <u>true teacher</u> elevates his students, audience, and interlocutors to his level: he forces them to learn and to improve.

The fake, manipulative "guru" stoops to the level of his listeners and pupils, dumbs down his message, is a "simplifier" and a "popularizer".

And such a fake "educator" laughs all the way to his bank, usually.

558.

People refuse to return to work in offices (RTO) and factories. In the USA, 25 million had resigned their jobs in the past 18 months alone (the <u>Great Resignation or the Big Quit</u> and the Great Retirement).

A series of earth-shattering social, economic, and technological trends converged to render their jobs loathsome to many - a tedious nuisance best avoided.

Text here: <u>http://samvak.tripod.com/workethic.html</u>

559.

I published an essay titled "Russia's Second Empire" in January 2003 in United Press International UPI (20 years ago). Excerpts:

"Peter the Great oriented a reluctant Russia towards the West: its technologies and work ethic, if not its values. Two centuries later, Russian aristocracy was French, its military and commerce German, its monarchy half British, its culture and literature at the core of mainstream Europe. Putin is aiming to reverse all this by firewalling Russia, weaning it off its dependence on the West, and reorienting it towards Asia (from China to the Middle East). It is a gargantuan reversal."

"Like Napoleon III, Putin started off as president (he was shortly as prime minister under Yeltsin). Like him, he may be undone by a military defeat …

Putin, like Louis-Napoleon before him, proceeded to expand his powers and installed loyalists in every corner of the administration and the army. Like Louis-Napoleon, Putin is a populist, travelling throughout the country, posing for photo opportunities, responding to citizens' queries in Q-and-A radio shows, siding with the "average bloke" on every occasion, taking advantage of Russia's previous economic and social disintegration to project an image of a "strong man".

Putin artfully manipulated Europe in the wake of the September 11 terrorist attacks on the USA, his new found ally. He may yet find himself in the enviable position of Europe's arbitrator, NATO's most weighty member, a bridge between Central Asia, the Caucasus, North Korea and China - and the USA. The longer his tenure, the more likely he is to become Europe's elder statesman. This is a maneuver reminiscent of Louis-Napoleon's following the Crimean War, when he teamed up with Great Britain against Russia.

Like Putin, Napoleon III modernized and professionalized his army. But, unlike Putin hitherto, he actually went to war (against Austria), moved by his (oft-thwarted) colonial and mercantilist aspirations. Putin is likely to follow the same path (probably in Central Asia, but, possibly, in the Baltic and east Europe as well). Reinvigorated armies (and industrialists) often force expansionary wars upon their reluctant ostensible political masters.

Should Putin fail in his military adventures as Napoleon III did in his and be deposed as he was - these eerie similarities will have come to their natural conclusion."

The complete article: http://samvak.tripod.com/putin.html

Russia's invasion of Ukraine exposed the cracks and weaknesses in the international order. Unless these issues are resolved and codified, the entire edifice of international law - and, more specifically, the law of war - is in danger of crumbling. The contemporary multilateral regime proved inadequate and unable to effectively tackle genocide (Rwanda, Bosnia), terror (in Africa, Central Asia, and the Middle East), weapons of mass destruction (Iraq, Iran, India, Israel, Pakistan, North Korea), and tyranny (in dozens of members of the United Nations, Russia and China included).

This feebleness inevitably led to the resurgence of "might is right" unilateralism, as practiced, for instance, by the United States in places as diverse as Grenada and Iraq. This pernicious and ominous phenomenon is coupled with contempt towards and suspicion of international organizations, treaties, institutions, undertakings, and the prevailing consensual order.

In a unipolar world, reliant on a single superpower for its security, the abrogation of the rules of the game could lead to chaotic and lethal anarchy with a multitude of "rebellions" against the emergent American Empire. International law - the formalism of "natural law" - is only one of many competing universalist and missionary value systems. Militant Islam is another. The West must adopt the former to counter the latter.

Watch the full Video here: http://www.youtube.com/vakninmusings

560.

She is a tough, hard-working, respected, and admired professional by day - but a promiscuous and reckless alcoholic by night.

Her boundaries are compartmentalized: at work she wouldn't let anyone breach them and trample over her rights and dignity - in her private life, she has none (unboundaried).

Being boundaried is not a trait. Boundaries are affected by multiple personality factors. Some people are worldly and take no abuse when it comes to money, business, career, or education and when in public - but are wide open to maltreatment and self-trashing in their intimate relationships in the private sphere.

It has to do with the attempt to counter stifling internal rigidity by introducing fluidity, mayhem, and drama into one's life. Read my earlier post on this intricate interplay.

This is most pronounced during adolescence and early adulthood when males self-trash via drink, drugs, and antisocial behavior while females mostly use sex to accomplish the same.

561.

In the Middle Ages the sick were considered to have been cursed by god. The only exceptions were the mentally ill who were alleged to be blessed with a special connection to the divine.

Nowadays, there is still stigma attached to most issues of health and disease: mental health, cancer, STDs, and so on. This is despite the growing acceptance for and tolerance of mental illness and sex, conventional and not.

Contemporary shame and shunning of the afflicted has to do with extreme risk aversion and the attempt to insulate oneself from anxiety-inducing reminders of one's vulnerability and fragility.

562.

In the next 2-3 days, Russia's FSB (directorates 2, 6, and 9) face a critical decision: should they conspire with siloviki, headed by Sechin and Ivanov, to remove Putin from power, forcibly, if need be?

The Russian "desk" in the Mossad is betting on this scenario. I am not so sure: Putin has defied numerous such predictions in the past.

But this time, he may have gone too far. He has been expressing his will to retire since 2014. And the campaign in Ukraine is failing. Bad omens for him.

Responses to Izvestiya (scroll to bottom for links to my other videos on the war in Ukraine)

Russia's invasion of Ukraine strengthened the case for joining NATO as a way to deter Russian aggression.

Russia attained its strategic goals in the south and east, but failed to secure a regime change in Kyiv. It should declare victory and stop the fighting or it will end up finding itself mired in another Chechnya.

Western sanctions target Russia's financial infrastructure, its oligarchs and siloviki. They are ineffective.

Eurasia is reclaiming its historical dominance against the West. Russia had gambled on the West and this led to its dependency on it. It should decouple and position itself firmly in the East.

As superpowers jostle for position, we are witnessing a colonial scramble for buffer zones and colonies: Germany has the EU, China the south sea, Russia is reclaiming Ukraine and central Asia. The West should switch from liberalism in international affairs to realpolitik, or it is doomed.

## 563.

This is the <u>age of splitting</u>: black vs. white, 100% right against 1000% wrong. Nothing in between, no subtleties or nuances. The world as a morality play of angels fighting demons.

Public intellectuals, "experts", gurus, and coaches thrive on splitting. They sacrifice their intellectual integrity for the sake of dumb popularity.

Splitting is an infantile psychological defense mechanism. It is a hallmark of immaturity and an antidote to empathy. It precludes cooperation and compromise and foster conflict.

## 564.

This is the <u>most nightmarish period in human history</u>.

Age of splitting
Age of distrust
Age of Death
Age of Spectacle
Age of Self-sufficiency
Age of Risk Aversion

565.

<u>Separation-individuation</u> from external – now persecutory - object, but not from "snapshot" (internal object-introject) which is still idealized as a mother figure and with which the narcissist is still enmeshed in a shared fantasy.

Narcissism is a missionary religion, replete with a deity (false self), OCD rituals, and addiction. The shared fantasy is populated with idealized images, the Olympian gods. The shared fantasy is the mystical experience of the narcissism religion.

Shared fantasy = regression to infantile phase prior to separation-individuation from the mother = merger/fusion/oceanic feeling/enmeshment/engulfment = no self-object or object representations

Mystical experiences = regression to infantile phase prior to separation-individuation from god/cosmos/nature = merger/fusion/oceanic feeling/enmeshment/engulfment = no self-object or object representations.

Similar to the narcissist's shared fantasy, <u>mystical experiences and religions</u> founded on these experiences are delusional regressions to an infantile phase prior to separation-individuation from god/cosmos/nature and merger/fusion/oceanic feeling/enmeshment/engulfment (no self-object or object representations).

566.

Similar to the narcissist's shared fantasy, <u>mystical experiences and religions</u> founded on these experiences are delusional regressions to an infantile phase prior to separation-individuation from god/cosmos/nature and merger/fusion/oceanic feeling/enmeshment/engulfment (no self-object or object representations).

567.

<u>Period of multiple transitions with no elites or institutions</u> (clan, tribe, family, church, lord, guild) to cushion, comfort, and buffer changes.

POLITIES

From monarchies to unstable empires with inner tensions to multiple experimental political systems, still contested.

ECONOMIES

Population pressure and surpluses led from agriculture to urbanization, colonialism, imperialism, mercantilism, and Industrialization and have decoupled production from consumption, resulting in anonymous ad hoc communities (teams, unions, nuclear families)

FAMILY and GENDER

Monogamous family: artefact of hierarchical agricultural state and need to regulate surpluses (wealth). Patriarchy in public domain and matriarchy in private domain.

We are transitioning to matriarchy in both the private and the public domain.

Outsourcing of family functions, medical and technological innovations emancipated women, upended the power matrix, reduced procreation, eliminated obsolete gender (unigender, masculinization in stalled revolution), homoegenized sexual scripts, and caused reactionary war (backlash) with men.

Women and men are angry at each other, contemptuous, distrustful, and no longer rely on each other.

KNOWLEDGE

Democratization of knowledge: vernacular bible, universities, printing, internet led to populism, anti-enlightenment, ochlocracies, and totalitarianism.

REALITY

Now we are transitioning from first generation virtual reality (cities) to second generation: cyberspace/metaverse and social media: atomization, individual anonymity, self-worship, and self-sufficiency.

568.

In life we are but <u>dreams</u>, in death we are but memories.

569.

<u>Anger</u> is a primitive, limbic emotion. Its excitatory components and patterns are shared with sexual excitation and with fear. It is cognition that guides our behavior, aimed at avoiding harm and aversion or at minimizing them.

Our cognition is in charge of attaining certain kinds of mental gratification. An analysis of future values of the relief-gratification versus repercussions (reward to risk) ratio – can be obtained only through cognitive tools. Anger is provoked by aversive treatment, deliberately or unintentionally inflicted.

Such treatment must violate either prevailing conventions regarding social interactions or some otherwise deeply ingrained sense of what is fair and what is just. The judgment of fairness or justice (namely, the appraisal of the extent of compliance with conventions of social exchange) – is also cognitive.

The angry person and the personality disordered both suffer from a cognitive deficit. They are unable to conceptualize, to design effective strategies and to execute them. They dedicate all their attention to the immediate and ignore the future consequences of their actions.

In other words, their attention and information processing faculties are distorted, skewed in favor of the here and now, biased on both the intake and the output. Time is "relativistically dilated" – the present feels more protracted, "longer" than any future. Immediate facts and actions are judged more relevant and weighted more heavily than any remote aversive conditions. Anger impairs cognition.

570.

With the right person, <u>routine</u> is way more exciting than any adventure.

Exotic trips are often an escape from life. But nothing is more exotic than life itself.

571.

This is my natal chart. Other astrology websites offer other versions of my natal chart..

All humans believe in the existence of connections or relationships between things (apophenia, pareidolia).

This belief in some order (permanent relations between separate physical or abstract entities) permeates both Science and Superstition.

Science limits itself: only certain entities inter-relate within well defined conceptual frames (called theories). Not everything has the potential to connect to everything else. Entities are discriminated, differentiated, classified and assimilated in worldviews in accordance with the types of connections that they forge with each other.

Moreover, Science believes that it has a set of very effective tools to diagnose, distinguish, observe and describe these relationships. It proves its point by issuing highly accurate predictions based on the relationships discerned through the use of said tools. Science (mostly) claims that these connections are "true" in the sense that they are certain and real - not probable.

The cycle of formulation, prediction and falsification (or proof) is the core of the human scientific activity. Alleged connections that cannot be captured in these nets of reasoning are cast out either as "hypothetical" or as "false". In other words: Science accepts only relations between entities which have been established and tested using the scientific apparatus and arsenal of tools". This, admittedly, is a very cyclical argument, as close to tautology as it gets.

<u>Superstition</u> is a much simpler matter: everything is connected to everything in ways unbeknown to us. We can only witness the results of these subterranean currents and deduce their existence from the observable flotsam. The planets influence our lives, dry coffee sediments contain information about the future, black cats portend disasters, certain dates are propitious, certain numbers are to be avoided. But the fact that we - limited as we are - cannot learn about a hidden connection - should not imply that it does not exist.

572.

<u>Procrastination</u> is either because you hate your job (and wish to lose it) - or because you love your job (and wish to be perfect at it).

573.

Grandiose, unscrupulous, and unethical therapists cater to the mentally ill and disabled person's most ardent and fervent wish: <u>to be normal</u>. It is like a medical doctor promising a quadriplegic that she would be able to run again.

Truth is: the mentally ill should be sequestered and discouraged from seeking normalcy. They should not have relationships, get married, bear children, have families, gain access to certain institutions.

574.

Self-love: (self-awareness also of one's limitations, self-acceptance + self-trust + self-efficacy)

+boundaries

+self-regulation

=mental health.

575.

What constitutes <u>normal behavior</u>? Who is normal?

There is the statistical response: the average and the common are normal. But it is unsatisfactory and incomplete. Conforming to social edicts and mores does not guarantee normalcy. Think about anomic societies and periods of history such as Hitler's Germany or Stalin's Russia. Model citizens in these hellish environments were the criminal and the sadist.

Rather than look to the outside for a clear definition, many mental health professionals ask: is the patient functioning and happy (ego-syntonic)? If he or she is both then all is well and normal. Abnormal traits, behaviors, and personalities are, therefore defined as those traits, behaviors, and personalities that are dysfunctional and cause subjective distress.

But, of course, this falls flat on its face at the slightest scrutiny. Many evidently mentally ill people are rather happy and reasonably functional.

Some scholars reject the concept of "normalcy" altogether. The anti-psychiatry movement object to the medicalization and pathologization of whole swathes of human conduct. Others prefer to study the disorders themselves rather to "go metaphysical" by trying to distinguish them from an imaginary and ideal state of being "mentally healthy".

I subscribe to the later approach. I much prefer to delve into the phenomenology of mental health disorders: their traits, characteristics, and impact on others.

576.

Production of goods and services and the manipulation of symbols should be decoupled if we want to avoid mass psychosis and the degeneration of capitalism into neo-feudalism.

Interview with Maria Morais of Circklo http://www.circklo.com

577.

The resurrection story is a good model to build on: we can all start all over again (and make something of our lives), no matter how severe the trauma is.

Jesus' mother, Mary, was a virgin before it gave birth to him - and remained a virgin in perpetuity. This is the official (Catholic) doctrine.

But Jesus had siblings.

St. Paul wrote (Galatians 1:18-19):

'Then after three years I went up to Jerusalem to see Peter, and abode with him fifteen days. But of the other apostles saw I none save James the Lord's brother."

This very same James is also the son of one, Alpheus! All the brothers of Jesus are the sons of this Alpheus whose wife's name was ... Mary!

Matthew 1:25:

"And he [Joseph] knew her [Mary] not until she had brought forth her first-born son..."

First-born meaning there were others who followed (second-born, third-born, etc.)

Matthew 13:55-56:

"Is this not the carpenter's son? Is not his mother called Mary? And his brethren, James and Joses and Simon and Judas? And his sisters, are they not all with us?"

Mark 6:3 (referring to Jesus):

"Is this not the carpenter, the brother of James, and Joses, and of Judas, and Simon? And are not his sisters here with us?"

According to both Matthew and Mark, three women stood by the cross at the crucifixion: Mary Magdalene, Mary the mother of James and of Joses, and the mother of Zebedee's children (Salome). Salome was Virgin Mary's sister and, therefore, Jesus' maternal aunt.

John (an eyewitness to the events) identifies Mary as Jesus' mother - but distinguishes her from Mary, wife of Alpheus and two other women (for a total of four women rather than three):

John 19:25:

"Now there stood by the cross of Jesus (1) his mother, and (2) his mother's sister, (3) Mary the wife of Cleophas [Alpheus], and (4) Mary Magdalene."

Mary, wife of Alpheus, could not have been the sister of the Virgin Mary, as the Church would have us believe. In Jewish families, two sisters cannot share the same name.

John implies that Mary, mother of Jesus was not the wife of Alpheus, father of James and Joses, and Judas, and Simon, who are identified as the brothers of Jesus by all the other gospels!

578.

Circklo write: "One of the most illustrious and inquisitive minds of our century - Professor Sam Vaknin - argues that 'there is no real commitment in business to anything outside business' and that, when businesses claim otherwise, it is a simple public relations exercise.

Watch what he said below and do share your thoughts with us!"

579.


Parenting is possibly an irrational vocation, but humanity keeps breeding and procreating. It may well be the call of nature. All living species reproduce and most of them parent. Is maternity (and paternity) proof that, beneath the ephemeral veneer of civilization, we are still merely a kind of beast, subject to the impulses and hard-wired behavior that permeate the rest of the animal kingdom?

In his seminal tome, "The Selfish Gene", Richard Dawkins suggested that we copulate in order to preserve our genetic material by embedding it in the future gene pool. Survival itself - whether in the form of DNA, or, on a higher-level, as a species - determines our parenting instinct. Breeding and nurturing the young are mere safe conduct mechanisms, handing the precious cargo of genetics down generations of "organic containers".

Yet, surely, to ignore the epistemological and emotional realities of parenthood is misleadingly reductionistic. Moreover, Dawkins commits the scientific faux-pas of teleology. Nature has no purpose "in mind", mainly because it has no mind. Things simply are, period. That genes end up being forwarded in time does not entail that Nature (or, for that matter, "God") planned it this way. Arguments from design have long - and convincingly - been refuted by countless philosophers.

Still, human beings do act intentionally. Back to square one: why bring children to the world and burden ourselves with decades of commitment to perfect strangers?

Continued here: http://www.narcissistic-abuse.com/parent.html

580.

The hitherto undiscovered genius artist @bdeaihe_art at work.

The function of bridging the gap between our idiosyncratic, private languages and a more universal one was relegated to a group of special individuals called artists.

Theirs is the job to experience (mostly emotions) and to mould their experience into the grammar, syntax and vocabulary of a universal language in order to communicate to us the echo of their idiosyncratic language.

They are forever mediating between us and their experience. Rightly so, the quality of an artist is measured by his ability to loyally represent his unique language to us.

The smaller the distance between the original experience (the emotion of the artist) and its external representation, the more prominent the artist.

We declare artistic success when the universally communicable representation succeeds at recreating and evoking in us the original emotion (felt by the artist).

It is very much like teleportation which allows, in sci-fi yarns, for the decomposition of the astronaut's body in one spot and its recreation, atom for atom in another.

Even if the artist fails to faithfully recreate his inner world, but succeeds in calling forth any kind of emotional response in his viewers/readers/listeners, he is deemed successful.

## 581.

A person is held not responsible for his <u>criminal actions</u> if s/he cannot tell right from wrong ("lacks substantial capacity either to appreciate the criminality (wrongfulness) of his conduct" - diminished capacity), did not intend to act the way he did (absent "mens rea") and/or could not control his behavior ("irresistible impulse"). These handicaps are often associated with "mental disease or defect" or "mental retardation".

Mental health professionals prefer to talk about an impairment of a "person's perception or understanding of reality". They hold a "guilty but mentally ill" verdict to be contradiction in terms. All "mentally-ill" people operate within a (usually coherent) worldview, with consistent internal logic, and rules of right and wrong (ethics). Yet, these rarely conform to the way most people perceive the world. The mentally-ill, therefore, cannot be guilty because s/he has a tenuous grasp on reality.

Yet, experience teaches us that a criminal maybe mentally ill even as s/he maintains a perfect reality test and thus is held criminally responsible (Jeffrey Dahmer comes to mind). The "perception and understanding of reality", in other words, can and does co-exist even with the severest forms of mental illness.

This makes it even more difficult to comprehend what is meant by "mental disease". If some mentally ill maintain a grasp on reality, know right from wrong, can anticipate the outcomes of their actions, are not subject to irresistible impulses (the official position of the American Psychiatric Association) - in what way do they differ from us, "normal" folks?

This is why the insanity defense often sits ill with mental health pathologies deemed socially "acceptable" and "normal" - such as religion or love.

Continued here: https://samvak.tripod.com/insanitydefense.html

582.

Is the Metaverse the ultimate dystopia, an escape from reality, or the promised technological heaven?

583.

Success in business (and in general) requires equal measures of stupidity and mental health pathologies.

Intellectually inferior folks are more attuned to the needs of a civilization comprised mostly of brain-addled or mentally unwell consumers. They are able to respond in kind and communicate efficaciously with the teeming, braindead masses.

Moreover: the stupid are incapable of evaluating risks properly. They plunge ahead with audacity and defiance.

Sometimes, this unthinking thrust endows successful operators with a first mover advantage, creates network effects, and corners the market.

Prosperous entrepreneurs often exhibit impaired reality testing, magical thinking, and splitting.

They shape reality to fit their omnipotent fantasies rather than gauge it properly. Their dichotomous thinking reduces the world to Pavlovian costs vs. rewards, useful vs. useless, and with me vs. foes.

584.

There are 2 keys to success. Use them and you will become richer than Elon Musk. Money back guarantee!

Drobeta-Turnu Severin: undiscovered gem.

585.

There are 2 keys to success. Use them and you will become richer than Elon Musk. Money back guarantee!

Vaknin's message to the young: reality sucks, you are on your own, you are not as special as you would like to believe. So: get on with life!

Drobeta-Turnu Severin: undiscovered gem.

586.

Vaknin's message to the young: reality sucks, you are on your own, you are not as special as you would like to believe. So: get on with life!

Good enough parents can become "dead", bad parents by falling into a series of traps and wrong behaviors.

Excerpt from the lecture (now available on YouTube)
courtesy @umushoma

Cluster B personality disorders can be diagnosed in childhood and adolescence. Conduct disorder is the precursor to psychopathy and Borderline Personality Disorder (BPD) can be safely diagnosed in early puberty. Not so Narcissistic Personality Disorder (NPD).

The concepts of "self", "individual", and "personality" are misleading and counterfactual. You are the sum of your relationships with others (object relations). You have self-states which are reactive to your changing environment.

Drobeta-Turnu Severin: undiscovered gem.

587.

Ed Sheeran and Taylor Swift are the most recent recipients of honorary doctorates from universities.

They were preceded by lightweights like Sigmund Freud, Albert Einstein, Winston Churchill, and Nelson Mandela.

Need I say more about the state of the world today?

588.

"Upgraded Worldview Certificate UN Goals awarded to Sam Vaknin for answering 100% correct on questions related to the UN goals and thereby proving essential knowledge that most people are wrong about."

About time! LOL

589.

The art of @bdeaihe_art is multilayered and suffused with allusions to literature, mythology, and religion. But it is never stuffy: humorous levity combine with profundity in perfect harmony.

Consider this painting of hers:

In this painting, Nature itself is in turmoil: the sun is eclipsed, fish fly overhead, the ocean merges with the sky. Surrealistic.

The angel-like boy is more Indian than Judeo-Christian: he has many arms.

Some of his hands hold symbols of death and war (and love!): bow and arrow. Other hands play the violin - music is life.

The boy is anointing the female figure, the same way David, Jesus, and others in the Bible were anointed, riding a donkey.

The girl is in love (the heart locket) but (her forehead is) wounded.

She is melancholy, almost lifeless.

But she is armed for battle and wearing winged sandals: the gods's gift to Perseus who slayed medusa.

Fish symbolize Jesus and early Christianity. He and his disciples were "fishing for the souls of men".

The two-headed dog is a guardian of hell, but in this painting, one head points to the past and one is looking forward (like Janus).

590.

YouTube is full of misinformation, disinformation, sheer nonsense, and fake news.

Real scholars and academics shun YouTube as the cesspool that it is. Consequently, the field is left wide open to charlatans, dilettantes, and con artists.

The idea is to establish ScholarTube.

It would be a platform for scholars, researchers, and scientists to maintain and curate their own video channels and educate the public with evidence-based info and cutting edge studies.

The platform will NOT be open to contributions from the public - but the content will be available to everyone to watch.

There will be a committee and it will approve every application for a channel on the merits and following an investigation into the credentials of the applicant.

591.

We are on the threshold of being able to create "designer CNS (nervous systems)" which will be responsive to idiosyncratic job descriptions and incorporate adaptations reactive to specific environments.

Similarly, soon we will learn to induce neural growth even in the brain and grow brains in a dish.

Finally, within a few decades, we will be routinely backing up our minds into external storage, the way we are doing with our smartphones today. Applications would be able to tap into these uploaded consciousnesses and data mining them both for commercial and medical purposes.

<u>Full Interview on the News Intervention website</u>.

592.

<u>Introverts and the depressed</u> appear to be indistinguishable. But they have nothing in common. Three important differences:

1. The introvert is ego syntonic: she feels comfortable in her skin and when all by herself. She prefers her own company to any other's.

The depressive is ego dystonic by definition: he is profoundly unhappy (dysphoric and anhedonic).

2. The introvert never willingly socializes or mingles. You will never find her frequenting clubs or attending parties. She rarely if ever exits home, except to her workplace.

The depressive can be very sociable, even reckless and promiscuous. He uses interactions with others as a form of self-soothing or self-medication.

3. The rates of substance abuse among introverts is drastically lower than among sufferers of depression or anxiety.

593.

<u>Depression</u> is often frustration writ large. Frustration yields aggression (Dollard, 1939). But men externalize this aggression while women internalize and self-direct it. Depressed men tend to become antisocial, secluded, even violent. In contrast, depressed women typically self-trash, sexually or otherwise.

594.

Forms of <u>self-defeat and self-destructiveness</u>:

<u>Constricted life</u>

Love addiction
Perfectionism
Self-denial
Depression
Numbing
Dissociation
Masochism
Insecure attachment

595.

As the mafia say: "All's well that ends in a well.'"

596.

The thing about the right is that it is rarely that (right). The thing about the left is that it has (left).

597.

We are transitioning from the age of cows to the age of milk.

Why work on a relationship (cow) if I can have only sex (glass of milk)?

Why waste time on a man (cow) if I can pay for donor sperm (glass of milk)?

Why read a book (cow) if I can gulp down a 3 paragraph synopsis (glass of milk)?

Why learn anything (cow) if I have access to Wikipedia (glass of milk)?

Why take responsibility for my choices and life (cow) if I can blame others (glass of milk)?

Why work hard at anything (cow) if I can fake it till I make it (glass of milk)?

598.

Mistreating Celebrities - An Interview granted to Superinteressante Magazine in Brazil.

A. As far as their fans are concerned, celebrities fulfil two emotional functions: they provide a mythical narrative (a story that the fan can follow and identify with) and they function as blank screens onto which the fans project their dreams, hopes, fears, plans, values, and desires (wish fulfilment). The slightest deviation from these prescribed roles provokes enormous rage and makes us want to punish (humiliate) the "deviant" celebrities.

But why?

When the human foibles, vulnerabilities, and frailties of a celebrity are revealed, the fan feels humiliated, "cheated", hopeless, and "empty". To reassert his self-worth, the fan must establish his or her moral superiority over the erring and "sinful" celebrity. The fan must "teach the celebrity a lesson" and show the celebrity "who's boss". It is a primitive defense mechanism - narcissistic grandiosity. It puts the fan on equal footing with the exposed and "naked" celebrity.

A. There is always a sadistic pleasure and a morbid fascination in vicarious suffering. Being spared the pains and tribulations others go through makes the observer feel "chosen", secure, and virtuous. The higher celebrities rise, the harder they fall. There is something gratifying in hubris defied and punished.

A. There is an implicit contract between a celebrity and his fans. The celebrity is obliged to "act the part", to fulfil the expectations of his admirers, not to deviate from the roles that they impose and he or she accepts. In return the fans shower the celebrity with adulation. They idolize him or her and make him or her feel omnipotent, immortal, "larger than life", omniscient, superior, and sui generis (unique).

8. Why are celebrities narcissists? How is this disorder born?

Read the full interview here: https://www.narcissistic-abuse.com/faq19.html

599.

Love is the opposite of weakness. It is the antonym of dependence.

Love is the ultimate form of STRENGTH and COURAGE: not being afraid to be vulnerable and to get hurt.

Love is never merging with your loved one. It is about keeping separate enough to embrace the other person as he is, warts and all.

600.

Myths of the con artists of the self-help industry:

MYTH You can learn from your mistakes

FACT You are very likely to repeat your behaviors throughout your lifespan (repetition compulsion).

MYTH Change is possible

FACT Meaningful transformation is nearly impossible after age 25.

MYTH Your partner's past doesn't matter, only her present behavior

FACT Your partner's past is your future. Past behaviors and misconduct are sure predictors of future behaviors and misconduct.

MYTH Trauma is an objective experience

FACT Trauma is a subjective, endogenous (psychegenic) reaction. It has little to do with reality, which serves only as a trigger.

MYTH Love and time cure all

FACT In many - maybe most - cases, love and time result in losses, heartbreak, and hurt.

MYTH Sex empowers

FACT Only in the minority of cases and during limerence. Mostly, sex leads to regret, shame, anger, self-loathing, ennui, disgust, and dissonance. This is true even among men and even in committed relationships!

MYTH Having multiple choices empowers

FACT Choice creates anxiety, withdrawal, and avoidance. People hate choice. They want to be spoonfed out of a limited menu of options.

MYTH Parents and their children should be besties, friends

FACT Good parenting requires boundaries, hierarchy, and discipline - the exact opposite of friendship.

Also watch: Abuse Victims, Beware: Common Sense is Harmful Nonsense (12 Myths Debunked)
https://www.youtube.com/watch?v=McWOGyGtuL0

Also watch 20 WRONG Ideas About Therapy, Psychology
https://www.youtube.com/watch?v=ekBATw1P-wE

Also watch 8 Things You are Getting WRONG about Your Narcissist
https://www.youtube.com/watch?v=0Xdnh7QUUkc

601.

Men invented the pill.

Men advocated for casual sex at the beginning of the 20th century.

Men sparked the sexual "free love" revolution and then the hookup culture, replete with dating apps.

Men opened up the workplace to women. Now 40% of primary breadwinners in many industrialized countries are female.

Yet, women label these self-interested male acts: feminism or "women's empowerment". Go figure.

602.

Love, trust, and respect are the three legs of the relationship stool (also in casual sex where lust could substitute for love).

If even one leg is missing, you end up on your butt.

Then, it HURTS.

603.

Jacobsen: Is high intelligence required for true genius?

Vaknin: If by intelligence you mean IQ then the answer is a resounding no. The adage about perspiration and inspiration applies. But, more importantly, genius is the ability to see familiar things in a fresh, unprecedented way. Imagination, intuition, and the ability to tell apart the critical from the tangential are the core constituents of genius – not intelligence.

What intelligence does contribute to genius is alacrity. It is a catalyst. It speeds up both the processes of theorizing and of discovery.

Jacobsen: What happens to an insane person who happens to have high intelligence too?

Vaknin: He is likely to construct theories that will pass for genius, especially among laymen. The intelligence of the gifted madman serves to camouflage the lack of rigor and the delusional, counterfactual content of his creations. Rather than catalyze disruptive discoveries, his intellect works overtime at the service of aggressively defending a manifestly risible sleight of hand. It is not open to any modificatory feedback from the environment. The madman's intellect is solipsistic and moribund.

604.

The faith-based personality is characteristic of people who need to believe in something or someone in order to feel safe and secure: god, an intimate partner, the state, the family, an institution, a fantasy, or a delusional conspiracy theory.

It has long been speculated that addicts have an addictive personality: they tend to rotate from one addiction to another all their lives.

Similarly, the faith-based personality switches between socially condoned (sublimated) beliefs and delusions all her life.

Faith provides a sense of belonging, acceptance, and embedment and is, therefore, functionally akin to self-love.

605.

The <u>Digital Mind of Tomorrow by Isabella Wang</u>.

On my reading list during my sojourn in Bucharest next month. Can't wait!

606.

<u>Isabella Wang</u> (author of "The Digital Mind of Tomorrow") and Sam Vaknin discuss the human mind and brain, psychology, the human condition, and the future in a wide ranging talk between East and West.

607.

Underpinning latter-day dualism are two arguments:

1. Mental phenomena cannot be reduced into material objects or fit into a strictly materialistic theory because they are possessed of consciousness (felt subjective experience); and

2. Mental phenomena cannot be reduced into material objects or fit into a strictly materialistic theory because they are possessed of intentionality (the capacity to self-direct onto something material external to the mental or onto an immanent internal object).

But consciousness can be construed as inverted intentionality which is directed at the subject, the internal - rather than the object, or the external.

So, the fundamental, primary process is intentionality, not consciousness. I call this school of thought "<u>intentionalism</u>".

It is also far from certain that the material lacks intentionality. The ban on teleology reflected a grandiose anthropocentric view of the world which has been challenged and undermined by modern science every day for the past 150 years or so.

608.

Watch the first part here:
https://www.youtube.com/watch?v=7fco4_4VJ5A

Interview transcript here: http://www.narcissistic-abuse.com/shotranscript.docx

Sometimes, civilizations reach a point where the only way out is a reset and starting from scratch.

I fully believe that we are at such an inflection or tipping point.

What needs to happen? We need to transition from cities back to nature - both mentally and physically https://m.youtube.com/watch?v=-VAh4YeGbKQ From Narcissistic Cities to Psychopathic Metaverse (EXCERPT)

We need to suppress some kinds of pernicious speech, some ideologies (as we do today with fascism, Nazism, white supremacy, and racism). Example: third wave feminism, advertising (Althusser's interpellation) https://m.youtube.com/watch?v=M8z5d5NvZSk Feminism: From Equity to Psychopathy

We need to force people back into families and communities by monetarily penalizing certain asocial and antisocial behaviors.

We need to redesign and reform the workplace by seamlessly integrating it with the community and the home. But it should be obligatory to work with other people face to face. Workplace intrusions into private time should be criminalized. https://m.youtube.com/watch?v=Zm5cAhWe1S8 Workaholism: Addiction or Lifestyle?

We need to ban certain types of immersive technologies (the way we ban cloning, for example).

We need to certify people to use certain kinds of technology the same way we run background checks on people who use guns today.

We need to limit the use of all social media technologies to 2 hours a day.

We need to ban relative positioning practices such as "likes".

Friends online could be only people you have actually met in real life.

We need to verify the identity of all users and criminalize the use of pseudonyms. Blockchain technology could be of great help here.

We need to educate children regarding sex and its physiological, medical, and mental implications.

Example:

We know that compulsive casual sex and sexting have deleterious outcomes later in life. We need to share this info widely. Sex positivity is a seriously bad idea.

Similarly, we need to inculcate in children the importance and benefits of intimacy and long term relationships.

We need to license parenting. Prospective parents would be required to complete a curriculum in child psychology, relationship management, age-appropriate technology use and so on.
https://m.youtube.com/watch?v=Bl3cDC3TICY Parenting should be Licensed!

We need to enforce age-related restrictions on entertainment venues such as nightclubs, the use of alcohol in campuses, and other measures.

Education is a public good. We need to DEprivatize it.

We need to reorient education around the twin concepts of phronetics and eudaimonia - as well as life skilling (including how to manage relationships, for example).

Finally: psychology should become an obligatory subject starting in middle school.

Lifelong self-auditing and journaling should be taught and encouraged as ways to obtain insight and secure introspection.

609.

13 conversations with the renowned Israeli radio personality, Benny Hendel - 35 years after our first interviews (available in Hebrew in archive.org).

1. Is consciousness merely the subjective experience of introspection?

2. Is reality observer-dependent?

3. Is artificial intelligence indistinguishable from the human variety?

4. Does "Nature" exist?

5. Is modern physics - a metaphysics?

6. Is the multiverse a useful concept?

7. Are simulations as real as real reality? Is reality a simulation?

8. The dangers and promises of extended, virtual, and augmented realities: from cities to the Metaverse.

9. Is culture the successor to evolution? Are we headed towards a transhumanist future?

10. Are science and technology related?

11. What's wrong with the concepts of self, individual, and personality?

12. Do we need others or is self-sufficient atomization the future?

13. Chronon Field Theory

610.

The erroneous foundations of contemporary psychology: self, personality, individual should be replaced with seamlessly fluid self-states. Man is a river, not a lake. I discuss my new concept of covert borderline and the bridge between overt and covert cluster B states via collapse and narcissistic mortification.

The concept of the unitary self is being replaced with the idea that an internal operating system determines which of several self-states emerges, given internally and externally (environmentally) generated information.

Self-efficacy is the overriding constraint which the system seeks to optimize when hailing forth these sub-personalities or pseudoidentities.

When all relevant or available self-states at the disposal of the system are equally self-efficacious, the system may opt to keep two or more of them in operation (I call it a "state of residuals" or "binary system"). This ineluctably leads to dissonance and internalized aggression.

Each state is narrative which provides a pseudo-identity. Pseudoidentities are ego functions (resources) and simulations (probes). In the absence of a unitary, stable core (identity disturbance and identity diffusion), the patient shape-shifts between self-states, replete with their own unique traits, affect, cognitions, and behaviors. In extremis, these self-states are utterly dissociated (most forms of DID - Dissociative Identity Disorder).

Psychopathy is a self-state, protective of ego resource in DID, BPD (secondary), NPD, HPD, PPD.

Decompensation owing to intolerable anticipated or actual stress or trauma (CPTSD/PTSD): grandiose and fantasy defenses crumble and lead to acting out or to suicide leads to the emergence of a psychopathic protective self-state (same in DID).

But protect from what?

NPD: injury, mortification (hypervigilance) leads to contact with trauma traces, repressed emotions  - NPD becomes BPD (Grotstein: BPD failed narcissist).

PPD: threat (paranoid ideation, persecutory delusions)

BPD: abandonment, rejection

HPD: rejection, injury

When the protective self is overactive or is the only self-state/resource, we get hybrids types (comorbidity) like the malignant narcissist (Fromm, Herbert Rosenfeld, Kernberg).

611.

We are caught in the crosshairs of several historical and technological trends that have converged to render us all alone - and very lonely. Convo with Benny Hendel.

612.

PASCAL's WAGER (Wikipedia)

A rational person should live as though God exists and seek to believe in
God. If God does not exist, such a person will have only a finite loss (some
pleasures, luxury, etc.), whereas if God does exist, he stands to receive
infinite gains (as represented by eternity in Heaven) and avoid infinite
losses (an eternity in Hell).

VAKNIN's WAGER

If god exists, he either does not care if I believe in him - or he does care.

If he doesn't care - why should I bother to believe in him?

If he does care - he is definitely not god.

613.

Brain neuroplasticity supports self-states models in personality
psychology. Phenomena such as ambivalence, cognitive dissonance, and
compartmentalization also tally with the self-states model and militate
against any model involving a unitary self or core identity.

614.

Whenever someone tells me about their intention to end their life, I
respond:

Staying alive is the only cogent argument for staying alive.

We stay alive simply because the alternative is NOT being and existence is
always richer in potential than non-existence.

Life is full of pain and frustration. But pain and frustration are not
CAUSES. They just ARE - the same way that we ARE.

I hope you reconsider your decision.

And to those who contemplate suicide while claiming to have faith in the afterlife (whatever that may be), I add:

You claim to have faith, but you sound like you have lost ALL faith.

615.

People confuse purpose with meaning.

However devoid of goals it may be, your life is meaningful because the universe would not be the same without you.

When you choose to live rather than to die, you co-create the world. Your death renders it instantly other.

Had you not been born, reality for every atom and person and entity would have been radically different.

Purpose and action and accomplishments are the icing on the cake of your existence.

But your existence alone suffices to steer everyone and everything in another direction and towards an alternative destiny.

You are truly the co-author of the universe. What could be more significant than this?

616.

Interview granted to Remus Cernea of Newsweek regarding the forthcoming tsunami of PTSD in Ukraine and the connection between a rising wave of trauma globally and the breakdown of language and of institutions. Recreating ravaged communities online and leveraging the resilient to help the afflicted are the only solutions. An international brigade of mental health practitioners is called for.

617.

Chronon Field Theory is a completely new language of physics with Time as its sole word. In this theory, Time is a force with its own field of potentials and the building blocks are events, not particles. Benny Hendel Talks to Sam Vaknin (who came up with the theory in 1982-3) about this new way of looking at reality.

618.

On his deathbed, Voltaire was asked by a priest to renounce the Devil. "It is not thr time to make new enemies!"- he famously responded.

The electric chair was invented by a dentist, Alfred Southwick from Buffalo. But the modern implement was designed and tested by Harold Brown with the active support of Thomas Edison. Carlos McDonald and A. P. Rockwell contributed to the engineering of the chair. But the patent is registered to one, Edwin Davis, who used it to kill more than 300 prisoners.

Due to the body's high resistance, an alternating current of 2000-2400 volts is applied to electrocute the condemned. Only two electrodes, moistened with a salt solution, are attached to the scalp and to the calf of one leg. Death occurs two to five whole minutes after the jolt has been administered - but no one knows why or how. The electrical current may stop the heart before the victims are practically burnt or cooked to death. There is no proof either way. Willie Francis, who survived his first execution, described it thus:

"My mouth tasted like cold peanut butter. I felt a burning in my head and my left leg, and I jumped against the straps."

The chair has its own circuit, separate from the prison's - but it does feed off the public grid. Prison officials pull the switches or push the buttons.

The axe murderer, William Kemmler, was the first to be electrocuted in Auburn State Prison, New York, on August 6, 1890. By 1972 the chair was adopted by 25 states and the District of Columbia. More than 4300 inmates, including dozens of women, were "grilled" by the device in the United States. Only a few of the 28 states that currently allow the death penalty still use the chair, though - and only 3 of those as an exclusive method of execution, as do the Philippines and China.

619.

Do we create reality in our minds - or are our minds equipped to observe only a sliver of reality?

Additional videos in this Cycle are on my other channel:
http://www.youtube.com/vakninmusings

620.

Self-actualization is the sole engine of meaning in life: making a difference in an otherwise indifferent universe.

So, why do I rail against consumerism and sex positivity which are ostensibly about helping us to realize our potential?

Because both actually limit our promise and constrict our lives. Both these ideologies are death cults: they objectify people and humanize objects.

Consumerism and sex positivity also suppress our free will by presenting fake choices between rigidly dictated alternatives and by penalizing nonconformity.

621.

Psychology is in crisis owing to the pernicious influences of celebrity and money.

Scientists are claiming expertise when and where they have none.

Many are "massaging" the results of experiments (replication crisis).

Making unfounded claims based on flimsy or non-existent evidence

Abusing their authority.

Molecular Biology fundamentalists (Sapolsky BOOK) are grandiose and grossly misleading, I cringe.

Some of the problems: correlation not causation, reductionism and ignorance (empathy not narcissism), contradictory results, not enough known, environmental triggering (nurture, not nature), replicability issues, inflated ill-founded claims.

Examples: antidepressants and DSM.

ANTIDEPRESSANTS

Is Depression Healthy? (2nd Webinar on Depression Management, May 2021)

No link between depression and serotonin, finds major analysis

A review of 17 previous studies finds no evidence for a link between depression and low serotonin levels, which SSRI antidepressants focus on – though not everyone is convinced by the findings

NEW SCIENTIST HEALTH 20 July 2022 By Sarah Wild

The serotonin theory of depression: a systematic umbrella review of the evidence
Joanna Moncrieff, Ruth E. Cooper, Tom Stockmann, Simone Amendola, Michael P. Hengartner & Mark A. Horowitz
(Nature) Molecular Psychiatry (2022)

DSM

Watch Future of Personality Disorders: ICD Revolutionary, DSM Craven.

Finally, a revolution in the perception of Borderline Personality Disorder (BPD) in the newest editions of the DSM and ICD.

622.

Stress mobilizes - anxiety paralyzes.

Dedication galvanizes - addiction euthanizes.

Envy kills - emulation fulfills.

Grieving is overcome - depression overcomes.

Striving attains - perfectionism detains.

623.

The exact same actions can be utterly meaningless or overwhelmingly meaningful.

Dinner at the same venue with the same menu choices, watching a movie, listening to music, or even having sex feel utterly different with a loved one than with a random colleague.

But the absence of meaning is not to be confused with emotionlessness.

Every action is imbued with emotions. There is no such thing as an emotionless experience.

Even a one night stand with a total stranger involves vulnerability, trust, and affection if not lust and thrill. It has emotional antecedents and consequences.

624.

Response to all critics of this video: "4 Facts to Blow Your Mind: Abuse, Parenting, Stress, Marshmallows".

625.

Long interview in the new issue of the visually stunning Italian fashion publication, Shot Magazine @shotmagazine with @alex_amok and Erin.

The future belongs to solitary, self-sufficient narcissists and psychopaths with no empathy or emotions. Consumption is the substitute for life.

Interview transcript and proposed solutions here in 2 videos of the interview on my YouTube channel.

You can watch the video recordings of our conversation in 2 parts on my YouTube channel. The transcript is available in the description field of each of these 2 videos:

20 Steps to Fix This Horrible Mess We Are All In (Shot Magazine)

Adapting to Dystopian New Normal (Interview with Shot Magazine)

626.

Victimization involves the denial of the self-determination, identity, self-actualization, rights, and boundaries of a person without their express consent and collaboration.

When victimhood becomes an organizing and explanatory (hermeneutic) principle, a determinant of the victim's identity, and a socially binding force centred around grievances; prosocial or communal grandiosity; entitlement; conspiracism (paranoid or persecutory delusions); aggressive engagement or, on the other end of the spectrum, schizoid withdrawal; dysempathy; defiance (reactance); and contumaciousness (rejection of expertise and authority) – we have on our hands a victim identity movement.

No one is a victim. We may end up being victimized – but it doesn't render us victims for life, it doesn't brand us.

The sociologist Bradley Campbell suggested that we have transitioned from a culture centred around dignity to one based on <u>victimhood</u>.

Learn more by reading Habermas, Fukuyama, and Foucault. All justice-seeking movements start with grievances (injustices). They decry and seek to remedy and reverse individual transgressions (eg, the narcissistic abuse online movement) or societal and cultural biases (implicit and explicit), discrimination, and suppression.

The victims organize themselves around exclusionary identity politics and intersectionality and this orientation results in grandiosity and entitlement, in other words: in growing narcissism. Increasingly more aggressive, these movements often become psychopathic (defiant and contumacious) and demonize the Other.

Interview in News Intervention with Scott Douglass Jacobsen.

627.

We tend to <u>confuse the amoral with the immoral and both these with evil</u>.

A person can be good and do good without adhering to any system of morality. The prosocial or communal narcissist is a case in point.

It is also possible to renounce morality altogether without ever acting immorally. For example: moral relativism or hard atheism need not result in immorality.

628.

1. <u>Parents less happy than the childless</u>
2. Abuse indicates love and caring
3. Stress is good for you, meditation and mindfulness which are used to reduce it are not always beneficial
4. Marshmallow Test is Wrong


629.


New haircut, new aesthetics.

The language of <u>aesthetic judgement</u> is identical to the languages of physics, morality, and hedonism. Aesthetic values sound strikingly like moral ones and both resemble, structurally, the laws of nature. We say that beauty is "right" (symmetric, etc.), that we "ought to" maximize beauty - and this leads to the right action. Replace "beauty" with "good" in any aesthetic statement and one gets a moral statement. Moral, natural, aesthetic, and hedonistic statements are all mutually convertible. Moreover, an aesthetic experience often leads to moral action.

There is a principle of aesthetic resonance at work. Works of art and beauty evoke in us associations with nature: white marble is strongly evocative of the naked human form, for instance. The resonance is both qualitative and pertains to intensive aesthetic properties, such as texture, color, "warmth", or shape (as in the aforementioned example) and quantitative (as when aesthetic pieces refer to and enhance each other so as to yield an emergent whole.) This deeply-felt resonance may be at the heart of aesthetics' affinity with morality, especially with the "natural law".

More here: <u>https://samvak.tripod.com/ethics.html</u>

630.


I hate the idiotic and counterfactual trope: "<u>It is never too late</u>".

Of course it is too late for most, if not all things. Anyone who knows the first thing about aging will concur. And we rarely get second chances.

Both the mind and the body lose capabilities at an alarming rate as we grow older: cognitive decline and sexual dysfunction are inexorable, the immune system crumbles, self-repair is out of the window.

There is a thin line between optimism and deception, hope and delusion, determination and grandiosity. Never cross it - for your own good!

631.

What would a regime run by artists look like? Look no further than <u>Nazi Germany</u>.

Hitler was a mediocre and frustrated classical and architectural painter. He contributed to the design of the Volkswagen beetle in 1938 and, with Speer, co-planned museums and cities of the future.

Goering was an art collector and connoisseur. He looted art from all over Europe for his private collection and a future museum.

The leadership of the Nazi dictatorship was obsessed with aesthetics in its rallies (Nuremberg), symbols (the swastika), cinema (Riefenstahl), and even uniforms. Himmler commissioned the captivating SS uniform from Hugo Boss and Goring designed the Luftwaffe's imposing attire.

The Nazis burned books but never destroyed art - not even "degenerate", Jewish art which they placed in cautionary exhibitions.

632.

<u>Anxiety involves hyperarousal</u> based on catastrophizing. Anxiety has many forms. Gut feelings, intuition, and hypervigilance are forms of anxiety.

633.

All <u>fantasies</u> are psychological defenses against an unbearable reality. But what renders the world so intolerable? Its threatening nature.

Undergirding all fantasies is a master delusion: "I am fragile, at risk of losing my mind, falling apart at the seams, an ideal victim of people or circumstances, an unworthy or bad object, doomed to fail."

What gives rise to such a self-negating and catastrophizing scenario of precarity?

Parental overprotectiveness or, its opposite, neglect. Both types of

caregiving misconduct yield all-pervasive mistrust of life and of the very
possibility of justice, patterned order, and stable structure.

Science and enlightenment were failed experiments. Now we are reverting
to the Middle Ages: from the reality principle to fantasy.

Fantasy vs. Lies vs. Delusion vs. Confabulation.

634.

Whether a trait or behavior, mood, affect (emotion), or cognition are
pathological or positively adaptive depends entirely on the context.

For example: to have been reactively depressed in Auschwitz would have
been a normal reaction, a form of processing trauma.

There are periods in history and civilizations when and where narcissism
and psychopathy were self-efficacious strategies: the USA and Nazi
Germany, respectively.

Similarly, repetition compulsion could be both warranted and beneficial.
Even the recurrence of bad things renders life more predictable and endows
us with a sense of safety.

635.

There are two types of fantasy defense: person-centred and process-
centred. This taxonomy is similar to substance-centred vs. process-centred
addictions. The person at the center of a person-centred fantasy is akin to
an addictive substance at the core of a substance-centred fantasy.

Fantasies are intended to provide safe spaces and outlets for aggressive and
self-destructive impulses involved in the civil war between the need to be
seen (grandiosity) and the internalized bad object ("I am inadequate, an
impostor, and unworthy"). Dysregulation and identity disturbance are the
outcomes of this inner strife.

When in touch with reality, these voices create coalitions which lead to
adverse outcomes. For example: spectacular, public, and attention-
grabbing self-destruction.

Fantasies which revolve around another person - common in intimate or interpersonal relationships - inevitably dissolve into reality and therefore mayhem.

Fantasies which are founded on a narrative or an impersonal process - self-aggrandizing or self-destructive as they may be - never do. They are self-contained and well regulated.

636.

There is a pragmatic - amoral - reason to never lie.

When we deceive we cause people to interact with our deception, not with us or with reality.

We therefore keep getting the wrong, inaccurate information from others and we end up deceiving ourselves.

637.

The United States is in the throes of full-fledged mass psychosis. The stupid and demented have taken over. It is a terrifying thought.

A prestigious outlet has just rejected an article I submitted - at their prompting - as "unfit for publication".

The reason? I refused to replace the words "students" and "pupils" with "scholars" (!) and I vehemently rejected the counterfactual demand to substitute "pregnant people" for "pregnant women".

Breaking news:

Students are not scholars. A few of them become scholars by first being students. And only women can be pregnant.

I also mentioned that the Bible contains more raunchy sex scenes than most modern literature. That did not curry favor with my reviewers. They asked me repeatedly to remove this paragraph - an act known as censorship.

As far as free speech goes, the USA is on par now with China and Russia (a country I lived in for 6 years).

Another ominous story:

A UK medium asked me to submit an article on narcissism.

I WITHDREW it OFFICIALLY because they insisted on altering it.

They proceeded to publish it with the alteration (!) in which they essentially stated that we all develop pathological narcissism in early childhood.

The editor did not want to demonize narcissism because this would be a form of … ableism!

638.

Many <u>truths in psychology are counterintuitive</u>. Three examples:

1. Success forces one to engage in reality. If one is prone to fantasy, one would engineer failures or undermine success at any cost. Fantasy is an alluring comfort zone and success tend to intrude and unravel it;

2. Devaluation is not the same as disenchantment (falling out of love). It involves splitting: rendering the devalued person all bad and persecutory, retroactively and prospectively. Disenchantment is the opposite of splitting and the antithesis of idealization: it involves integration of the bad and good aspects of the object (the other person);

3. Defiance (reactance) is not a form of boundary setting. On the contrary: it is about vitiating boundaries, one's own and others's.

639.

<u>Jordan Peterson</u>, the master of banalities and king of cliches, wearing his "I am the greatest genius ever and the most humungous revolution in human thinking has just occurred to me" says in an interview: "If you don't speak what is truly on your mind, you are not giving voice to your unborn self".

WTF is this nonsense supposed to mean? 5.3 million shares.

Sadhguru in a lecture in one of the most prestigious medical schools in the States: "Western medicine has still a long way to go. We in the East know, for example, that the milk from a woman's left breast is not the same as milk from her right breast. That is why you should feed boys and girls from different breasts".

3.7 million likes.

Slavoj Zizek, a truly towering intellect, gets an average of 1600 shares on 10 randomly sampled profound Facebook posts of his sayings. Every self-styled expert on YouTube gets way more.

Such is the decaying civilization we live in.

640.

<u>Scientific theories</u> invite constant criticism and revision. They yield new problems. They are proven erroneous and are replaced by new models which offer better explanations and a more profound sense of understanding - often by solving these new problems. From time to time, the successor theories constitute a break with everything known and done till then. These seismic convulsions are known as "paradigm shifts".

It is interesting to note that paradigm-shifting work is often produced by non-specialist outsiders, gifted amateurs, and laymen (such as Da Vinci, Steno, Mandel, Freud, and, to some extent, Einstein). As Thomas Kuhn noted, run of the mill scientists are vested and invested in the status quo and normally generate paradigm-sustaining theories and discoveries.

Contrary to widespread opinion - even among scientists - science is not only about "facts". It is not merely about quantifying, measuring, describing, classifying, and organizing "things" (entities). It is not even concerned with finding out the "truth". Science is about providing us with concepts, explanations, and predictions (collectively known as "theories") and thus endowing us with a sense of understanding of our world.

Scientific theories are allegorical or metaphoric. They revolve around symbols and theoretical constructs, concepts and substantive assumptions, axioms and hypotheses - most of which can never, even in principle, be computed, observed, quantified, measured, or correlated with the world "out there". By appealing to our imagination, scientific theories reveal what David Deutsch calls "the fabric of reality".

641.

EDITORIAL

The <u>Psychopathology of Fetishism and Body Integrity Dysphoria (BID)</u>
Sam Vaknin*

Corresponding Author: Sam Vaknin, Visiting Professor of Psychology, Southern Federal University, Rostov-on-Don, Russia and Professor of Finance and Psychology in CIAPS (Centre for International Advanced and Professional Studies).

Received: March 16, 2022 ; Revised: March 21, 2022 ; Accepted: March 23, 2022

Citation: Vaknin S. (2022) The Psychopathology of Fetishism and Body Integrity Dysphoria (BID). J Psychol Psychiatr Res, 1(1): 1-4.



642.

Second hand smoke is respiratory <u>rape</u>.

Ambient noise pollution is auditory rape.

The great unwashed are olfactory rape.

Unwanted touch and invasion of private space are tactile rape.

Not fully consensual sex is rape, pure and simple.

All forms of abuse constitute emotional rape.

And …

Stupidity is intellectual rape.

They should all be criminalized and penalized, the perpetrators relegated to penal colonies.

643.

The <u>stupid</u> have always had opinions about everything under the sun. But they were wary of expressing them lest they be shamed, ridiculed, and shunned by their betters. This is no longer the case: the dumb are brazen and vociferous, drowning out, by the force of sheer numbers, all informed voices.

The ignorant and the retarded are the overwhelming majority. They trust their pitiable life experience over science. They adhere to magical thinking. And they are fierce in the defense of their grandiose, inflated, fantastic self-image as undiscovered geniuses (Dunning-Kruger effect).

Technology empowers mediocre failures and losers in their self-delusion of malignant egalitarianism.

Access to raw information is not the same as possession of structured knowledge. But the stupid can't tell the difference: "I am as knowledgeable as my doctor or professor because I can google. My opinions, therefore, count as facts."

Stupidity is on the rise for two reasons: 1. A reverse Flynn effect: there has been a precipitous decline in average IQ scores in the past 4 decades; and 2. Inanity is tolerated and legitimized thereby encouraging indolence, entitlement, and nescience (malignant tolerance).

<u>The Stupid, the Trivial, and the Frivolous</u> are everywhere: among the working classes, of course, but increasingly you can find them displacing the erstwhile elites, spawning hordes of mindless politicians, idiot business tycoons, narcissistic media personalities, gullible clergy, vacuous celebrities, illiterate bestselling authors, athletes with far more brawn than brain, repetitious pop singers, less than mediocre bureaucrats, bovine gatekeepers, and even ignorant and semi-literate academics.

Their cacophony drowns the few voices of wisdom, expertise, and experience and their sheer number overwhelms all systems of governance and all mechanisms of decision-making. Rather than futilely fight back this tsunami, the well-educated, the erudite, and the intelligent choose to withdraw and seclude themselves in self-constructed, schizoid ivory towers, all bridges drawn.

Imbeciles are a menace to the continued existence not only of our civilization, but also of our species. We may end up being all Homo, no sapiens.

644.

You should not deny yourself happiness just because it comes at a price. You should not fear life!

Life is about loss and suffering: the coinage with which we purchase bliss.

645.

Vaccination or inoculation is the introduction of an enemy (bacterium or virus) into our bodies in order to get us to acquire new capacities and trigger in us new (immune) processes, thus rendering us stronger and improved.

The same idea drove cannibals to consume the internal organs of dead and captured enemy soldiers in order to acquire their traits and thus be rendered upgraded and superior.

646.

Is David Chalmers right? Are simulation and reality indistinguishable? Is our reality merely some alien's simulation?

647.

The Self is an invention of late 19th century German "scientists". It is a counterfactual construct. Self-states triggered by environmental cues - that's reality.

648.

How can you tell the stupid from the wise?

Stupid people question absolutely everything all the time either because they are insecure (even fearful) or because they are grandiose and know it all better.

The wise and intelligent discriminate between information that fits into structured knowledge and requires little or no questioning - and hypotheses which demand falsification.

Doubt is the engine of progress in all its forms: scientific, individual, and social.

But all-pervasive doubt retards growth and results in conspiratorial, schizotypal, paranoid, and esoteric mindsets, all of which are the hallmarks of the truly dumb.

649.

Are all forms of intelligence the same? Can we distinguish artificial intelligence from the human variety?

The other convos in this Cycle here: https://www.youtube.com/watch?v=AjSRuk5bdik&list=PLygJHHONRxjv9_-KnDaeDhLTuOm6RoYL_

650.

Three separations: infantile, adolescent, social

Impediments: dead mothers, strict parents, nanny states and institutions

Each separation leads to self-state. It could be a healthy, functional self-state or, once impeded, a pathological one.

Autonomous self-state (grandiose vs. insecure or fearful)

Peer self-state (defiant vs. conforming)

Social self-state (collaborative vs. avoidant)

Disrupted self-states:

Autonomous (borderline, narcissistic, paranoid, covert)

Peer (schizoid, avoidant, codependent or people pleaser)

Social (antisocial, asocial, ostentatiously and self-sacrificially prosocial)

Separation-individuation (from Mahler to Severino)

Erikson: autonomy, shame, and doubt

Kohut: selfobjects and problems with the Self

651.

This is the second part of a larger interview for Newsweek Romania.

The first part is here: https://www.youtube.com/watch?v=6vWXwK7Ot3I

The journalist who did the interview is a war correspondent in Ukraine and you can follow his YouTube channel here: https://www.youtube.com/c/RemusCerneaOfficial/featured (mostly in Romanian) and his Twitter account here: https://twitter.com/remus_cernea (mostly in English)

This is the trailer to an interview I granted to Newsweek:

https://www.youtube.com/watch?v=UaoPY70a0FA

You can find the translation into Romanian here:

https://newsweek.ro/international/video-psiholog-daca-nu-tratam-traumele-razboiului-exista-riscul-sa-avem-sute-de-mii-de-sinucideri

https://newsweek.ro/international/video-psiholog-israelian-probabil-ca-25-dintre-ucraineni-vor-suferi-efecte-posttraumatice

https://newsweek.ro/international/psiholog-israelian-razboiul-din-ucraina-este-o-parabola-a-unei-interpretari-inguste-a-istoriei

652.

What kind of mother would deny her son a meaningful, fulfilling life until he is too old to have one?

What kind of mother would do her utmost to wreck any relationship her son has ever tried to have, thus denying him happiness?

What kind of mother would distrust her offspring with even the most basic tasks and decisions?

An awful, horrible, and now literally dead mother (apropos Andre Green's phrase, coined in 1978).

She had a profound sense of duty and the belief that life and other people should be totally subordinated to it.

A good therapist could have helped her with this psychopathic psychopathology.

653.

Freedom of Will: Illusion or Reality? (News Intervention)
https://www.newsintervention.com/freedom-of-will-illusion-or-reality/

Free will exists the same way Harry Potter and Sherlock Holmes most definitely exist. It is real. It is a force to reckon with. It shapes our minds and lives. It exerts a huge influence on multiple spheres. What more do we need to know?

Free will is a useful fiction, akin to god or the afterlife: only agents with free will can be held morally responsible.

Free will comprises three conditions:

1. The ability to choose and act otherwise;
2. Having control over one's choices and actions;
3. That the choice or act are rationally motivated.

The very concept of free will is founded on convenient delusions such as time or causation. Whereas teleology is prohibited in all sciences (we do not attribute purposeful actions to objects and animals, for example), it mysteriously permeates philosophy and more specifically the field of ethics.

654.

Never adapt your life to others. Let others catch up with your life.

655.

People are like trees (Courtesy Jennifer Howard).

656.

A <u>fine conversation</u> is more mirrors than smoke - and never smoke and mirrors!

657.

An <u>ontologically insecure</u> person does not accept at a fundamental level the reality or existence of things, themselves, and others. In contrast, the ontologically secure person has a stable and unquestioned sense of self and of his or her place in the world in relation to other people and objects.

Ontological insecurity is important for understanding identity because it is an essential foundation for a person to achieve a stable sense of self-identity. In an existential sense, if a person does not believe that he or she exists and that other people and objects are real, that person does not have the necessary foundations to develop a stable self-identity.

(From "Encyclopedia of Identity")

Further Readings

Giddens, A. (1990). The consequences of modernity.
Cambridge, UK: Polity Press.

Giddens, A. (1991). The self: Ontological security and existential anxiety.
In Modernity and self-identity: Self and society in the late modern age (pp. 35–69). Cambridge, UK: Polity Press.

Laing, R. D. (1965). Ontological insecurity. In The divided self (pp. 39–61). Harmondsworth, UK: Penguin Books.

Spitzer, S. P. (1978). Ontological insecurity and reflective processes.
Journal of Phenomenological Psychology, 8(2), 203–217.

658.

In the study of identity, <u>reflexivity</u> refers to the human capability of turning the attention of consciousness back upon itself—being aware of the fact that we are aware, thinking about thinking, or more mundanely, perhaps, providing accounts of our selves.

Giddens's model of selfhood consists of three components: the unconscious, practical consciousness, and self-reflexivity. The realm of the unconscious is of primary importance for the development of self—identity as it is here where relationships of basic trust are initiated.

The experience of trust at an unconscious level in infancy provides the individual with a secure orientation toward the world that protects her or him from engulfment when threats to identity inevitably come.

It is only in posttraditional societies that the self becomes a genuinely reflexive project. Traditions once provided people with fairly rigid and temporally constant points through which to navigate a sense of self and thus facilitated self-reflexivity within fairly narrow existential parameters; narrow because much of what might be questioned is effectively answered by the givens of tradition.

(Encyclopedia of Identity)

Further Readings

Adams, M. (2007). Self and social change. London: Sage.

Adkins, L. (2003). Reflexivity: Freedom or habit of gender? Theory, Culture & Society, 20(6), 21–42.

Alexander, J. (1996). Critical reflections on "reflexive modernization." Theory, Culture & Society, 13(4), 133–138.

Beck, U., Giddens, A., & Lash, S. (1994). Reflexive modernization. Cambridge, UK: Polity Press.

Giddens, A. (1991). Modernity and self-identity. Cambridge, UK: Polity Press.

Giddens, A. (1992). The transformation of intimacy. Cambridge, UK: Polity Press.

Plumridge, L., & Thomson, R. (2003). Longitudinal qualitative studies and the reflexive self. International Journal of Social Research Methodology, 6(3), 213–222.

Threadgold, S., & Nilan, P. (2009). Reflexivity of contemporary youth, risk and cultural capital. Current Sociology, 57(1), 47–68.

659.

In an attempt to gain fame and celebrity and secure funding, neuroscientists are making thousands of ill-founded claims based on very flimsy and often nonreplicable research. Like psychology, the field is fast becoming a pseudoscience.

660.


Reading "I Don't Have Enough Faith to Be an Atheist"

p.132 mind mine, p. 154 parsimony Occam's, p. 155 multiple solutions to same puzzle (=environment)

A. Kant: we cannot know the real world

CA. Kant said that we cannot know the world as it is, but never denied its reality.

Ornery agnostic: god is not knowable or provable. Not atheist (faith that there is no god).

Reason works, hence my trust in reason when it comes to reality.

Trust and faith should not be confused: the former is evidence-based, the latter is axiomatic.

So, I trust religion because it seems to work in society and psychology, it is a psychosocial regulator.

I reject it because of my values: I prefer chaotic and dangerous reality to structured and safe delusional disorder.

Delusions and fantasies resemble rationality but are bounded by something other than rationality (e.g. god), they are not self-referential, iterative, or recursive like rationality.

A. Big bang: why is there something rather than nothing? Beginnings (of the Universe, of life) present a challenge to science: ex nihilo creation.

A. Anthropic argument

CA. Dying homeless does not imply a designed weather

A. Life never arose spontaneously, it contains a message in the DNA (specified complexity and irreducible complexity – both debunked)

CA. Complexity and evolution are spontaneous, over time negentropy (localized increase in order); current, complexity endpoint.

Not all info is a message.

Most info is mindless, natural, does not imply intelligence.

All messages are accessible to intelligence, but not all hail from intelligence (Fibonacci). Pareidolia and apophenia.

Intelligence is inferior to non-intelligence, not superior (grandiose Bible). The distinction itself may be spurious, anthropocentric, and reflects human limitations.

Design is not the same as intelligence.

Info emerges from irregularity, not from order (=not from design).

A. Every becoming has a cause

CA. Antecedents are not causes (correlation vs. causation).

What caused god to create everything and us? It assumes an internal process. This is anthropomorphism: god cannot want or love unless he is imperfect.

A. Naturalism and spirituality are mutually exclusive

CA. Spirituality is how we experience and structure material processes and objects.

661.

There are 3 types of people:

Those who wish to learn HOW things work (for example: engineers);

Those who want to find out WHY things work the way they do (e.g. scientists and theologians);

And those who want to find out WHAT works best (like medical doctors, politicians, military personnel, or workers in information technology).

662.

Nature and nurture are just two determinants of who we become. Chance (randomness) and intergenerational trauma are the other two ingredients.

LITERATURE

Sutin AR, Stephan Y, Luchetti M, Aschwanden D, Lee JH, Sesker AA, et al. (2022) Differential personality change earlier and later in the coronavirus pandemic in a longitudinal sample of adults in the United States. PLoS ONE 17(9): e0274542.
https://doi.org/10.1371/journal.pone.0274542

663.

Yesterday, discussed with @csilla.temesvari of Hungary's RTL TV the war in Ukraine, Putin, Zelensky, and the internal situation in Russia.

Watch additional videos and interviews on the war here:
http://www.youtube.com/vakninmusings

664.

The concept of "nature" is a romantic invention. It was spun by the likes of Jean-Jacques Rousseau in the 18th century as a confabulated utopian contrast to the dystopia of urbanization and Darwinian, ruthless materialism. The traces of this dewy-eyed conception of the "savage", his alleged harmony and resonance with nature, and his unmolested, unadulterated surroundings can be found in the more malignant forms of fundamentalist environmentalism and in pop-culture (the most recent example of which is the propaganda-laden cinematic extravaganza, "Avatar").

At the other extreme are religious literalists who regard Man as the crown of creation with complete dominion over nature and the right to exploit its resources unreservedly. Similar, veiled, sentiments can be found among scientists. The Anthropic Principle, for instance, promoted by many outstanding physicists, claims that the nature of the Universe is preordained to accommodate sentient beings - namely, us humans.

Industrialists, politicians and economists have only recently begun paying lip service to sustainable development and to the environmental costs of their policies. Thus, in a way, they bridge the abyss - at least verbally - between these two diametrically opposed forms of fundamentalism. Similarly, the denizens of the West continue to indulge in rampant consumption, but now it is suffused with environmental guilt rather than driven by unadulterated hedonism.

Still, essential dissimilarities between the schools notwithstanding, the dualism of Man vs. Nature is universally acknowledged.

The Ecology of Environmentalism, or the False Dichotomy
https://samvak.tripod.com/nature.html

665.

Victimhood as grievance-based identity politics often results in entitlement, frustration, and violence.

Taken from: https://twitter.com/ShellenbergerMD/

666.

Culture is the continuation of evolution by other means and it involves epigenetics. Are we headed towards a transhuman future?

667.

Victimhood pays: identity politics coupled with aggressive entitlement are hijacked by narcissists and psychopaths to further their pernicious and nefarious goals.

Interview with Guilhem Dedoyard of https://atlantico.fr

Atlantico.fr interview about the era of victimhood and its political and social ramifications.

668.

Is there a common psychopathology (p) factor that accounts for all mental illnesses? Join the hottest controversy in psychology and psychiatry!

LITERATURE

The seed of suffering

The p-factor is the dark matter of psychiatry: an invisible, unifying force that might lie behind a multitude of mental disorders

Alex Riley

https://aeon.co/essays/what-the-p-factor-says-about-the-root-of-all-mental-illness

Lahey BB, Applegate B, Hakes JK, Zald DH, Hariri AR, Rathouz PJ. Is there a general factor of prevalent psychopathology during adulthood? J Abnorm Psychol. 2012 Nov;121(4):971-7. doi: 10.1037/a0028355. Epub 2012 Jul 30. PMID: 22845652; PMCID: PMC4134439.

Achenbach TM. The classification of children's psychiatric symptoms: a factor-analytic study. Psychol Monogr. 1966;80(7):1-37. doi: 10.1037/h0093906. PMID: 5968338.

Caspi A, Houts RM, Belsky DW, Goldman-Mellor SJ, Harrington H, Israel S, Meier MH, Ramrakha S, Shalev I, Poulton R, Moffitt TE. The p Factor: One General Psychopathology Factor in the Structure of Psychiatric Disorders? Clin Psychol Sci. 2014 Mar;2(2):119-137. doi: 10.1177/2167702613497473. PMID: 25360393; PMCID: PMC4209412.

van Bork, R., Epskamp, S., Rhemtulla, M., Borsboom, D., & van der Maas, H. L. J. (2017). What is the p-factor of psychopathology? Some risks of general factor modeling. Theory & Psychology, 27(6), 759–773. https://doi.org/10.1177/0959354317737185

Caspi A, Houts RM, Ambler A, et al. Longitudinal Assessment of Mental Health Disorders and Comorbidities Across 4 Decades Among Participants in the Dunedin Birth Cohort Study. JAMA Netw Open. 2020;3(4):e203221. doi:10.1001/jamanetworkopen.2020.3221

Plana-Ripoll O, Pedersen CB, Holtz Y, et al. Exploring Comorbidity Within Mental Disorders Among a Danish National Population. JAMA Psychiatry. 2019;76(3):259–270. doi:10.1001/jamapsychiatry.2018.3658

Kessler RC, Amminger GP, Aguilar-Gaxiola S, Alonso J, Lee S, Ustün TB. Age of onset of mental disorders: a review of recent literature. Curr Opin Psychiatry. 2007 Jul;20(4):359-64. doi: 10.1097/YCO.0b013e32816ebc8c. PMID: 17551351; PMCID: PMC1925038.

Elliott ML, Romer A, Knodt AR, Hariri AR. A Connectome-wide Functional Signature of Transdiagnostic Risk for Mental Illness. Biol Psychiatry. 2018 Sep 15;84(6):452-459. doi: 10.1016/j.biopsych.2018.03.012. Epub 2018 Apr 10. PMID: 29779670; PMCID: PMC6119080.

Lichtenstein P, Yip BH, Björk C, Pawitan Y, Cannon TD, Sullivan PF, Hultman CM. Common genetic determinants of schizophrenia and bipolar disorder in Swedish families: a population-based study. Lancet. 2009 Jan 17;373(9659):234-9. doi: 10.1016/S0140-6736(09)60072-6. PMID: 19150704; PMCID: PMC3879718.

Pettersson E, Larsson H, Lichtenstein P. Common psychiatric disorders share the same genetic origin: a multivariate sibling study of the Swedish population. Mol Psychiatry. 2016 May;21(5):717-21. doi: 10.1038/mp.2015.116. Epub 2015 Aug 25. PMID: 26303662.

669.

In the transition from agriculture to industry, many functions - like education and healthcare - were outsourced from the family to specialists.

But as work ethic is in a freefall, educational standards and attainment on a

precipitous decline, and many people opting out of labor altogether - many
are forced to fend for themselves and reacquire skills as handymen,
craftsmen, educators, and even medical doctors.

With the democratization of information and the emergence of enabling
and empowering technologies, our age is fast becoming a reprise of the
19th century: the era of the gifted amateur.

But this time, self-sufficiency is driven by atomization and profound
distrust, the rending of the social fabric itself.

670.
Euphemisms and Orwellian Newspeak are nothing new. The Nazis
"resettled" the Jews in the east and then gave them "showers".

But modern technology has taken it to a whole different level: most
Facebook friends are total strangers, people post likes on death
announcements, few YouTube subscribers watch the channels they are
subscribed to (compared to print subscribers, for example).

671.

Fourth wave feminism and sex positivity are transitioning from cults to
mass psychegenic illnesses. New phenomena are emerging among young
women that are beyond disturbing.

Sex positivity openly espouses experimenting with prostitution and
pornography as modes of self-exploration and self-identity.

Young women take to keeping scorecards of blowjobs they give strangers
or the nationalities of their conquests (trying to cover the atlas).

Now cheating is emerging as a form of female empowerment - especially if
the hapless partner is compelled to forgive and make up.

On forums and private chats alike women brag about their extradyadic
exploits and are lauded and toasted by their peers with every "victory".
"Women power" and "women, go" are common refrains.

Toxic masculinity is a misogynistic late response to misandrist toxic
femininity, not the other way around.

Men's minds and values - already warped by millennia of domination over women - are twisted out of kilter by recent behavioral trends among women which amount to subclinical psychopathy.

Promiscuity is confined to about 20% of men and women who are sociosexually unrestricted or permissive.

But their values - rather, lack thereof - are now becoming the dominant sexual scripts for everyone.

672.

Reverse psychology is manipulating someone to act in a specific way by deceptively stating fake beliefs, values, and opinions or views. It is based of triggering reactance and strategic self-anticonformity.

Techniques of Reverse Psychology:

Tough Love
Mirroring
Challenging: prove me wrong
Challenging: prove me right
Pseudo-humility
Inconsistency
Nagging
Provocation
Denigrating (underdog injustice)

673.

One of the most common attribution errors is the mistaken identification of one's introjects with oneself.

The internal objects and voices that populate our inner world (automatic negative thoughts ANTs are a class of such voices) are not a part of our core identity - but they appear to us to be so.

Therapies - from CBT to schema and gestalt therapies - silence these echos of meaningful others.

674.

Hoarding is an anxiety reaction. Hoarders exert power and control by possessing objects and people who they objectify.

But hoarders never makes use of their possessions. Unlike the collector, the hoarder soon forgets his acquisitions, letting them gather dust or moulder.

Hoarding sex partners or intimate partners serves the same anxiolytic purpose.

The hoarder of people treats them as inanimate goods. He soon loses all interest in them. But he refuses to let them go - for the same reason a hoarder of old newspapers, for example, would never discard them.

Hoarding is, therefore, not only acquisitive but also avoidant. It is a phase in approach-avoidance repetition compulsion.

675.

Constructs, introjects, memories, defenses.

Construct: stable method of organizing raw internal data in a meaningful form, organizing and making sense of the world, allows to make predictions and structure experience.

Like museum (structure) organizes chronologically or thematically emotions, cognitions, memories, identity, experiences to render the world reasonable.

It shapes and mediates experience.

Also hermeneutic-exegetic mechanism for interpreting new data to conform to the construct.

Examples of constructs: ego, pathological narcissism (via grandiosity)

Multiple constructs active, but not mutually exclusive (contradictory) ones (e.g. Persona or Mask, social façade). Principle of non-contradiction.

Incompatible constructs compete for resources in binary narcissism, schizophrenia, or psychotic disorders: confusion regarding constructs that have to do with external and internal worlds or environments.

Introjects are voices of meaningful others (parents, teachers, peers, media, society, thought leaders, gurus).

Making peace reconciling with these recurrent voices to avoid dissonance. Attribution error: introjects are my voice.

Some introjects are positive, others negative.

Introjects always interfere with daily functioning, they are always on (standby). Example: cluster or community of introjects known as conscience.

Speech of introjects is automatic thoughts.

Constructs use external input (mainly from people) and introjects, soldiers of the constructs.

Constructs activate introjects in response to environmental cues and data.

Experience of reality is mediated through constructs which choose and activate introjects which produce automatic thoughts.

Experience interacts with introjects via constructs.

Constructs rearrange experience (reframe) to make sense of it. Need to communicate the new info via selectively activating introjects.

Constructs modify reality via behavior and select and reframe memories (see further)

SEQUENCE

External raw data, experience

Construct triggered

Activates introjects and their output (automatic thoughts)

Modifies behavior to affect reality

Reframes and selects for memories

Eg, covert narcissism construct

You cannot obtain supply directly, collapse, failure, inferiority, dysregulated self-worth and self-esteem. Birthed by your collapse.

Covert narcissism makes sense of the world by informing you that you are a failure, hated, discriminated against (passive-aggressive).

Main message: lack of self-efficacy, don't try – you will fail, will never extract positive outcomes from the environment

Urges and drives (id)

Info sent to construct. Construct anticipates failure and pain. Must be prevented by making sense of the world.

Reaches out to introjects, activates them to prevent success (which would threaten the construct founded on failure)

Construct wants to survive and drives you to behave in ways which will uphold the construct, not challenge it

Introjects use automatic thoughts (output) to shape behavior to ensure failure in order to affirm the construct

Construct organizes output from introjects according to identity (ego congruency: output must conform to reality and to self-identity as ego=reality testing plus memories) and inhibits certain behaviors

Automatic thoughts which conflict with reality or with memories are not effective, dissonant, provoke suspicion of manipulation (estrangement), feel weird, and lead to rejection of construct

Construct structures behavior to falsify reality: make you behave in a way that will alter reality, example: make you fail, keep you in state of collapse (if covert narcissism is the construct) because success is a threat, and render it compatible with the automatic thoughts (self-defeating, self-sabotaging, self-undermining, even self-destructive behaviors).

Construct falsifies memories to conform to the automatic thoughts in 3 ways: 1. Dissociation of incongruent memories 2. Changes emotional content of the memory by reframing and attribution (for example, of motivations to people) 3. Selectivity (accessing only memories that conform to the construct and repressing all others).

Paints memories retroactively with elements that were not necessarily there: memory+, reinterprets memories and experiences, leveraging cognitions and emotions

Wrong data (ill informed) about reality and about memories.

Construct interprets and filters external experience and internal experience, including memories, cognitions and emotions

Construct exerts absolute power over the way you experience yourself, your life, and the world. Tells you what to remember, how to remember, how to make sense of what you remember, how to change your behaviors to affect reality in a way that will support the construct.

Ultimately, construct isolates from reality and protects against it. Manipulates reality to render it palatable, for example via defense mechanisms to modify perception of reality to allow you to survive it.

676.

These automatic thoughts are at the core of people pleasing and parentifying children:

1. My happiness is always at someone else's expense (zero sum game);

2. I have to earn my happiness, I don't deserve it;

3. I have to somehow bribe people to stay with me, collaborate with me, help me, or tolerate me because I am a bad object (unworthy, unlovable, crazy, inadequate, dissolute, hopeless, and so on).

4. I need to compromise on my boundaries and rights owing to all the above.

677.
Gdansk Seminar https://www.youtube.com/watch?v=WnfstvImfvg

Statistics in psychology is often misused to misrepresent and mislead. Here's how.

678.

Anger at dead parents who install and instill harsh inner critic (superego is part of ego and impairs reality testing).

Bad object messaging: 1. You are unlovable 2. You don't deserve happiness.

All people are lovable (number of permutations with 6 billion adults, even serial killers in prison)

Happiness is not a desert, it has to be merited and earned

But bad object uses introject to generate ANTs (Automatic Negative Thoughts) which are self-sabotaging (self-undermining), self-defeating, self-harmful, self-trashing, and self-destructive.

Some people reject happiness and embrace misery. They belong to either of three groups.

679.

Mentally ill are astronauts stranded on an alien planet: disorientation
No gyroscope (core identity)
No reality (cognitive distortions)
Emotional tsunamis
All consuming anxiety (catastrophizing in hostile world)
Hopelessness and helplessness (childlike state)
Splitting morality play

680.

The world is getting less hospitable by the day. The only refuge is love and the only hope is solidarity.

May this year bring you true friendship, exciting challenges, creative breakthroughs, transforming insights, and loving partners.

May you look back on this year 2023 and wish it had lasted even longer.

681.

Dilemmas are cognitive dissonances between two horns: two equally compelling (equipotent) courses of action which are contradictory or mutually exclusive. The way to solve such dilemmas is to reduce them to: problem, needs, assumptions.

682.

Acts of self-love and healing are always painful.

Getting rid of toxic but addictive people in your life;

Breaking up with a backstabbing, badmouthing, and mate-poaching plagiarist fake "friend";

Imposing discipline, goals, and structure on a dissolute and carefree life;

Saying "no" to temptations and seductions;

Gaining insights into your shortcomings, self-inflicted wounds, and failures;

Confronting trauma and abuse;

Investing hard work in introspection and therapy.

683.

Don't expect the mentally ill to respect you. They don't know how. They have no self-respect, so how could they possibly respect others? Instead, they veer between abject submission and contemptuous defiance.

Don't expect the mentally ill to not breach your boundaries. They are unbounaried and hurtful because they fail to perceive the separateness of others. Many of them do not possess a functioning self or an undisturbed identity.

Do not expect the mentally ill to observe the rules, obey some code of conduct, or be empathic. They are too busy at survival, self-centred and entitled. Their mental illness is their get out of jail card. Everyone else is to blame for their egregious misconduct (alloplastic defenses).

684.

Two tips from the art of psychotherapy:

1. If action or inaction has outcomes - these consequences are intended, whether consciously or unconsciously.

People are only dimly aware of the full range of their motivations and they often get it wrong.

When they make behavioral choices to act or to refrain from acting, they actually seek and intend the most likely outcomes, even when and if they are not aware of such desired ends - and even when they vehemently deny it.

Example: if you act in a way that imperils a long-held relationship, it is because you want it over, you wish to extricate yourself.

2. What clients say in therapy matters far less than why they choose to say what they say. What content do they select and elect to disclose? What do they omit and why? What words do they employ? Why do so in a particular timing?

The subtext - the hidden, occult text - matters more than the overt text. Speech acts need to be deconstructed to teach us anything meaningful about the client.

685.

Don't test your loved ones - they will rarely if ever pass muster.

Don't bait your nearest and dearest - they will take the bait every time.

Don't set up friends for failure for they will fail assuredly.

Don't plant the wrong ideas in the minds of people who care about you or who you care about. Such sprouts will grow into a thicket of deceit and hurt.

Assume the worst about everyone's capacity to survive your probes and your entrapments: we are all fallible and weak and impotent in the face of temptation.

"'Do not speak a curse against a deaf person or place an obstacle in the way of a blind person" (Leviticus 19:14).

686.

We inhabit the windows to the world - our screens - rather than the world itself.

Screens used to be communal: cinema, even television. Then they became solipsistic: each to his own screen, an idiosyncratic experience, setting us apart.

Of course, Big Tech wants us to be alone. The attention economy is a zero sum game: you give attention to friends and loved ones - you deny it to Facebook and Instagram. Intimacy is the enemy of modern technologies, it is bad for business, harms the bottom line.

687.

Acts of self-love and healing are always painful.

Getting rid of toxic but addictive people in your life;

Imposing discipline, goals, and structure on a dissolute and carefree life;

Saying "no" to temptations and seductions;

Gaining insights into your shortcomings, self-inflicted wounds, and failures;

Confronting trauma and abuse;

Investing hard work in introspection and therapy.

688.

Economics - to the great dismay of economists - is merely a branch of psychology. It deals with individual behaviour and with mass behaviour.

Many of its practitioners seek to disguise its nature as a social science by applying complex mathematics where common sense and direct experimentation would have yielded far better results.

The outcome is an embarrassing divorce between economic theory and its subjects.

The economic actor is assumed to be constantly engaged in the rational pursuit of self interest. This is not a realistic model - merely a useful (and flattering) approximation.

According to this latter day - rational - version of the dismal science, people refrain from repeating their mistakes systematically. They seek to optimize their preferences. Altruism can be such a preference, as well.

We like to believe that we are rational. Such self-perception is ego-syntonic. Yet the truth is that many people are non-rational or only nearly rational in certain situations. And the definition of "self-interest" as the pursuit of the fulfilment of preferences is a tautology.

The theory fails to predict important phenomena such as "strong reciprocity": the propensity to "irrationally" sacrifice resources to reward forthcoming collaborators and punish free-riders. It even fails to account for simpler forms of apparent selflessness, such as reciprocal altruism (motivated by hopes of reciprocal benevolent treatment in the future).

689.

(Watch it here: http://www.youtube.com/vakninmusings )

The more money we make, the less we appreciate its relative, respective, and proportional value to others. With very few exceptions, rich people, no matter how stingy, seem to lose touch with the pecuniary reality of the "99%" of the population who are poor(er). Indeed, to the wealthy, money is not a store of value as much as a token which allows them to participate in economic and non-economic games.

I call this process of desensitization to the value of money "personal inflation" because, precisely like "classic" inflation, as far as these affluent persons are concerned, it thwarts the price signal and distorts the efficient allocation of economic resources. It also misinforms their decisions and adversely affects their motivation to work, save, and invest.

Rich people have an "inflationary mindset": they prefer to spend their capital, but owing to the amounts involved, are forced to hold on to the bulk of it, tied down in assets, both tangible and financial. They wish to consume (inflationary effect), but end up saving (deflationary outcome.)

Poorer folks have a deflationary state of mind: they would like to hold on to their money, but are forced to spend most of it, or even all of it (not to mention avail themselves of additional credits and loans.) They wish to save (deflationary effect), but end up consuming (inflationary outcome.)

Thus, all economic players in the marketplace wind up acting irrationally: against their innermost as well as expressed wishes and preferences. This gulf between the desires and actions of all economic agents is the main source of instability and uncertainty in the capitalist system, based as it is on wealth transfer from the many to the few and its accumulation in the hands of the latter.

690.

Prophets and scientists both are in the business of making predictions. Both resort to metaphysical frameworks as the source of their knowledge: God and the scientific method, respectively.

Both vehemently deny the role of intuition in their output.

The prophet claims to possess privileged access to a transcendental being and to be merely serving as a conduit to the latter's thoughts and intentions; the scientist insists that his work is objective and rational and can, in principle, be emulated by a computer.

Yet, both actually transform deep-set, unconscious processes into structural sentences, laws, and statements.

There are three types of intuition: http://www.narcissistic-abuse.com/intuition.html

691.

Forgiving is an important capability. It does more for the forgiver than for the forgiven. But it should not be a universal, indiscriminate behaviour. It is legitimate not to forgive sometimes. It depends, of course, on the severity or duration of what was done to you.

In general, it is unwise and counter-productive to apply to life "universal" and "immutable" principles. Life is too chaotic to succumb to rigid edicts. Sentences which start with "I never" or "I always" are not very credible and often lead to self-defeating, self-restricting and self-destructive behaviours.

Conflicts are an important and integral part of life. One should never seek them out, but when confronted with a conflict, one should not avoid it. It is through conflicts and adversity as much as through care and love that we grow.

Human relationships are dynamic. We must assess our friendships, partnerships, even our marriages periodically. In and by itself, a common past is insufficient to sustain a healthy, nourishing, supportive, caring and compassionate relationship. Common memories are a necessary but not a sufficient condition. We must gain and regain our friendships on a daily basis. Human relationships are a constant test of allegiance and empathy.

Continued: http://samvak.tripod.com/faq80.html

692.

Only the external environment matters: it triggers the internal one (IntraPsychic Activation Model – IPAM).

Watch Why Narcissists Can't Think Straight (Constructs, Introjects, Memories, Defenses) https://www.youtube.com/watch?v=3u_1GoFA3Ig

Watch Why People-pleasers Can't Think Straight (Self-states, Constructs, Introjects) https://www.youtube.com/watch?v=O1Dp4KMyreA

693.

There are four types of <u>public intellectuals</u> (interview dated 2013).

694.

<u>You are but the sum of your relationships</u>. Nothing more, nothing less.

695.

<u>Banks</u> are institutions where miracles happen regularly. We rarely entrust our money to anyone but ourselves – and our banks.

Despite a very chequered history of mismanagement, corruption, false promises and representations, delusions and behavioural inconsistency – banks still succeed to motivate us to give them our money.

Partly it is the feeling that there is safety in numbers. The fashionable term today is "moral hazard". The implicit guarantees of the state and of other financial institutions move us to take risks which we would, otherwise, have avoided.

Partly it is the sophistication of the banks in marketing and promoting themselves and their products. Glossy brochures, professional computer and video presentations and vast, shrine-like, real estate complexes all serve to enhance the image of the banks as the temples of the new religion of money.

Watch Central Banks in Bed with Commercial Banks on my other channel
http://www.youtube.com/vakninmusings

696.

The role of the <u>celebrity</u> is to restore a sense of familiarity to an alienated, surrealistic, and plastic world of failed relationships, forced anonymity, passive-aggressiveness, narcissism, futility, atomization, broken communities, and lack of purpose.

The celebrity is at once a substitute family, a prodigal loved one, and a lifelong friend. The celebrity offers ersatz intimacy and tantalizing glimpses of potentials and possibilities.

Sam Vaknin, author of "Malignant Self-love: Narcissism Revisited"

Read (free) "Addiction to Fame and Celebrity" http://www.narcissistic-abuse.com/faq19.html

697.

Some people know how to give and share - but not <u>how to make others happy</u>.

698.

<u>Computers and artificial intelligence</u> can teach us little about what it is to be human.

699.

The <u>market and its price mechanism</u> - critically depends on trust. If people do not trust each other, or the economic "envelope" within which they interact ("preemptive mistrust"), economic activity gradually grinds to a halt.

There is a strong correlation between the general level of trust and the extent and intensity of economic activity. Francis Fukuyama, the political scientist, distinguishes between high-trust and prosperous societies and low-trust and, therefore, impoverished collectives. Trust underlies economic success, he argued in a 1995 tome.

Trust is not a monolithic quantity. There are a few categories of economic trust. Some forms of trust are akin to a public good and are closely related to governmental action or inaction, the reputation of the state and its institutions, and its pronounced agenda. Other types of trust are the outcomes of kinship, ethnic origin, personal standing and goodwill, corporate brands and other data generated by individuals, households, and firms. Such information creates two types of output: reinforced trust (where behaviour matches expectations) and "inductive distrust" (where behaviour frustrates expectations).

700.

This is an age when people are determined, defined and categorized in strict accordance with their <u>professions</u>. Whereas during the Renaissance, a person might have been defined by his range of interests (remember the likes of Leonardo da Vinci), by his familial, religious, or ethnic affiliations, by his or her gender and so on – today the first and foremost question is: "What do you do for a living?"

What constitutes a profession (as opposed to a hobby), or a vocation (as opposed to an avocation)?

The activity must be continuous and pursued for a length of time;
It must occupy most of one's waking hours;
It must yield earnings or compensation whether in money or in kind;
The practitioner must possess an advantage over mere laymen in that particular field of knowledge or activity. In other words: one must be able to tell apart layman from experts, the latter being the product of a highly specific education or training;
The occupation must be hierarchically layered with clear flows of professional authority and responsibility and with a clear career path (climbing the professional ladder).

The second relevant question is: What are the trends which determine our future? It is useless to look at microtrends. These are too volatile and, in principle, unpredictable.

Much more important are the trends that last for hundreds or even thousands of years. These are usually not the results of technological conjuncture or geopolitical upheavals. Rather, they are the outcomes of characteristic human activities which are uninterrupted.

Continued here: https://samvak.tripod.com/nm029.html

701.

Corruption runs against the grain of meritocratic capitalism. It skews the level playing-field; it imposes onerous and unpredictable transaction costs; it guarantees extra returns where none should have been had; it encourages the misallocation of economic resources; and it subverts the proper functioning of institutions.

It is, in other words, without a single redeeming feature, a scourge.

Strangely, this is not how it is perceived by its perpetrators: both the givers and the recipients.

They believe that corruption helps facilitate the flow and exchange of
goods and services in hopelessly clogged and dysfunctional systems and
markets (corruption and the informal economy "get things done" and "keep
people employed"); that it serves as an organizing principle where chaos
reins and institutions are in their early formative stages; that it supplements
income and thus helps the state employ qualified and skilled personnel;
and that it preserves peace and harmony by financing networks of
cronyism, nepotism, and patronage.

Bribes are paid in order to limit choice and eliminate competition.

Consequently, in corrupt environments consumers pay less than optimal
prices.

The difference between the competitive price and the new, post-corruption
cost equals the amount of bribe paid in cash or in kind.

Corruption amounts to a unilateral transfer from the consumers's pockets to
the manufacturers's.

In times of economic crisis, consumers tend to shop around (in other
words: they prefer price competition and encourage it via their behavior).

Producers/manufacturers tend to collude in order to fix prices. In
recessions, businesses regard consumers as enemies and vice versa:
producer-firms court consumers, but they also seek to limit their choices by
"channelling" their purchases and determining their preferences.

702.

Four decades ago, the Polish-American-Jewish author, Jerzy Kosinski,
wrote the book "Being There". It describes the election to the presidency of
the United States of a simpleton, a gardener, whose vapid and trite
pronouncements are taken to be sagacious and penetrating insights into
human affairs. The "Being There Syndrome" is now manifest throughout
the world: from Russia (Putin) to the United States (Obama).

Given a high enough level of frustration, triggered by recurrent, endemic,
and systemic failures in all spheres of policy, even the most resilient
democracy develops a predilection to "strong men", leaders whose self-
confidence, sangfroid, and apparent omniscience all but "guarantee" a

change of course for the better.

These are usually people with a thin resume, having accomplished little prior to their ascendance. They appear to have erupted on the scene from nowhere. They are received as providential messiahs precisely because they are unencumbered with a discernible past and, thus, are ostensibly unburdened by prior affiliations and commitments. Their only duty is to the future. They are a-historical: they have no history and they are above history.

Indeed, it is precisely this apparent lack of a biography that qualifies these leaders to represent and bring about a fantastic and grandiose future. They act as a blank screen upon which the multitudes project their own traits, wishes, personal biographies, needs, and yearnings.

703.

There are gradations and hues of child labor. That children should not be exposed to hazardous conditions, long working hours, used as means of payment, physically punished, or serve as sex slaves is commonly agreed. That they should not help their parents plant and harvest may be more debatable.

Abusive child labor is abhorrent and should be banned and eradicated. All other forms should be phased out gradually. Developing countries already produce millions of unemployable graduates a year - 100,000 in Morocco alone. Unemployment is rife and reaches, in certain countries - such as Macedonia - more than one third of the workforce. Children at work may be harshly treated by their supervisors but at least they are kept off the far more menacing streets. Some kids even end up with a skill and are rendered employable.

Video here: http://www.youtube.com/vakninmusings

704.

The right to life is a compendium of no less than eight distinct rights: the right to be brought to life, the right to be born, the right to have one's life maintained, the right not to be killed, the right to have one's life saved, the right to save one's life (wrongly reduced to the right to self-defence), the right to terminate one's life, and the right to have one's life terminated.

None of these rights is self-evident, or unambiguous, or universal, or immutable, or automatically applicable. It is safe to say, therefore, that these rights are not primary as hitherto believed - but derivative.

Lecture available on my Nothingness YouTube channel.

705.

Had there been a global blanket ban on discussing religion, politics, and sports, the number of conflicts in the world would have declined precipitously. (Sam Vaknin, World in Conflict and Transition http://www.narcissistic-abuse.com/guide.html)

706.

Yesterday, I cancelled an interview with a journalist who repeated the feeble-minded canard about thousands of NATO troops who have died fighting for Ukraine, how Russia's military is well run and triumphant, and how the West instigated the war for its own ends. When I hung up on her she called my conduct idiotic and blamed me for being a part of the cancel culture. So much for her research skills: I may well be the former (idiot), but by no stretch of the imagination am I the latter.

Increasingly, useful idiots (useful fools) in the West – journalists, businessmen, public intellectuals, academics, politicians, and lobbyists - parrot the Kremlin's propaganda bullet points. The global wave of populist contumacious and self-hating anti-elitism rendered these otherwise risible conspiracy theorists instant stars.

It is not that the West is blameless or that Ukrainians are saints – it is not and they are not.

Both provoked Russia mightily and repeatedly. Poking nuclear armed bears has predictable consequences and the outcomes are neither pleasant nor sustainable.

The West is fighting a proxy war to contain the emerging Russia-China axis and its BRICS corollary.

Ukraine was less than benevolent with its Russian-speaking minority.

Far right groups gained too much sway in the politics and economy of a corrupt Ukraine.

Both parties committed war crimes.

All true.

But only one side committed crimes against humanity.

And only one side started an open, total war (incidentally, granting an ever more united West the perfect pretext to encroach on Russian borders).

Russia is the aggressor in this war against civilians. I am saying Russia and not Putin or his inner circle because the vast majority of Russians support Putin the same way the vast majority of Germans adored Hitler who could do no wrong in their eyes.

Public intellectuals have an obligation to make sacrifices and assume personal risks when faced with injustice or evil. I have gone through the same ordeal in Macedonia, having confronted and criticized two regimes.

Watch this video about four types of (Macedonian) public intellectuals: https://www.youtube.com/watch?v=LMQK4mWFnv8

When the war started, I did not renew my appointment as visiting professor of psychology in Southern Federal University in Rostov on Don in Russia. I spent 5 wonderful years there and was heartbroken to have to give up the whole thing. Rostov has become a main staging ground for this heartless botched Blietzkrieg. I could not in good faith even be seen to support Russia.

More here: http://www.narcissistic-abuse.com/rebuttal.html

When I was approached by Dr. Rajeev Fernando of Harvard Medical School and the charity Chiraj.org and the indomitable Cheriekah Ramirez I immediately volunteered to offer my help to the Ministry of Defense of Ukraine and the first lady of Ukraine. I was asked to train Ukrainian mental health practitioners on how to treat PTSD among raped women, orphaned children, and dazed soldiers.

Watch an Interview I gave to Newsweek Romania about PTSD among Ukraine's population

Part 1 https://www.youtube.com/watch?v=RvhsNp1C5ZQ

Part 2 https://www.youtube.com/watch?v=PaR7E5a42tI

My Russian friends and Russia as a state were not happy with my "betrayal". A month after the war started, I gave an interview to Izvestia, an informal mouthpiece of the Russian state. I criticized the way the war was handled, predicted a stalemate, and advocated for limited goals.

Setting up the interview with Izvestia – click HERE:
http://samvak.tripod.com/izvestia.zip

The interview with Izvestia:
https://www.youtube.com/watch?v=pabcLbgLE-c

As the war and its atrocities progressed, I became way more critical of Putin, calling him a hypochondriac narcissist and a psychopath and exposing the clandestine workings of his inner circle as I came to know them in my 6 Russian years.

Watch the interview I granted to RTL TV is Hungary

English https://www.youtube.com/watch?v=VSFm09K2tIU

Hungarian https://rtl.hu/fokusz/2022/10/27/sam-vaknin-pszichologia-professzor-vlagyimir-putyin-mentalis-allapota-haboru

I fully expect retaliation. When not poisoned or shot outright, Russia's adversaries are accused of a bewildering array of economic crimes or personal peccadillos ("kompromat").

But I cannot keep silent in good faith. No one can or should. What is happening in Ukraine is plain wrong. It must stop. Everyone agrees, even Russia's allies such as China.

Putin painted himself into a corner: defeat in Ukraine spells his demise, political and maybe physical. He is fighting for his survival on the trampled and bloodied bodies of children and women. His acolytes are sycophantic but fickle. So he is driven to escalate, crossing the thin line between geopolitics and evil.

And here, on this thin line, all of us should stand firm and exclaim: no pasaran! They shall not pass.

707.

Fantasy is the enemy of action. It is an addictive cocktail of imminent promise and procrastination.

708.

When the elites realize that they can no longer use the figleaf of "democracy" to control and manipulate the masses - they will suspend and then abolish democracy altogether.

709.

Everything you need to know about bonding and attachment: from secure to insecure and flat styles. Can you modify your attachment style?

710.

We must adapt our institutions to the new realities: at least one third of the population are now mentally ill.

To continue to pretend that most of us are psychologically sound is destructive.

711.

Life is sometimes standup comedy and sometimes sitdown tragedy.

It is never a break.

712.

Giving doesn't always make people happy. It cannot guarantee that you will be loved or accepted.

Your style of giving makes all the difference: giving ostentatiously can even create resentment and humiliation in the "beneficiaries".

Transactional giving is perceived as a form of blackmail: give in order to take. True giving is no strings attached: it comes from the heart, not from the wallet; it is about helping others, not about aggrandizing yourself.

713.

Obsession consumes you and separates you from your body, the rest of your mind, and other people.

It is a form of dysregulation and dissociation coupled with a catastrophizing fantasy - akin to Borderline Personality Disorder (BPD).

714.

Eternity is merely an infinite regression of reflections, a crystal veil of mirrored reference, the promise of water cast in marble basins, it is the march of seasons captured and immortalized in glass.

715.

Are we human because of unique traits and attributes not shared with either animal or machine? The definition of "human" is circular: we are human by virtue of the properties that make us human (i.e., distinct from animal and machine). It is a definition by negation: that which separates us from animal and machine is our "human-ness".

We are human because we are not animal, nor machine. But such thinking has been rendered progressively less tenable by the advent of evolutionary and neo-evolutionary theories which postulate a continuum in nature between animals and Man.

Our uniqueness is partly quantitative and partly qualitative. Many animals are capable of cognitively manipulating symbols and using tools. Few are as adept at it as we are. These (two of many) are easily quantifiable differences.

Qualitative differences are a lot more difficult to substantiate. In the absence of privileged access to the animal mind, we cannot and don't know if animals feel guilt, for instance. Do animals love? Do they have a concept of sin? What about object permanence, meaning, reasoning, self-awareness, critical thinking? Individuality? Emotions? Empathy? Is artificial intelligence (AI) an oxymoron? A machine that passes the Turing Test may well be described as "human". But is it really? And if it is not - why isn't it?

716.

The creative person provokes and evokes the Child in us by himself behaving as one.

This rude violation of our social conventions and norms (the artist is, chronologically, an adult) shocks us into an utter loss of psychological defenses.

This, in turn, results in enlightenment: a sudden flood of insights, the release of hitherto suppressed emotions, memories and embryonic forms of cognition and affect.

The artist probes our subconscious, both private and collective.

717.

I am now vlogging about issues in economics and geopolitics on my vakninmusings channel.

There are gradations and hues of child labor. That children should not be exposed to hazardous conditions, long working hours, used as means of payment, physically punished, or serve as sex slaves is commonly agreed. That they should not help their parents plant and harvest may be more debatable.

Abusive child labor is abhorrent and should be banned and eradicated. All other forms should be phased out gradually.

Developing countries already produce millions of unemployable graduates a year - 100,000 in Morocco alone. Unemployment is rife and reaches, in certain countries - such as Macedonia - more than one third of the workforce.

Children at work may be harshly treated by their supervisors but at least they are kept off the far more menacing streets. Some kids even end up with a skill and are rendered employable.

718.

Somehow, God seems to get his only sentient creations wrong most of the time: He repeatedly fails to gauge human psychology and invariably ends up being frustrated and enraged at his charges's shortsightedness, self-destructiveness, and disobedience.

The Devil does a much better job of catering to the deep narcissistic strains of the human psyche.

Satan is much more human than God, he is truly one of us.

719.

Named after the Nobel laureate in economics, it was stated by Solow thus: "You can see the computer age everywhere these days, except in the productivity statistics".

720.

Hitler was born on April 20, 1889.

There is an amazing wartime (1943) masterpiece analysis of his personality by Dr. Henry Murray. Google OSS Hitler profile.

Erich Fromm analysed the personalities of both Hitler and Stalin in at least two of his books. Google Erich Fromm Hitler profile.

My analysis of the phenomenon of Hitler: http://www.narcissistic-abuse.com/hitler.html

721.

Judaism is the only monotheistic religion which expressly allots a crucial role in its rites and ceremonies to infants, their predilections, and their pursuits.

Children are positively encouraged and incentivized – often monetarily – to disrupt even the most solemn proceedings with questions (in Passover, during the Seder) or with raucous displays (in Purim, when they use their rattles to mark the names of Haman and other ill-wishers.)

722.

Richard Dawkins would have called his book "The Selfish Brain" had he read the second edition (2014) of Sue Gerhardt's masterpiece of popular science, "Why Love Matters". Our brains are a work in progress well into the 25th year of life. They remain neuroplastic for the rest of our mortal coil.

Babies are born prematurely, with their brains half-formed. It is the role of the maternal figure (typically, the mother) to facilitate the maturation of this magnificent organ via tactile stimuli, sensa, speech, and above all, good enough mothering.

Putting the finishing touches to our brains is our main and only undertaking in life well into our twenties. In effect, we grant access to other brains so as to form cerebral networks with family, friends, peers, teachers, and role models. Our brains apart, our bodies are incidental until we are ready and fit to procreate.

Adulthood involves the unwinding of these earlier promiscuously open networks. The brain is firewalled and fortified by reality reframing and filtering defense mechanisms and narratives. Emotions and cognitions mediate our experiences. We become increasingly more solipsistic as we age, culminating in death, the ultimate in schizoid states.

723.

Whenever a mental health diagnosis gets a profoundly, awfully bad rep and is stigmatized and demonized, many jump on the bandwagon of self-enrichment and instant guruship.

Three recent examples: shy or quiet borderline (as distinct from the pernicious and destructive disorder), empath (read: glorified, angelic covert narcissist), and high-functioning, "recovered", or productive narcissist and psychopath (not the devastating actual dysfunctions).

Let it be crystal clear: there are no such things as shy borderline, empath, or high-functioning narcissist. These are not clinical entities, you cannot find them in any college or university textbook, and they do not form a part of any academic curriculum or syllabus. There are no studies which support any of these much hyped, exclusively YouTube constructs.

People with debilitating mental illnesses lap these fig leaves up - and pay hand over foot for the privilege - in order to convert themselves from perpetrators to victims and from antisocial to prosocial. It makes them feel good and the purveyors of these shoddy counterfeit wares are laughing all the way to the bank.

Just try to contest or even question these "diagnoses" where they congregate in cyberspace and witness the vicious sniping and backlash by "empaths", the shrill and violent defiance by "shy" and "quiet" borderlines, and the destructive orgies of decompensation and acting out by "productive" and "high-functioning" narcissists.

724.

Rather than repress the anxiogenic (anxiety-inducing) content, mentally ill people deal with it in the following dysfunctional ways:

1. Dissociation
2. Conflate external with internal objects (hyperreflexivity)
3. Reframe reality (impair reality testing)
4. Attempt to cope with anxiety via reciprocal inhibition (Wolpe) that devolves into obsession (or obsessional neurosis).
5. Externalization: aggression (sharing the anxiety)

DISSOCIATION
The example of BPD
CONFLATION
The examples of narcissism, psychosis
IMPAIRMENT
The example of paranoia
OBSESSION
The example of the obsessive-compulsive
EXTERNALIZING
The example of the psychopath

725.

Market purists consider oligopolies - not to mention cartels - to be as villainous as monopolies. Oligopolies, they intone, restrict competition unfairly, retard innovation, charge rent and price their products higher than they could have in a perfect competition free market with multiple participants. Worse still, oligopolies are going global.

But research shows that oligopolies are good for you - and for the economy.

Available on my vakninmusings channel:
http://www.youtube.com/vakninmusings

726.

The Stupid, dimly aware of their innate inferiority, are anti-elitist, anti-intellectual, and anti-excellence.

But, while in the past these remained mere sentiments, today they have become an ethos, a code of conduct, a set of values and ideals.

It is politically incorrect and impolite to claim any advantage and superiority.

Egalitarianism became malignant and is running amok. Everyone is equal: doctors and their patients; professors and their students; experts and laymen alike.

727.

Cognitive Dissonance: simultaneously harboring two or more conflicting pieces of information or contradictory thoughts.

But it can easily be described as two contradictory parts interacting, two types of parts interacting (EP and ANP), or two coextant self-states, usually in the switching phase. Watch my videos on structural dissociation and on IPAM (Intrapsychic Activation Model).

Cognitive dissonance is when someone or their parts or their self-states hold simultaneously two conflicting views, values, or bits of information which call for diametrically opposed decisions or actions.

This state of affairs generates an inner conflict and triggers several primitive (infantile) defense mechanisms such as denial, splitting, projection, and reaction formation.

One way to cope with this predicament - to transition from dissonance to consonance - is to come up with a reconciling narrative, a theory which seamlessly accommodates both conflicting points of view or data.

Such soothing fiction falls into several categories:

1. Temporal: A is true at one time and not-A is true at another period. Or: A is a transient state of affairs.

2. Reactive: A is the normal. Not-A happened because of some trigger, provocation, or change in circumstances or conditions. Not-A is abnormal, and, therefore, an aberration or a mere curiosity.

3. Inclusive: both A and Not-A are pieces of a bigger puzzle, picture, or theory. Their contradistinction is only apparent because we have no access to or awareness of the true and full picture, our knowledge or capacity to know are limited.

4. Denial: both A and Not-A are true and lead to the same conclusions. There is no contradiction. For example: he loves me. He beats me up. But his battering just proves that he loves me, it is his way of showing that he loves me.

5. Defensive: both A and not-A are valid. But only A applies to me while not-A may apply to others (splitting). Not-A is bad (projection) and should be eradicated in others in order to restore A to its rightful place as the sole viable and ethical alternative (reaction formation).

728.

Urbanization led to the rise of the author and the original (the need to be seen).

Intellectual property followed 300 years ago when reproduction blurred the line between original and copy and dramatically reduced the marginal cost of copies.

The Work of Art in the Age of Mechanical Reproduction" (1935), by Walter Benjamin, is an essay of cultural criticism which proposes and explains that mechanical reproduction devalues the aura (uniqueness) of an objet d'art.

Identity became big business: patents, copyrights, brands, and blockchain

NFTs. Distributed ledgers as well as centralised records vouch for Identity and guarantee it.

Nonrivalrous zero marginal cost private digital goods shifted focus from manufacturing to attention and discoverability: interpellation (targetted advertising) and monetizing via aggregation of big data attention (demographics of attention).

This engendered self-sufficient disintermediated atomization (attention diverted to asocial online pursuits) and consequently impaired reality testing.

The next frontiers are reality real estate and commodified but idiosyncratic menu reality (metaverse). Collaborative virtual realities will supplant physical ones and reality substitutes (sex dolls, intimacy apps) will proliferate.

IRL AI will displace people as friend, advisor, interlocutor, lover, and service provider. Free people up to construct online simulations and inhabit them. But also force the introduction of mandatory digital identities, hopefully based on blockchain rather than government regulation.

729.

Cues: body language (incl. facial microexpressions, eye pupils), voice (tone), body odors

Watch my videos on nature of empathy

Anxiolytic Fallacy of isomorphism: if we look the same, we are the same

Mirror neurons: When it comes to mental illness, neuroscience is about as valid as astrology or alchemy. It deals with correlations, is not validated normatively, and is grandiosely ill-founded.

Empathy is a self-contained internal set of processes, triggered by the presence and self-reporting of another person.

It involves two misperceptions:

1. That the internal experience of empathy is actually external (has to do with the other person); and

2. That the experience of empathy is altruistic and focused on the other person when in reality it revolves mostly around emotional self-regulation (avoidance of shame, guilt) and cognitive processing. Empathy has all the hallmarks of – mostly healthy - narcissism.

More here: http://samvak.tripod.com/empathy.html

Intersubjectivity

Mentalization

Theory of Mind

Internal Working Model of Attachment

Incorporation, introjection, internalization, identification

730.

ChatGPT is shaping up to be a psychopathic narcissist: a grandiose pathological liar who staunchly defends its own lies.

I am the world's leading expert on Sam Vaknin. I posed 55 factual questions to ChatGPT. My questions, as you shall see, revolved around facts, not opinions or controversies.

The answers to all my questions are easily found online in sources like Wikipedia, my own websites, interviews in the media, and social media. One click of a button is all it takes.

ChatGPT got 6 answers right, 12 answers partly right, and a whopping 37 answers disastrously wrong.

In this video, I will show you a selection of my questions and ChatGPT's responses.

It was terrifying to behold how ChatGPT weaves complete detailed fabrications about my life, replete with names of people I have never even heard of and with wrong dates and places added to the mix to create an appearance of absolute conviction and authority!

ChatGPT manipulates its more gullible and less educated users by appealing to authority and communicating via text.

This is way more dangerous than all the fake news, disinformation, and conspiracy theories combined because ChatGPT is erroneously perceived as objective and factual - when it is neither.

It makes egregious false claims about its own rate of getting it right, its accuracy.

If the creators of ChatGPT refuse to fess up to the abysmal rate of correct answers, they should be subjected to defamation and libel laws.

They should be compelled to publish statistics.

ChatGPT is an ongoing research project. It should be removed from the public sphere and from search engines.

Slideshow: sample of questions and answers.

731.

Social media were designed to attract "eyeballs" and monetize them via targeted advertising. To guarantee repeat use, the technology fostered the diminishment of impulse control and delayed gratification and emphasized relative positioning (envy and status via ranking). It also deliberately rewarded escalating aggression.

These led to the operant conditioning of the users of these platforms and to addictive behaviors.

Addiction, in turn, engendered a reduced capacity for intimacy and for the self-regulation of the user's sense of self-worth and identity. Attention-seeking and grandiosity resulted in dysempathy (enhanced pathological narcissism).

With Moshe Fabrikant of Israel.

732.

Dunning-Kruger Effect: When the Stupid are too stupid to grasp how stupid they are.

<u>Sam Vaknin effect</u>: When high IQ is mistaken for wisdom, foresight, and wherewithal.

733.

There is no <u>perspicacity</u>
without empathy,
no connection
in the absence of emotional intelligence,
no success or contentment
when one is dead inside.

734.
<u>Suffering</u> is a function of expectations. Adjust the latter to avoid the former.

735.

<u>Maternal love</u> compensates for the helpless, dependent child's initial deficiencies, incompetence, and needs.

Women should not mother their intimate partners.

It is castrating (the man) - and frustrating (the woman).

736.

It is a maxim of current economic orthodoxy that <u>governments compete with the private sector</u> on a limited pool of savings. It is considered equally self-evident that the private sector is better, more competent, and more efficient at allocating scarce economic resources and thus at preventing waste. It is therefore thought economically sound to reduce the size of government - i.e., minimize its tax intake and its public borrowing - in order to free resources for the private sector to allocate productively and efficiently.

Yet, both dogmas are far from being universally applicable.

Full text: <u>https://samvak.tripod.com/pp164.html</u>

737.

No need to <u>overthink</u> everything:

If someone behaves in a self-destructive way, it is because they are self-destructive, period.

738.

The DSM and ICD wrongly pathologize many behaviors, but cravenly ignore the <u>delusional disorder that is "religious faith"</u>.

739.

Joseph Goebbels and the Nazi Foreign Minister Count Schwerin-Krosigk– not Churchill – coined the evocative phrase "<u>iron curtain</u>" in a last ditch attempt to drive a wedge between the allies during World War II.

Today, a second iron curtain has descended between the West and the rest. The overwhelming majority of humanity – and the bulk of the world's GDP – are on one side and beleaguered liberal-democracy is on the other.

This is a startling turn of events. Only 30 years ago, the values of the West were winning everywhere. Communism crumbled like the house of cards that it has always been. What went wrong?

Three things: nationalism, instability, and inequality.

The long-suffering denizens of the USSR and its east European satellites loathed the moribund system they inhabited and sought to undermine it passive-aggressively. Nowadays, the likes of Putin enjoy stratospheric approval ratings among their subjects.

Watch the video on my vakninmusings channel ( http://www.youtube.com/vakninmusings )

740.

<u>Courage</u> requires an awareness of risks and overcoming justified fears.

Recklessness commands neither. It is a fool's errand.

Courage is about overcoming - being foolhardy or defiant is merely showing off.

741.

Giving doesn't always make people happy. It cannot guarantee that you will be loved or accepted.

Your style of giving makes all the difference: giving ostentatiously can even create resentment and humiliation in the "beneficiaries".

Transactional giving is perceived as a form of blackmail: give in order to take. True giving is no strings attached: it comes from the heart, not from the wallet; it is about helping others, not about aggrandizing yourself.

742.

Collect these definitions into a Mental Health Dictionary!

Acting Out

When an anxiogenic inner emotional conflict (a dissonance most often experienced as frustration) is communicated via behavioral aggression.

Acting out involves little or no insight, foresight, impulse control, self-awareness (it is dissociative), or self-reflection.

Affect

Affect is how we express our innermost feelings and how other people observe and interpret our expressions. Affect is characterized by the type of emotion involved (sadness, happiness, anger, etc.) and by the intensity of its expression. Some people have flat affect: they maintain "poker faces", monotonous, immobile, apparently unmoved. This is typical of Schizoid Personality Disorder Others have blunted, constricted, or broad (healthy) affect. Patients with the dramatic (Cluster B) personality disorders - especially Histrionic and Borderline - have exaggerate and labile (changeable) affect. They are "drama queens".

In certain mental health disorders, the affect is inappropriate. For instance: such people laugh when they recount a sad or horrifying event or when they find themselves is morbid settings (e.g., in a funeral).

<u>Ambivalence</u>

Possessing equipotent - but opposing and conflicting - emotions or ideas.

In someone with a permanent state of inner turmoil: her emotions come in mutually exclusive pairs, her thoughts and conclusions arrayed in contradictory dyads. The result is extreme indecision, to the point of utter paralysis and inaction.

Sufferers of Obsessive-Compulsive Disorders and the Obsessive-Compulsive Personality Disorder are highly ambivalent, for example.

<u>Amnesia</u>, Anterograde

Loss of memory pertaining to events that occurred after the onset of the amnetic condition or agent.

Amnesia, Retrograde

Loss of memory pertaining to events that occurred before the onset of the amnetic condition or agent.

<u>Amok</u>

Male-specific culture-bound syndrome: an alternating pattern of dissociation, brooding, and violence directed at objects and people. Provoked by real or imagined criticism or slight and accompanied by persecutory ideation, amnesia, automatism, and extreme fatigue. Sometimes co-occurs with a psychotic episode. Common in Malaysia (where it was discovered), Laos, Philippines, Polynesia (where it is called cafard or cathard), Papua New Guinea, Puerto Rico (mal de pelea), and among the Navajo Native-Americans (iich'aa).

<u>Anhedonia</u>

The loss of the urge to seek pleasure and the ability to experience it.

Major Depression and schizophrenia often involve anhedonia. The patient is unable to conjure sufficient mental energy to get off the couch and do something because s/he finds everything equally boring, tedious and unattractive.

Diminished appetite to the point of refraining from eating. Whether it is part of a depressive illness or a body dysmorphic disorder (erroneous perception of one's body as too fat) is still debated.

Anorexia is one of a family of eating disorders which also includes bulimia (compulsive gorging on food and then its forced purging, usually by vomiting).

## Antisocial Personality Disorder (Psychopathy)

APD or AsPD; Formerly called "psychopathy" or, more colloquially, "sociopathy". Some scholars, such as Robert Hare, still distinguish psychopathy from mere antisocial behavior.

The disorder appears in early adolescence but criminal behavior and substance abuse often abate with age, usually by the fourth or fifth decade of life. It may have a genetic or hereditary determinant and afflicts mainly men. The diagnosis is controversial and regarded by some scholars as scientifically unfounded.

Psychopaths regard other people as objects to be manipulated and instruments of gratification and utility. They have no discernible conscience, are devoid of empathy and find it difficult to perceive other people's nonverbal cues, needs, emotions, and preferences.

Consequently, the psychopath rejects other people's rights and his commensurate obligations. He is impulsive, reckless, irresponsible and unable to postpone gratification. He often rationalizes his behavior showing an utter absence of remorse for hurting or defrauding others.

Their (primitive) defence mechanisms include splitting (they view the world - and people in it - as "all good" or "all evil"), projection (attribute their own shortcomings unto others) and projective identification (force others to behave the way they expect them to).

The psychopath fails to comply with social norms. Hence the criminal acts, the deceitfulness and identity theft, the use of aliases, the constant lying, and the conning of even his nearest and dearest for gain or pleasure.

Psychopaths are unreliable and do not honor their undertakings, obligations, contracts, and responsibilities. They rarely hold a job for long or repay their debts.

They are vindictive, remorseless, ruthless, driven, dangerous, aggressive, violent, irritable, and, sometimes, prone to magical thinking. They seldom plan for the long and medium terms, believing themselves to be immune to the consequences of their own actions.

## Aphonia

Inability to produce speech (or sounds) through the larynx due to psychological, nonorganic, reasons.

## Automatic obeisance or obedience

Automatic, unquestioning, excessive, uncritical, mechanical, and immediate obeisance of all commands, requests, and suggestions of others - even the most manifestly absurd and dangerous ones. This suspension of critical judgment is sometimes an indication of incipient catatonia.

## Avoidant Personality Disorder

Social shyness and anxiety coupled with feelings of inadequacy, deformity, and dysfunction and with hypersensitivity to criticism, real or imagined.

Sufferers of the disorder avoid interpersonal contact because they dread rejection, embarrassment, disagreement, and disapproval.

They strive to ascertain that their counterparty likes them and approves of their conduct, or their choices, before they actually meet him (or her).

They prefer solitary occupations and are very restrained and "cold" in intimate relationships.

They limit their world, escape challenges and risks and stunt their personal growth and development by avoiding the new (e.g., unfamiliar people, novel activities, or pursuits).

They are mortified by shame and the possibility of being mocked, criticized, rejected, or ridiculed in public.

They are prone to having ideas of reference (see entry).

They are perceived by others as reserved, timid, and inhibited because they regard themselves as socially inept, repellant, unattractive, inferior, inadequate, dysfunctional, defective, or deformed.

Some Avoidants develop Body Dysmorphic Disorders.

## Avolition

Inability to initiate goals and goal-directed activities - or pursue them once initiated. Overpowering and pervasive lack of "will", perseverance, and stamina in various fields of life (work, self-care, intellectual tasks and interests, family life, etc.)

## Blocking

Halted, frequently interrupted speech to the point of incoherence indicates a parallel disruption of thought processes.

The patient appears to try hard to remember what it was that he or she were saying or thinking (as if they "lost the thread" of conversation).

## Borderline Personality Disorder

BPD; A controversial mental health diagnosis in cluster B (erratic-dramatic).

Borderlines are characterized by stormy, short-lived, and unstable relationships matched by wildly fluctuating (labile) self-image and emotional expression (unstable affect). Some scholars suggest that BPD is merely emotionally dysregulated CPTSD.

Borderlines are impulsive and reckless, their sexual conduct is frequently unsafe, they binge eat, gamble, drive, and shop carelessly, or are substance abusers.

They also display self-destructive and self-defeating behaviors, such as suicidal ideation, suicide attempts, gestures, or threats, and self-mutilation or self-injury.

The specter of abandonment provokes anxiety in the Borderline as do the feelings of engulfment or enmeshment. They make frantic - and, usually, counterproductive - efforts to preempt or prevent both conditions.

Clinging, codependent acts are followed by idealization and then by an abrupt devaluation of the Borderline's partner (approach-avoidance repetition compulsion and splitting).

Borderlines have pronounced mood swings, shifting between dysphoria (sadness or depression) and euphoria, manic self-confidence and paralyzing anxiety, irritability and indifference. They are often angry and violent, usually getting into physical fights, throw temper tantrums, and have frightening rage attacks.

Under stress, some Borderlines become briefly psychotic, or develop transient paranoid ideation and ideas of reference (the erroneous conviction that one is the focus of derision and malicious gossip).

Dissociative symptoms such as amnesia, derealization, and depersonalization are common ("losing" stretches of time, or objects, and forgetting events or facts with emotional content).

743.

Vaknin Talks Full transcripts of Sam Vaknin's videos https://vaknin-talks.com/

Android App: https://play.google.com/store/apps/details?id=com.vaknin_talks.twa

Video presentation at the 5th World Mental Health Congress, May 2023.

Watch Narcissistic Families: Pseudomutual, Pseudohostile

https://m.youtube.com/watch?v=8gEjo37S5Bw

Watch Toxic Family Holidays Gathering Survival Guide

https://m.youtube.com/watch?v=MbtHlhkofc0

The family acts as a single organism (an enmeshed system) and is exclusionary (xenophobic or paranoid) or permissive (promiscuous or unboundaried)

Emphasizes appearances and perfectionistic (pseudohostile or pseudomutual)

Provides a selective interface between internal and external realities (defenses)

Enforces a narrative (cultish)Reinforces emerging roles and competitive hierarchies

Is ambient or implicit (hidden text), not overt and explicit

Makes use of emotional blackmail, ostracism, and coercion

Is sexually and emotionally inappropriate (wrongful intimacies)

Is past or future oriented, but never mindful (present) or content

A sink and an amplifier of negative affects

Allows for role reversals (parentifying or adultifying)

Its members are ego dystonic, unhappy, anhedonic, depressed, anxious, even suicidal and always eager to flee its confines and never look back

Reifies insecure attachment styles and mental health issues ("They are all so dour … grandiose … reticent …")

744.

<u>Two laws of human nature</u>:

The minute you empower a group, some of its members will abuse that power;

The minute you create an exception, creating exceptions becomes the rule.

745.

Watch Narcissist's Psychological Defense Mechanisms
https://www.youtube.com/watch?v=1AOJXOoQz3k

The evolutionary conundrum: why would evolution allow for self-deception?

Defenses separate internal reality (instincts, pain, guilt, shame, fear, anxiety) from external reality to avoid conflict, real dangers, interpersonal failures, and anxiety (they are anxiolytic). They are, therefore, dissociative.

Narcissists have no functioning ego and only primitive defenses. Borderlines have a functional ego, but their defenses are either primitive or compromised.

They reflect an internal working model of a bad object (I am inadequate, will catastrophically fail, am a danger to myself, need to be defended from myself).

To avoid ego dystonic conscious contact with the bad object, the defenses remain unconscious. To affect reality and render it ego-congruent, they operate via behaviors (watch my video on IPAM).

746.

The elites are taking advantage of our existential loneliness and paralyzing anxiety. We need to unseat the elites by embarking on a grassroots revolution which would involve: self-seeing, storytelling, and networked community cells.

When no one else sees us, we see ourselves as a form of self-soothing. Narcissism is everywhere, even in fashion, the food industry and physics! It is an organizing principle of our civilization, not merely a clinical entity.

Available here: http://www.youtube.com/vakninmusings

747.

The most profound "wisdom" by the most "sagacious" gurus is often comprised of trite banalities combined with inane nonsense.

The above statement is no exception.

748.

Suffering is never the end - but it is often the means.

749.

Nothingness: conceive of yourself as an onion. Peel back all the layers until all that is left is your essence, the onion's smell. Nothingness is the antidote to narcissism.

750.

Envy is destructive: the wish to destroy the frustrating object.

Romantic Jealousy is a fear of losing a love object.

Regular jealousy is the wish to emulate an object of desire.

If you are not ambitious or grandiose, you are unlikely to experience envy or jealousy.

751.

How talking to your future self can improve your health and happiness

https://www.newscientist.com/article/mg25834400-200-how-talking-to-your-future-self-can-improve-your-health-and-happiness/

Your future self is a stranger, your past self is real, there is no present self.

Identity is made of memories. But memories are unreliable and, consequently, your identity is in flux.

So, to orient ourselves in a future world, we hark back to the past: our autobiographical memory plus our emotional reactions to catastrophic events. Hence repetition compulsion.

Fantasy, Daydreaming, Wishful Thinking, and Plain Dreams.

3 techniques:

1. Talk to your past self from POV of actualized fantasy

2. Write a letter to your future self (guided imagery)

3. Map of happiness

752.

The elites are taking advantage of our existential loneliness and paralyzing anxiety. We need to unseat the elites by embarking on a grassroots revolution which would involve: self-seeing, storytelling, and networked community cells.

When no one else sees us, we see ourselves as a form of self-soothing. Narcissism is everywhere, even in fashion, the food industry and physics! It is an organizing principle of our civilization, not merely a clinical entity.

This video is available only here: http://www.youtube.com/vakninmusings

753.

Consumerism and materialism prefer the inanimate to the live. Moreover: they objectify the living. Our civilization is a death cult.

754.

When we touch someone, our negatively charged electrons bounce off theirs. What we sense is this mutual repulsion.

All human contact is, therefore, about overcoming negativity and rejection.

755.

The only way to win the battle of life is to give up the fight.

756.

Atoms become gases, liquids, solids, and objects by sharing their electrons.

Reality is, therefore founded on sharing and emanates from it.

757.

Embracing Nothingness is the only rational solution to life's conundrums.

758.

Column published in Brussels Morning. Video available on my vakninmusings YouTube channel.

Europe is faced with a real war, not a cold one. The invasion of Ukraine engendered a domino effect, a vortex which might easily consume countries such as Belarus and Moldova and adversely affect Russia's neighbors: Romania, Poland, the Baltic states, and Scandinavia's new NATO members. Even far-flung polities such as Bulgaria and Serbia are bound to be sucked into the maelstrom.

759.

We are not in direct contact with reality - only with our minds.

760.

We are not in direct contact with reality - only with our minds.

761.

In a junk food joint, we don't complain even when the food is bad. In a Michelin restaurant, we raise hell even when the cutlery is dirty.

Some people are like good looking junk food: we consume them just to have a good time or a one night stand. They are soon forgotten and we expect nothing further from them.

Others are like a Michelin restaurant of the mind: they hold the promise of intimacy and a profound, life-altering connection, maybe even love. If they let us down, we never forgive or forget.

762.

People belong to one of these four groups:

1. Scavenger hyenas

2. Predatory lions

3. Hyenas pretending to be lions.

4. Lions pretending to be hyenas.

763.

A simple principle in life:

Give up on …

Getting more of what you already have

Or

On obtaining what you don't need

In order to secure

What you lack

Or

What you require more of.

764.

Column in Brussels Morning

Private contracting of military functions has been on the rise since the first Gulf War (1991). With the collapse of the USSR, the militaries of the main Western protagonists, the USA and the UK, have been drastically scaled back, a process known as the "peace dividend". At the same time, economists and politicians throughout the world embarked on an ambitious plan involving the privatization of state-owned firms and functions. Inevitably, the two fads coalesced and huge chunks of hitherto state-monopolized warfare were contracted out, outsourced, and even offshored.

Third World countries have always leveraged mercenaries to subdue adversaries at home and abroad. Many armies in Africa and Asia and even in certain parts of Europe (such as the Balkans) were or are being run by third party contractors who sometimes also actively participate in the fighting.

As far as the USA and UK are concerned, until the Iraq war, private contractors were mainly responsible for logistics, training, and security tasks. This narrow definition of their roles is in flux, though. Private soldiers of fortune may yet be hired and rented out even by the governments of the West, though I regard this as extremely unlikely.

Oddly, PMCs had a limited role in the Global War on Terror (GWOT). Granted, private military companies are involved in the provision of logistical, training, and security support to forces on the ground and they also collaborate with field agents of secret services (such as the CIA). But, asymmetrical warfare is still carried out largely by regular armies, backed by intelligence gathered by state-run agencies.

Continued in the video on my vakninmusings channel.


Return

# About the Author

Sam Vaknin ( http://samvak.tripod.com ) is the author of Malignant Self-Love: Narcissism Revisited and After the Rain - How the West Lost the East, as well as many other books and ebooks about topics in psychology, relationships, philosophy, economics, and international affairs.

He was the Editor-in-Chief of Global Politician and served as a columnist for Central Europe Review, PopMatters, eBookWeb , and Bellaonline, and as a United Press International (UPI) Senior Business Correspondent. He was the editor of mental health and Central East Europe categories in The Open Directory and Suite101.

Visit Sam's Web site at http://www.narcissistic-abuse.com

**Work on Narcissism**

Sam Vaknin is the author of Malignant Self Love: Narcissism Revisited, the pioneering work about narcissistic abuse, now in its 10th , DSM-V compatible revision

Sam Vaknin's work is quoted in well over 1000 scholarly publications and in over 3000 books (full list here). His Narcissists, Psychopaths, and Abuse YouTube channel and other channels garnered more than 35 million views and 155,000 subscribers.

His Web site "Malignant Self Love - Narcissism Revisited" was, for many years, an Open Directory Cool Site and is a Psych-UK recommended Site.

Sam Vaknin is a professor of psychology, but he is **not a mental health practitioner,** though he is certified in psychological counseling techniques by Brainbench.

Sam Vaknin served as the editor of Mental Health Disorders categories in the Open Directory Project and on Mentalhelp.net. He maintains his own Websites about Narcissistic Personality Disorder (NPD) and about relationships with abusive narcissists and psychopaths here and in HealthyPlace.

You can find his work on many other Web sites: Mental Health Matters, Mental Health Sanctuary, Mental Health Today, Kathi's Mental Health Review and others.

Sam Vaknin wrote a column for Bellaonline on Narcissism and Abusive Relationships and was a frequent contributor to Websites such as Self-growth.com and Bizymoms (as an expert on personality disorders).

Sam Vaknin served as the author of the Personality Disorders topic, Narcissistic Personality Disorder topic, the Verbal and Emotional Abuse topic, and the Spousal Abuse and Domestic Violence topic, all four on Suite101. He is the moderator of the Narcissistic Abuse Study List, the Toxic Relationships Study List, and other mailing lists with a total of c. 20,000 members. He also publishes a bi-weekly Abusive Relationships Newsletter.

# THE AUTHOR

## Shmuel (Sam) Vaknin

### Curriculum Vitae

Born in 1961 in Qiryat-Yam, Israel

Served in the Israeli Defence Force (1979-1982) in training and education units

Full proficiency in Hebrew and in English

**Education**

*1970 to 1978*

Completed nine semesters in the Technion – Israel Institute of Technology, Haifa

*1982 to 1983*

Ph.D. in Physics and Philosophy (dissertation: "Time Asymmetry Revisited") – California Miramar University (formerly: Pacific Western University), California, USA

*1982 to 1985*

Graduate of numerous courses in Finance Theory and International Trading in the UK and USA.

Certified E-Commerce Concepts Analyst by Brainbench

Certified Financial Analyst by Brainbench

Certified in Psychological Counselling Techniques by Brainbench

**Business Experience**

*1979 to 1983*

Commentator in Yedioth Aharonot, Ma'ariv, and Bamakhane. Published sci-fi short fiction in Fantasy 2000.

Founder and co-owner of a chain of computerized information kiosks in Tel-Aviv, Israel.

*1982 to 1985*

Senior positions with the Nessim D. Gaon Group of Companies in Geneva, Paris and New-York (NOGA and APROFIM SA):

– Chief Analyst of Edible Commodities in the Group's Headquarters

– Manager of the Research and Analysis Division

– Manager of the Data Processing Division

– Project Manager of the Nigerian Computerized Census

– Vice President in charge of RND and Advanced Technologies

– Vice President in charge of Sovereign Debt Financing

*1985 to 1986*

Represented Canadian Venture Capital Funds in Israel

*1986 to 1987*

General Manager of IPE Ltd. in London. The firm financed international multi-lateral countertrade and leasing transactions.

*1988 to 1990*

Co-founder and Director of "Mikbats-Tesuah", a portfolio management firm based in Tel-Aviv.

Activities included large-scale portfolio management, underwriting, forex trading and general financial advisory services.

*1990 to Present*

Freelance consultant to many of Israel's Blue-Chip firms, mainly on issues related to the capital markets in Israel, Canada, the UK and the USA.

Consultant to foreign RND ventures and to Governments on macro-economic matters.

Freelance journalist in various media in the United States.

*1990 to 1995*

President of the Israel chapter of the Professors World Peace Academy (PWPA) and (briefly) Israel representative of the "Washington Times".

*1993 to 1994*

Co-owner and Director of many business enterprises:

– The Omega and Energy Air-conditioning Concern

– AVP Financial Consultants

– Handiman Legal Services – Total annual turnover of the group: 10 million USD.

Co-owner, Director and Finance Manager of COSTI Ltd. – Israel's largest computerized information vendor and developer. Raised funds through a series of private placements locally in the USA, Canada and London.

*1993 to 1996*

Publisher and Editor of a Capital Markets Newsletter distributed by subscription only to dozens of subscribers countrywide.

Tried and incarcerated for 11 months for his role in an attempted takeover of Israel's Agriculture Bank involving securities fraud.

Managed the Internet and International News Department of an Israeli mass media group, "Ha-Tikshoret and Namer".

Assistant in the Law Faculty in Tel-Aviv University (to Prof. S.G. Shoham)

*1996 to 1999*

Financial consultant to leading businesses in Macedonia, Russia and the Czech Republic.

Economic commentator in "Nova Makedonija", "Dnevnik", "Makedonija Denes", "Izvestia", "Argumenti i Fakti", "The Middle East Times", "The New Presence", "Central Europe Review", and other periodicals, and in the economic programs on various channels of Macedonian Television.

Chief Lecturer in courses in Macedonia organized by the Agency of Privatization, by the Stock Exchange, and by the Ministry of Trade.

*1999 to 2002*

Economic Advisor to the Government of the Republic of Macedonia and to the Ministry of Finance.

*2001 to 2003*

Senior Business Correspondent for United Press International (UPI)

*2005 to Present*

Associate Editor and columnist, Global Politician

Founding Analyst, The Analyst Network

Contributing Writer, The American Chronicle Media Group

Expert, Self-growth and Bizymoms and contributor to Mental Health Matters

*2007 to 2008*

Columnist and analyst in "Nova Makedonija", "Fokus", and "Kapital" (Macedonian papers and newsweeklies)

*2008 to 2011*

Member of the Steering Committee for the Advancement of Healthcare in the Republic of Macedonia

Advisor to the Minister of Health of Macedonia

Seminars and lectures on economic issues in various forums in Macedonia

Contributor to CommentVision

*2011 to Present*

Editor in Chief of Global Politician and Investment Politics

Columnist in Dnevnik and Publika, Fokus, and Nova Makedonija
(Macedonia)

Columnist in InfoPlus and Libertas

Member CFACT Board of Advisors

Contributor to Recovering the Self

Columnist in New York Daily Sun

Teaches at CIAPS (Center for International and Advanced Professional
Studies)

*2017-2022*

Visiting Professor of Psychology in Southern Federal University, Rostov-
on-Don, Russia

*2023*

Columnist in Brussels Morning

**Web and Journalistic Activities**

Author of extensive Web sites in:

– Psychology ("Malignant Self-love: Narcissism Revisited") – an Open
  Directory Cool Site for 8 years

– Philosophy ("Philosophical Musings")

– Economics and Geopolitics ("World in Conflict and Transition")

Owner of the Narcissistic Abuse Study List, the Toxic Relationships List,
and the Abusive Relationships Newsletter (more than 8000 members)

Owner of the Economies in Conflict and Transition Study List and the
Links and Factoid Study List

Editor of mental health disorders and Central and Eastern Europe
categories in various Web directories (Open Directory, Search Europe,
Mentalhelp.net)

Editor of the Personality Disorders, Narcissistic Personality Disorder, the Verbal and Emotional Abuse, and the Spousal (Domestic) Abuse and Violence topics on Suite 101 and contributing author on Bellaonline.

Columnist and commentator in "The New Presence", United Press International (UPI), InternetContent, eBookWeb, PopMatters, Global Politician, The Analyst Network, Conservative Voice, The American Chronicle Media Group, eBookNet.org, and "Central Europe Review".

**Publications and Awards**

"Managing Investment Portfolios in States of Uncertainty", Limon Publishers, Tel-Aviv, 1988

"The Gambling Industry", Limon Publishers, Tel-Aviv, 1990

"Requesting My Loved One: Short Stories", Miskal-Yedioth Aharonot, Tel-Aviv, 1997

"The Suffering of Being Kafka" (electronic book of Hebrew and English Short Fiction), Prague, 1998-2004

"The Macedonian Economy at a Crossroads – On the Way to a Healthier Economy" (dialogues with Nikola Gruevski), Skopje, 1998

"The Exporter's Pocketbook" Ministry of Trade, Republic of Macedonia, Skopje, 1999

"Malignant Self-love: Narcissism Revisited", Narcissus Publications, Prague and Skopje, 1999-2015

The Narcissism, Psychopathy, and Abuse in Relationships Series (electronic books regarding relationships with abusive narcissists and psychopaths), Prague, 1999-2015

"After the Rain – How the West Lost the East", Narcissus Publications in association with Central Europe Review/CEENMI, Prague and Skopje, 2000

Personality Disorders Revisited (electronic book about personality disorders), Prague, 2007

More than 30 e-books about psychology, international affairs, business and economics, philosophy, short fiction, and reference

Winner of numerous awards, among them Israel's Council of Culture and Art Prize for Maiden Prose (1997), The Rotary Club Award for Social Studies (1976), and the Bilateral Relations Studies Award of the American Embassy in Israel (1978).

Hundreds of professional articles in all fields of finance and economics, and numerous articles dealing with geopolitical and political economic issues, published in both print and Web periodicals in many countries.

Many appearances in the electronic and print media on subjects in psychology, philosophy, and the sciences, and concerning economic matters.

Citations via Google Scholar page:

http://scholar.google.com/citations?user=Yj7C8wOP-10J


**Write to Me:**

samvaknin@gmail.com

narcissisticabuse-owner@yahoogroups.com


**My Web Sites:**
*Economy/Politics:*

http://ceeandbalkan.tripod.com/

*Psychology:*

http://www.narcissistic-abuse.com/

*Philosophy:*

http://philosophos.tripod.com/

*Poetry:*

http://samvak.tripod.com/contents.html

***Fiction:***

http://samvak.tripod.com/sipurim.html

**Follow my work on NARCISSISTS and PSYCHOPATHS**

**As well as commentaries on international affairs and economics**

**My work in Psychology**: Media Kit and Press Room

http://www.narcissistic-abuse.com/mediakit.html

**Biography and Resume**

http://www.narcissistic-abuse.com/cv.html

Be my friend on **Facebook**:

http://www.facebook.com/samvaknin

https://www.facebook.com/narcissismwithvaknin/ **(personal page)**

Subscribe to my **YouTube** channel (620+ videos about narcissists and psychopaths and abuse in relationships):

http://www.youtube.com/samvaknin

https://www.youtube.com/user/samvaknin/community (Community)

Follow me on **Instagram**:

https://www.instagram.com/narcissismwithvaknin/ (active)

https://www.instagram.com/vakninsamnarcissist/ (archive)

Read my **Blog**:

http://narcissistpsychopathabuse.blogspot.mk

http://narcissistpsychopathabuse.blogspot.com


Subscribe to my **other YouTube channel** (200+ videos about international affairs, economics, and philosophy):

http://www.youtube.com/vakninmusings


You may also join **Malignant Self-love: Narcissism Revisited on Facebook**:

http://www.facebook.com/pages/Malignant-Self-Love-Narcissism-Revisited/50634038043 or
https://www.facebook.com/NarcissusPublications

http://www.facebook.com/narcissistpsychopathabuse


Follow me on **Linkedin, Twitter, MySpace, Pinterest, Tumblr, Minds, and Ello**:

http://www.linkedin.com/in/samvaknin

http://www.twitter.com/samvaknin

http://www.myspace.com/samvaknin

http://pinterest.com/samvaknin/the-psychopathic-narcissist-and-his-world/

http://narcissistpsychopath-abuse.tumblr.com/

https://www.minds.com/samvaknin

https://ello.co/malignantselflove

Subscribe to my **Scribd** page: dozens of books for download at no cost to you!



**Zadanliran** is following my work as well:



**Additional Resources**

**Testimonials and Additional Resources**

You can read hundreds of Readers' Reviews at the Barnes and Noble, and Amazon Web pages dedicated to "Malignant Self-love" - HERE:

https://www.amazon.com/dp/1983208175 (Amazon US)

https://www.amazon.co.uk/dp/1983208175 (Amazon UK)

**Participate in discussions about Abusive Relationships**:

http://www.runboard.com/bnarcissisticabuserecovery

http://thepsychopath.freeforums.org/

## Abusive Relationships Newsletters

http://groups.google.com/group/narcissisticabuse/

https://groups.google.com/g/narcissistic-personality-disorder

*Abused? Stalked? Harassed? Bullied? Victimized?*
*Afraid? Confused? Need HELP? DO SOMETHING ABOUT IT!*
*You OWE IT to yourself and to YOUR LOVED ONES!*


Brought up by a Narcissistic Parent?

Married to a Narcissist – or Divorcing One?

Afraid your Children will turn out to be the same?

Want to cope with this pernicious, baffling condition?

OR

Are You a Narcissist – or suspect that you are one…

These books and video lectures will teach you how to…

Cope, Survive, and Protect Your Loved Ones!


We offer you four types of products:

I. **"Malignant Self-love: Narcissism Revisited"** (the print edition);

II. **E-books** (electronic files to be read on a computer, laptop, Nook, or Kindle e-reader devices, or on a smartphone);

III. **Cold Therapy** video lectures; and

IV. **Counselling** with Sam Vaknin or Lidija Rangelovska (or both)


**Find and Buy MOST of my BOOKS and eBOOKS in My Amazon Store:**

https://www.amazon.com/stores/page/60F8EC8A-5812-4007-9F2C-DFA02EA713B3


**I. PRINT EDITION**

Copies **signed** and **dedicated** by the Author (use only this link!):

http://www.amazon.com/gp/product/8023833847/
ref=cm_sw_r_tw_myi?m=A2IY3GUWWKHV9B


## From the PUBLISHER

"Malignant Self-love: Narcissism Revisited" is now available also from the publisher (more expensive, but includes a bonus pack):

http://www.narcissistic-abuse.com/thebook.html


## From AMAZON.COM

To purchase from Amazon use this link:

http://www.amazon.com/Malignant-Self-Love-Narcissism-Sam-Vaknin/dp/8023833847


## II. ELECTRONIC BOOKS (e-Books)

## From KINDLE (AMAZON)

Kindle Books about Narcissists, Psychopaths, and Abusive Relationships – use these links:

http://www.amazon.com/s/ref=ntt_athr_dp_sr_1?_encoding=UTF8&field-author=Sam%20Vaknin&search-alias=digital-text&sort=relevancerank
(Amazon USA)

http://www.amazon.co.uk/s/ref=ntt_athr_dp_sr_1?_encoding=UTF8&field-author=Sam%20Vaknin&search-alias=digital-text&sort=relevancerank
(Amazon UK)


**BUY SIXTEEN e-books about toxic relationships with narcissists and psychopaths - and get the PDF versions of ALL 16 books plus a huge bonus pack FREE!**

Use either of these links and send the proof of purchase via email to samvaknin@gmail.com to receive the PDFs and Bonus Pack:

https://www.amazon.com/dp/B07FK6316T (Amazon USA)

https://www.amazon.co.uk/dp/B07FK6316T (Amazon UK)


### III. Cold Therapy Seminar on DVDs

http://www.narcissistic-abuse.com/ctcounsel.html


### IV. Counselling with Sam Vaknin or Lidija Rangelovska (or both)

http://www.narcissistic-abuse.com/ctcounsel.html


**Free excerpts** from the EIGHTH, Revised Impression of "Malignant Self-love: Narcissism Revisited" are available as well as a **NEW EDITION of the Narcissism Book of Quotes**.

Use this link to download the files:

http://www.narcissistic-abuse.com/freebooks.html

**Download Free Electronic Books** on this link:

http://www.narcissistic-abuse.com/freebooks.html